The Second Wave

ISAAC HECKER STUDIES
IN RELIGION AND AMERICAN CULTURE

THE SECOND WAVE:

Hispanic Ministry and the Evangelization of Cultures

Allan Figueroa Deck, S.J.

Paulist Press
New York/Mahwah

Material from *La Morenita: Evangelization of the Americas* by Virgil Elizondo is reprinted by permission of the Mexican-American Cultural Center, San Antonio.

Cover photo by Al Antczak/The Tidings. Cover design by Tim McKeen.

Text design by Ellen Whitney

Library of Congress Cataloging-in-Publication Data

Deck, Allan Figueroa, 1945–
 The second wave : Hispanic ministry and the evangelization of
cultures in the United States / Allan Figueroa Deck.
  p. cm. — (Isaac Hecker studies in religion and American
culture)
 Bibliography: p.
 ISBN 0-8091-3042-4 : $9.95
 1. Church work with Hispanic Americans. 2. Hispanic Americans.
I. Title. II. Series.
BV4468.2.H57D43 1989
261.8'34868073—dc19   88-38792
                  CIP

Published by Paulist Press
997 Macarthur Boulevard
Mahwah, NJ 07430

Printed and bound in the
United States of America

Contents

Dedicatión

**Para el Arzobispo
Tomás Alberto Clavel
(1921–1988),
nuestro querido e inolvidable
"Archie."**

Acknowledgments

This book is the fruit of ten years of ministry among Hispanics in the diocese of Orange in California. Those ten years were made possible through the encouragement of my Jesuit superiors and the confidence of the first bishop of Orange, the late William R. Johnson. During that decade I was exposed to several areas of ministry—a *barrio* parish, the diocesan office of Hispanic ministry, community organizing projects, and advocacy on behalf of undocumented immigrants. It was a delight during those years to have worked with Archbishop Tomás A. Clavel, former archbishop of Panama and vicar for the Hispanic community of Orange.

I am especially indebted to my mother Amparo Figueroa Deck and my grandmother, Armida Ochoa Figueroa, for introducing me to the peculiar beauty and power of Mexican Catholicism. The Hispanic community at Our Lady of Guadalupe Parish (Delhi) in Santa Ana, California, where I served as pastor were my teachers in the ways of Hispanic Catholicism as well.

Over the years I benefited from ongoing dialogue on Hispanic ministry issues with my sister, Armida Deck, C.S.J., and my friend and colleague Teresita Basso, P.B.V.M. Similarly, my Jesuit brothers Tacho Rivera, Don Kolda, Michael Mandala, Jerry Helfrich, Frank Gallagher, George Casey, George Wanser, Gerald Phelan, and Robert Fambrini were a source of support and insight.

The overall concept of this book was the result of several conversations with Marcello de Carvalho Azevedo, S.J., researcher and writer at the Brazilian Development Institute (IBRADES) in Rio de Janeiro, Brazil, and professor of missiology at the Pontifical Gregorian University in Rome. His careful reading and advice were crucial in helping me give substance to my many reflections and concerns. I am deeply indebted to him for his encouragement and professionalism.

The support and scholarly dedication of the Gregorian University's Faculty of Missiology has played a large part in the production of this study. A debt of gratitude is due especially to Prof. Ary A. Roest Crollius, S.J., former chairman of that faculty, for making possible my studies in Rome.

In the year and a half that it took to produce this work I was fortunate to have received the advice and assistance of Dominic Maruca, S.J., rector of the Collegio San Roberto Bellarmino in Rome; Stephen Pisano, S.J., superior of the Jesuit Community at the Pontifical Biblical Institute in Rome; and Terrance Mahan, S.J., superior at Manresa Retreat House in Azusa, California.

I am grateful, as well, to Eleuterio and Linda Rodríguez whose friendship has been a source of strength and perseverance for me in the task of research and writing.

Many thanks are due to my colleagues at The Jesuit School of Theology at Berkeley, especially to T. Howland Sanks, S.J., who encouraged me to tackle this project, and to John A. Coleman, S.J., for his valuable editorial advice and boundless enthusiasm.

In the task of typing the manuscript I was ably assisted by Laura Hernández. The editing of the text and the final copy were made possible through the excellent services of James Kraft and Mary-Sharon Moore.

Allan Figueroa Deck, S.J.
The Jesuit School of Theology
    at Berkeley
May 5, 1988

Foreword

This book is a fascinating adventure into the core pastoral challenges and questions of today which actually started in 1492. The problematic is nearly 500 years old; the true pastoral response only now begins to be formulated. This is not to say that the people have been totally ignored or that nothing has been done in evangelization and pastoral ministry. Much has taken place and much is going on today. But have the ultimate questions and creative responses of a true Incarnational pastoral ministry been formulated? Allan Deck dares to go to the very core of today's pastoral challenge and presents it in the context of our contemporary U.S. culture. The problematic is rooted in ancient Mexico but the formulation of the response must take place in the United States of today.

The Second Wave comes to us at the very dawn of 1992, the 500th anniversary of the meeting and encounter of two totally distinct worlds, of two totally distinct humanities. Neither one had ever suspected the existence of the other and their respective worldviews were completely different. From the beginning, they were fascinated with each other, but instinctively they seemed to have known that they would not be able to co-exist. One had to give way to the other.

The Mexicans appeared to have been abandoned by their ancestral gods while the European Christians, armed with superior weapons of war, appeared to be protected and favored by their gods. It was a battle of the gods being played out through their human subjects—like a massive puppet show which was being handled from on high. On the one hand, one sees the highly individualistic and possessive world of western civilization as exemplified by Hernan Cortez: conquest was their mission and gold appeared as their true God. On the other hand, one is drawn by the collective and religious world of the Indians, the seductive world of beauty, predetermined order, and the ritual celebration of the masses.

It is my conviction that we do not yet sufficiently appreciate the great clash-encounter which started in 1492 when two totally different worlds—as different as Mars most probably is from planet earth—discovered one another. It was the beginning of the new world of modern European men and women wherein one would be defined through power and wealth. It was the final days of the old world of myth and harmony. The new world of Europe would destroy the ancient world of Mexico and impose itself as the New World. What was not destroyed of the old world was reduced to silence.

There is no other example of such magnitude in the history of humanity with the possible example of the encounters in prehistoric Europe between the Cro Magnons and the Neanderthals. But the Mexican drama can be studied historically and its results observed today. The consequences of the painful encounter appear to be ever present throughout Latin America. They are not spoken about, because the conquered Indian was silenced by the conquest, but they are definitely there to see.

The Europeans were scandalized by the brutal human sacrifices of the Indian world, while the Indians were scandalized by the brutality of the Europeans. Those who were horrified by human sacrifices were not at all bothered by the useless killings of their own wars of conquest. Those who highly valued individuality did not hesitate to take advantage of the collectivity of the Indians and enslave them into hordes of faceless servants—even branding them like cattle.

Thus the new world of Europe conquered the ancient world of Mexico and named it that which Europe was just beginning to become: The New World! Yet the ancient world of mystery, myth, harmony and cosmic communion continued to fascinate and captivate the captors and executioners of the ancient world. They were drawn into it as a strong magnet pulls objects into its realm of power. Reason was captivated by the world of the transrational which was ever so real yet beyond its powers to comprehend.

The challenge of Hispanic ministry started when the Europeans arrived on the soil of these lands. Yet the missioners, saintly and exemplary as they were, were too entrapped in their own worldview to be able to rise to the ultimate challenge of the evangelization of cultures and religions totally distinct from their own—not better or worse, not more or less saintly or sinful, not superior or inferior, but definitely different. Yet like all cultures with their religious expressions, the native Mexican culture was truly in need of evangelization just as much as the western culture of Europe was in need of evangelical reform and renewal. The mistake was that, rather than evangelize, the attempt was made to eliminate and replace the native culture with the culture and religious expression of Spain. In the name of the gospel, which is the word of life, cultures were destroyed. The true evangelization of culture as clearly outlined by Pope Paul VI is still one of the greatest challenges of the church today. It cannot take place without a lot of humility and a willingness to die to one's own cultural absolutes, to one's own household gods.

The new world of European thought, rationalism, planned order, doctrinal Catholicism and individual salvation (both worldly through wealth and spiritual through the sacraments of the church) imposed itself upon Mexico and the Mexicans but never penetrated into the depth of the collective soul of Mexico. The colonial church and later on the church of today's Mexico have often lived and ministered on the margins of the Mexican religious ethos without seeming to appreciate it or incorporate it into its liturgical life. The masses of the people are very Catholic, but the European-based Catholicism of the majority of the clergy and religious often remains in a world of its own, profoundly distant from the Catholicism of the masses of the faithful.

Why then are the people Christian-Catholic? It is obvious and simple: God's direct intervention through the apparition of Our Lady at Tepeyac which became known and promulgated through the mediation of a poor, low class Indian named Juan Diego. Our Lady of Guadalupe—La Morenita del Tepeyac—countered the rationally planned evangelization and catechetical practices of the early missioners. Their attempts at evangelization were truly outstanding, but incomprehensible to the cosmovision of the ancient Indian world. Her words are beautiful and moving but quite secondary to her very presence. In her one becomes absorbed by the ancient images, symbol and myth which have given life to previous generations and which will give life to generations to come. In her one is in communion with the cosmos and with one another, with the present and with the eternal, with the individual and the collectivity. In her, one is truly and fully alive.

It is she who understood, appreciated, and introduced into Mexican Catholicism the mythical-symbolic element of the religious experience of the Mexican worldview while at the same time introducing into the Mexican religious world the finest elements of the gospel message brought over by the missioners. In her and through her mediation, the two radically opposing worldviews, solidly grounded on their religious symbols, became fused into a new religious symbol truly combining elements of both. The evangelical dialogue which permits the true incarnation of the gospel and the birth of the local church started and continues in Our Lady of Guadalupe.

It is she who started the evangelical dialogue in the Americas. Through her, the word was incarnated into the cosmovision of the ancient religions of the Americas. It would no longer be the word of foreigners, but the eternal word making itself present and alive in the midst of the local people. It is through her and the mediation of Juan Diego and his descendants in the persons of the poor, oppressed, marginalized and silenced masses of Mexican society that the gospel has continued to penetrate the innermost soul of Mexicans and Mexican Americans. The Mother of the true God insisted that Juan Diego be her trusted messenger. He became the first true evangelizer of the Americas.

It is no wonder that during his 1987 visit to the USA, Pope John Paul II stated that the only way to come to the Americas was through Our Lady of Guadalupe. Furthermore, it is this continuity with the luminous world of the past which mediated reality through myth and symbol that we as Mexican and Mexican American Christians have the most to offer to today's world where the limitations of rational and systematic theology and catechesis are becoming more and more evident. It is not to say that we do not need critical thought and theology, but it is to say that it is not sufficient. The rational needs the transrational to enter the world of mystical communion while the transrational needs the rational to avoid becoming a world of empty rituals and senseless magic. Neither one is sufficient to fulfill the total person. Both need one another. Maybe the synthesis which was started with Guadalupe but which has not yet been achieved by the church can began to come about today. This is the challenge that Allan Deck poses in this book.

This work is a marvelous collection and synthesis of the best Latin American and North American thought woven together into a beautiful mosaic. It clearly presents the beauty and the ugliness, the dreams and the nightmares, the disappointments and the aspirations, the obstacles and the challenges, the obvious and the unsuspected, the pains and the joys, the struggles and celebrations which together make up the incredible complexity of Hispanic ministry today. As one reads this fascinating work, one is gradually led through the long and arduous journey of generations of Mexicans and Mexican Americans who have struggled to live in spite of the multiple forces of death which have always surrounded us. Death has not been able to prevent us from believing in life.

The Second Wave of Allan Deck should not be read by anyone who is seeking easy answers and a simple "how to" manual of Hispanic ministry. But this book is definitely a must for anyone who truly wants to be an intimate part of the Hispanic's struggle for life in its fullness. Without addressing the challenging questions that Father Deck poses, well-meaning ministers can easily hurt and destroy the Hispanics instead of being true partners in the Hispanics struggle for life in the USA.

This is a masterful work which in a very professional and compassionate way introduces the reader to the challenges and depth of Hispanic ministry. The ultimate question: How to reconcile the western world of individualism, materialism and rational thought (with logical pastoral planning, defined goals and clearly stated pastoral plans) with the ancient Mexican world of *divina providencia* (which appears as magical ideas to the outsider), mystery, and myth which are the effective cause of our communion with God and God's effective intervention in our lives? This challenge has never been faced before and has led to the ongoing separation and even antagonism between church celebrations and teachings and the religious life of the people.

It is amazing how in the person of the Hispanic poor, who are struggling to survive in a highly materialistic, individualistic, technological and hedonistic society, our dominant culture is questioned and challenged. In relation to the values of the gospel, who needs to change whom? Who needs to evangelize whom? Who needs to convert whom to whose way? Are we of the dominant culture seeking to evangelize while in effect we should first be seeking to be converted as individuals and as a people?

As the gospel is full of unsuspected surprises, so is Allan's work. The key to effective Hispanic ministry, as the very core of today's challenge to evangelize the Hispanics, is the evangelization of North American culture itself. It is the ministers of evangelization who come from the North American cultural reality who first of all need to be evangelized in relation to the materialism, individualism and hedonism of North American culture. To the degree that we neglect to evangelize North American culture, we will never truly evangelize the Hispanics in this country. Rather, we will impose the values of North American culture in the name of the gospel. In seeking to offer them life, we will in effect be calling them to death.

From an analysis of a very particular and well defined local situation, Allan arrives at what is probably the most universal challenge of today's church: the evangelization of the materialistic-individualistic cultures of the western world, commonly known as the Christian world. It is the traditional mission-sending cultures who need to evangelize their own if they are to become true the witness of the gospel values of Jesus. The cultures our American ministers seek to evangelize are often, at the level of core gospel values, far closer to the gospel then the ministers themselves. And it is the culture with its core cultural values which is the deepest carrier of the ultimate message of the messenger. Hence if the gospel values are not core values of the culture of the ministers, no matter how great the minister may be, that minister is really more an obstacle to the gospel.

Deck's book revolves around two core elements of Hispanic ministry: the need to recognize in a positive way the religous expressions and ethos of the mestizo Hispanics, and the need to strive for the conversion of the core values of the western world. Neither has been a part of Hispanic ministry before. While citing some of the efforts currently going on, Allan clearly points the way to the fantastic task ahead of us. It's a great challenge and we cannot delay. It is our task and our privilege to take part in the building of something truly new—the church of the Americas.

Virgil Elizondo
Feast of Our Lady of Guadalupe, 1988

Introduction

The migration of millions of Latin American and Asian-Pacific peoples to the United States since World War II—the "second wave"—is a fact of extraordinary importance for U.S. society. For the Roman Catholic Church of the United States the Latin American part of that second wave constitutes a sea change whose implications are only now emerging. This second immigrant experience promises to be every bit as significant, if not more significant, than the first one whose memory and meaning is rapidly fading from mainstream U.S. Catholics.

U.S. Catholics have become comfortable with their hard-earned identity. Sons and daughters of the teeming masses—the "first wave"—that disembarked in the last century or early in this one, they achieved acceptance in a predominantly Protestant and rather anti-Catholic country. The struggle was long and often bitter. World War II gave these immigrants and their offspring an opportunity to demonstrate their Americanism. They performed their civic and patriotic duties with distinction. By and large they ceased speaking their native languages. And by 1960 the United States was able to elect a Catholic president. Roman Catholics were becoming "as American as apple pie."

The traditional Catholic ethnic groups—Irish, German, Italian, and Slavic—were mainstreaming. That meant cultural as well as social class change. They were becoming like the other Americans. The importance of this adaptation was often stressed by bishops and pastors alike (at least by the late nineteenth century). They perceived a need for the Church to Americanize if ever it were to significantly influence U.S. society.

Just as U.S. Catholics and their bishops, priests, and men and women religious were becoming comfortable with their hard-earned status, the second wave was already well on its way. In some respects the difficult conditions and demands of a century before were once

1

again asserting themselves. The cultural and social class conflicts of bygone times were again ignited. The identity of the U.S. Catholic Church was again becoming that of the outsiders, the marginal, and the poor.

At this moment in time, consequently, the U.S. Catholic Church is schizophrenic, caught between two identities. One is the achievement of the mainstreaming process; the other is the result of a new migration that shows no sign of abating. This migration will transform that Church by the next century into a predominantly Hispanic American institution just as today it is predominantly Irish American.

There is a temptation to brush aside the immensity of the challenge implied by this second wave. Many observers are consoled by the fact that sooner or later these immigrant groups do mainstream and become "just like us." Such a view presupposes a static context. But the fact is that the United States has changed and so has the Church especially in these past forty years. Consequently the level and nature of the participation of Hispanics in the U.S. Church and society is being determined by complex and often unanalyzed trends in Church and society. An intelligent response to the Hispanic presence, therefore, requires attention to the facts and their implications. It also means interpreting those facts and events in terms of the sources of our faith—scripture, tradition, and the remarkable body of ecclesial reflections that constitute the post-Vatican II magisterium.

This book is written with the conviction that what is done to promote the effective pastoral care of Hispanics today will determine to a degree still not fully appreciated the vitality and effectiveness of the U.S. Catholic Church of the twenty-first century. There can be no greater priority for the Church, her priests, pastoral ministers, and teachers than the flesh and blood people who will constitute the majority of the Catholic faithful in the United States in the very near future. Those people shall be of Hispanic origin and it is likely, moreover, that they will be poor and relatively powerless.

There is another circumstance that requires consideration here. The psychological space within which the U.S. Catholic Church gears up to face this new challenge is not that of a uniformly immigrant Church as was the case a century ago. Now there is a "we" and a "they." The loyalties and sensibilities of many U.S. Catholics are no longer grounded in their ancient Catholic cultures and in the vivid memory of the trauma of migration. The effort needed to bridge the gap between this new American way of being Catholic and the more rooted, ancient way of Hispanic Catholicism is considerable. That gap hardly existed in those initial decades of conflict that ultimately gave rise to today's Church.

Perhaps even more significant is the fact that the U.S. Catholic Church is being asked to confront this challenge at a time of internal crisis. The consequences of the relatively rapid renewal process set in motion by the Second Vatican Council are only now being fully felt. One of the consequences is a new and still untested understanding of ministry in the Church. There is, as well, a serious crisis in vocations to the ministerial priesthood and to the religious life. The clerical institution that has been unquestionably at the heart of Catholic life for centuries is under siege. And one can only speculate on where this development will lead.

The point is that there are many profoundly serious issues facing the U.S. Catholic Church at this point in time. Surely one may take them to be part of a growth process; others may interpret them as signs of decline. In any event, the challenge of the Hispanic presence with all its ramifications comes precisely at a time of uncertainty. Resources—human and material—to cope with the challenge may not be as plentiful. There may be a lack of courage under these circumstances. And, what is worse, there is a certain amount of psychological fatigue among Church leaders who increasingly experience limitations in terms of resources, finances, morale, and ability to lead. The past twenty years since the close of Vatican II has been a time of exhausting change on many fronts, especially in the Church. A mature and creative response to the Hispanic presence requires a great deal of energy. Frankly, there are some signs that the energy is not there. The vigorous and often effective outreach of evangelical Protestant groups to Hispanics compared to the sometimes lackluster outreach of Catholic parishes and schools to the same group is a case in point. The persistent denial of the presence of Hispanics in their parishes on the part of some pastors in the face of considerable proof to the contrary is not so rare even at this late date. The inflexibility and feet-dragging of some seminaries and religious houses of formation in adapting to the needs of Hispanic candidates is a much commented perception. Realistically one may even ask whether the will to reach out and serve these newcomers is there.

Many statements have been made by the bishops themselves about the central importance of Hispanic ministry in the United States. The most recent is the National Pastoral Plan for Hispanic Ministry. This ministry has surely gained wide recognition by almost all sectors of the U.S. Church. Nevertheless, there continues to be a chasm between what is being preached and proposed and what is really happening. The proliferation of projects in Hispanic ministry and the allocation of funds for various activities is certainly better than the benign neglect that had heretofore characterized the response of many parishes, dioceses, seminaries, and religious congregations to the Hispanic presence. Practical responses, projects, and activities initiated in response to the challenge, however, may not be based upon a thoughtful analysis of the reality. They may prove themselves to be quite ineffective, misguided, or inadequate. The failure to evaluate may perpetuate errors and, even worse, lead to disillusionment among pastoral workers. It is my conviction that that is the case—not always, but enough to raise concern. Nothing less than the well-being of the Church to come is at stake.

This work, then, is an effort to move Hispanic ministry and pastoral care beyond the level of anecdote and unanalyzed response. It hopes to provide a fuller but by no means complete account of the numerous practical and theoretical questions that Hispanic ministry poses to the watchful and reflective pastoral agent. For much too long a time these questions have either been ignored or dealt with in a superficial manner. Clichés and nostrums have unfortunately abounded. Narrow ideology, pet theories, and unanalyzed assumptions have hindered ministerial effectiveness.

One of the serious limitations faced by those who would do reflection upon the pastoral reality of Hispanics in the U.S. Church is the appalling dearth of serious social science data about it specifically with regard to Hispanic religious attitudes and practices. Literature on the participation and interaction of Hispanics within Church contexts is almost totally lacking. If, indeed, one is dealing here with a major if not *the* major issue for the U.S. Catholic Church of the next century, then such a lack of knowledge and insight is nothing less than astounding. The following study, therefore, is only a tentative effort to outline the major issues and give background that sheds light on the reality. It provides clues and suggestions for further research in innumerable areas.

The "see-judge-act" methodology for pastoral planning has been adopted for the national pastoral planning process (the Tercer Encuentro Nacional Hispano de Pastoral). The Pastoral Plan was the result. While providing a rich variety of resources, analyses, and proposals, this Plan needs to be complemented by more in-depth appraisals, differentiations, and realistic evaluations of what has been done in the past. Efforts to apply this plan at the regional and diocesan levels appear to be stymied by a lack of clarity about the real issues, a failure to appropriate the experiences of the past, and the persistence of different and even conflicting agendas among the pastoral workers themselves. While the present work does not pretend to provide the answers to the what and how of Hispanic ministry in the future, it does offer signposts and suggestions that might be useful in confronting the challenge more intelligently. It ought to be read along with the bishops' National Pastoral Plan for Hispanic Ministry.

At the very outset it must be stated that the use of the word Hispanic is problematic. It is an umbrella term that simply does not do justice to the heterogeneity of the people in question.[1] There is really no adequate term to cover the various national groups and the several generations that constitute this "pluriverse" of Latin American origin in the United States. The levels of assimilation to the U.S. environment and social class distinctions are varied. Consequently it is hard to generalize about these people. The failure to distinguish among the several Hispanic groups in the U.S. leads to a false sense of security and sometimes betrays a kind of mental laziness. Recently some Hispanic groups have been promoting the word "Latino" as more appropriate. That term, however, is just as problematic.

The term of reference for this study, nevertheless, is Hispanics of Mexican origin in California. These people continue to be the single largest Hispanic group in the country, and the author is most familiar with them. While it is risky and methodologically unsound to draw conclusions for the many U.S. Hispanic groups from an analysis of the Mexican origin cohort, it is reasonable to begin someplace, especially with the largest and most historically rooted of the various Hispanic communities. More detailed studies of the various groups along the lines of the present one are required if Hispanic ministry is to achieve the level of coherence and conceptual clarity it deserves.

The present study unfolds in the following way. The first chapter provides a demographic and social science interpretation of the reality. The second chapter tries to highlight significant elements in the complex historical and cultural background of Hispanics of Mexican origin in California. Chapter three gives a phenomenology, profile, and inventory of pastoral practices in Hispanic ministry in California. The method here is fundamentally descriptive and the range of situations extensive. Chapter four isolates key issues that emerge in the analysis of the pastoral praxis. This chapter stresses the urgency of developing a critical sense of the dominant U.S. culture as well as of the dependent Hispanic cultures—a dual sociocultural analysis—if the Church's primordial task of evangelization is to be adequately served. The fifth chapter returns again to the pastoral reality, to the level of praxis, in an effort to clarify goals, objectives, and strategies in light of the key theoretical issues raised in the previous chapter.

There are several core concepts that inspire this book. The first is the notion of evangelization in the rich and nuanced sense embraced by Pope Paul VI's *Evangelii Nuntiandi*. It has to do with conversion, but not in some simplistic sense. Rather, evangelization means change that is both personal and social. The second core concept is inculturation as developed in the rich body of literature in the magisterium and in theology, especially missiology, today. A third key notion is liberation or commitment to transformative action, social justice, in the world. Such activity, as the Bishops' Synod of 1971 taught, is an integral dimension of the Church's mission. The pastoral ministry of Pope John Paul II has powerfully enhanced and dramatized this conviction of Catholic social teaching. A fourth concept is secularization and modernization.

The vast literature on these themes is extremely relevant to grasping the context within which Hispanics find themselves today in the U.S. For they are inexorably caught up in the complex dynamics of secularization and modernity. The issues here need to be assessed, the process understood, if ministry is to proceed with a minimum of realism. Finally, the role of the people's popular religiousness is affirmed and stressed. In a sense the effectiveness of ministry with Hispanics depends more upon a positive and respectful understanding of their popular religion than on any other single factor. For that is where they are. That *is* their religion in most cases. A sound catechesis must begin there. The ongoing hostility of today's pastoral agent, the priest, the director of religious education, the deacon, or the lay minister to various manifestations of people's popular religion is nothing less than scandalous. An effort is made to explain why.

A final issue stressed especially in chapter four is the lack of real cultural awareness on the part of U.S. Catholics across the board. One cannot evangelize when one is immersed unreflectively in one's own culture. Evangelization means the relativization of one's culturally acquired norms, values, and feelings. The failure to develop such a transcultural sensitivity means that a great deal of Americanization masquerades as evangelization in the U.S. Catholic Church. As the nation becomes even more pluralistic as the new century dawns there is need to assert a Catholic identity rooted in the gospel. Such an identity if authentically pursued will undoubtedly bring committed U.S. Catholics into conflict with many values and norms being promoted as American. By the same token responses to the Hispanic presence can gratuitously assume that what is at stake is Hispanicizing U.S. culture. This author's conviction is that U.S. culture needs to be evangelized. That means going beyond cultures to the heart of Christ's message that is always in some regards new, surprising, and countercultural.

The schizophrenia noted above needs to be pondered. One segment of the U.S. Church—the mainstream and especially the more progressive in that mainstream—is courageously striving to relate the Catholic heritage to U.S. values such as egalitarianism, democracy, individualism, and women's rights. The other segment—the second wave communities with their third world traditionalism—has a much different background and agenda at this point in time. Marshaling the energies of the U.S. Church to respond to the Hispanic presence means in the final analysis proposing a vision for being Catholic and North American in years to come. Hispanic ministry can only be a part of the larger picture, the dialogical process, which is the evangelization of U.S. culture across the board. As long as there is confusion about and ignorance or disregard of the cultural question there can be no really coherent pastoral planning of any kind.

What is proposed in this work, then, is only part of a larger picture which is the interaction between religion and culture in a nation undergoing rapid change in almost every area of its existence. The way that the Hispanic presence impacts the life of the Catholic Church and how that Church responds is only one act—albeit an especially crucial one— in the drama of the U.S. Church and society in these closing years of the twentieth century.

1 | Hispanics in the United States: An Overview

Faithfulness to the spirit of the Second Vatican Council, especially to the Council's Pastoral Constitution on the Church in the Modern World *Gaudium et Spes*, requires that students of Hispanic ministry begin their study in an inductive manner. The Church's mission in the world requires faithful and prayerful attention to the "signs of the times" as they are identified and clarified by the human sciences. The contexts within which the people of God find themselves are the proper object of inquiry for pastoral agents who must scrutinize those realities in the light of gospel truths.[1]

This opening chapter is concerned, then, with providing an overview of the current situation of Hispanics in the United States as it is revealed in demographic and socioeconomic data. Since the data indicate that one of the formative experiences of Hispanics in this country has been their condition as immigrants, a second part of the chapter attempts to synthesize the pertinent facts about that immigration. In a third section the pattern of Hispanic immigrations to the U.S. and the subsequent integration of the people into the North American milieu are viewed in comparison with the patterns of previous immigrant groups. Differing social science perspectives—functionalist and Marxist—are discussed here, finally, in terms of their contrasting interpretations of the reality.

Demographic and Socioeconomic Data

The U.S. Census for 1985 reported 16,900,000 persons of Hispanic origin in the United States. That is an increase of 2,300,000 (16 percent) over the 1980 figure of 14,600,000. If one takes into account that there are between three and five million undocumented Hispanic immigrants in the U.S. and that the vast majority of these are not counted in the census, then it is reasonable to infer that the Hispanic population of the U.S. is somewhere between twenty and twenty-two million.[2]

Of the approximately twenty million Hispanics, half are below the age of 25—almost seven years younger than the median age for the entire U.S. population which is 31.9 years. The families of these Hispanics are larger than the average U.S. family: 28.7 percent according to the 1985 Census had five persons or more, while only 14.9 percent of all U.S. families had such a number of family members. The Hispanic population, then, is large, young, and one of the most rapidly growing segments of the U.S. population.[3] In the decade of the 1970s, for instance, the Hispanic population grew by 61 percent, while the entire U.S. population grew by only 11.5 percent.[4]

The specifically Mexican origin cohort of the Hispanic population is growing even faster than the entire Hispanic population. In the decade of the 1970s the Mexican origin group grew from 4.5 million to 8.7 million—an increase of 93 percent. The Mexican population constitutes more than 60 percent of the entire U.S. Hispanic population.[5]

In California, the Mexican origin population in 1980 was 3,637,000 out of 4,543,770 Hispanics, or approximately 80 percent of all California Hispanics. The Hispanic population of California in turn constitutes 31 percent of the entire U.S. Hispanic population and 41 percent of the entire Mexican origin population. Approximately 20 percent of California's entire population of twenty-five million is Hispanic.[6]

The Mexican origin population is even younger than the Hispanic, the median age being 21.9 years rather than the 25 years as already mentioned. The Mexican families are also slightly larger than the other Hispanic families, averaging 3.74 members per household rather than 3.48 for the entire Hispanic and 2.75 for the entire U.S. population.[7]

The Hispanic population of the U.S. is concentrated in five states: California, Texas, New York, Florida, and Illinois. These five states account for 71 percent of all U.S. Hispanics. It is true, however, that Hispanics are increasingly present in every one of the fifty states and in the District of Columbia. Their numbers are growing in places that historically have had little to do with Hispanics such as Oregon and Washington, and in such faraway places as Alaska.[8]

After the Mexican origin group, the second largest Hispanic group is Puerto Rican. It is concentrated in the New York and New Jersey areas, with some presence in the Midwestern industrial states, especially the Chicago area. There are approximately 1.5 million Puerto Ricans in the U.S. The third largest Hispanic community is the Cuban which is concentrated in South Florida. There are approximately one million Cuban Americans.[9]

Another important fact is that 88 percent of the Hispanic population live in urban areas. Only the Asian population is more urbanized (91 percent). Of these millions of urban Hispanics, moreover, 58 percent reside in inner cities. Even when Hispanics suburbanize they do not necessarily move to more affluent neighborhoods, but rather to *barrios* that are found tucked between middle-class suburbs throughout southern California, for example.[10]

In recent years the life expectancy of U.S. Hispanics appears to be improving. There is a convergence in mortality patterns between the Anglo and Hispanic populations. The life expectancy for males in both populations is approximately seventy years, and for females, seventy-eight years.[11]

A fact of special importance is the number of households headed by a woman alone. For Hispanics the number is 20 percent, or one in five households headed by a woman. Given that pay scales for women are considerably lower than for men, this statistic is also related to the number of Hispanics below the poverty level which is 25 percent, or one in four Hispanics.[12] Also related to poverty is the educational level of Hispanics. It is the lowest in the nation with 56.7 percent of Hispanics not having a high school degree. Similarly, Hispanics have the smallest percentage of any group in the country with at least a college degree.[13]

Hispanic men of Mexican origin have the highest percentage of their members in the labor force of any group in the United States. Almost 80 percent of the males are working, while only 49.3 percent of the females are working outside the home. Perhaps a factor here is the likelihood of their having young children at home. Nevertheless, the unemployment rate among the same group is high: 8.7 percent for the males and 9.9 percent for the females. This is compared to the unemployment rate for white males and females, which is 5.7 percent.[14] In terms of occupational distribution, 78.9 percent of the Mexican origin population in the U.S. is blue collar. This is the highest percentage of any group in the nation. Conversely, the smallest cohort of white-collar workers are Hispanics of Mexican origin.[15] Contrary to popular conceptions, a relatively small percentage of Hispanics of Mexican origin are involved in agricultural labor. It does not exceed 6 percent of that labor force. The vast majority of Hispanic workers of Mexican descent are in factory and service work.[16]

As these statistics suggest, the Mexican origin population receives the lowest wages of any group in the country. The median annual income of white males, for example, is $13,029; for Mexican origin males, $8,888. Especially noticeable is the median annual income of Mexican origin females, which is $4,556. Only the Puerto Rican females have a lower annual median income.[17]

The implications of these data for the United States Catholic Church are far-reaching. The 1986 *Official Catholic Directory* estimates the Catholic population of the United States to be 52.5 million. A conservative estimate of the Hispanic population of the U.S. as mentioned above is in excess of twenty million. How many of these Hispanics are baptized Catholics? There is not any totally reliable study of this available, but the estimates range from a low of 75 percent to a high of 95 percent. If one takes the middle road and considers 85 percent of the Hispanics to be baptized Catholics, then approximately eighteen million of the 52.5 million U.S. Catholics are Hispanic, that is, 34 percent.[18] In some areas of the nation Hispanics already constitute a majority of the Catholics—California, Texas, Arizona, and New Mexico, for instance. In nine of the twelve dioceses of California, Hispanics constitute a majority of the Catholics. This is especially true of the archdiocese of Los Angeles, the most populous archdiocese of the nation, where the Hispanic Catholic population is in excess of 70 percent of the entire Catholic population.[19]

Given the relatively higher fertility rate among Hispanic women, the larger family size, and the projections of continuing immigration from Mexico and Central America, the Hispanics are predicted to become the majority of U.S. Catholics sometime early in the twenty-first century.

Mexican Immigrants in California: A Summary of Current Knowledge

This part of chapter one is concerned with assessing in greater detail the current knowledge regarding immigration by Mexican Hispanics specifically to California. One of the more recent studies of Mexican immigration to California is that of McCarthy and Valdez. They prepared an executive summary of a project sponsored by the California Roundtable, an organization of ninety leading corporations which studies current issues with broad public policy ramifications for California. The report published by the Rand Corporation in November 1985 is entitled *Current and Future Effects of Mexican Immigration in California.*

One of the more revealing discoveries of the Rand Corporation research is the underlying dynamic of Mexican immigration. According to their findings, there are three kinds of Mexican immigrant: short-term, cyclical, and permanent. The research found that short-term immigrants enter for approximately ten to twelve weeks, then return to Mexico. Cyclical immigrants, on the other hand, leave their families in Mexico but stay in California for longer periods of time and return to Mexico on a fairly regular basis. Permanent immigrants, in contrast to the first two groups, bring their families with them and establish more or less permanent residence in California. Each one of these categories contains both documented and undocumented workers. But the permanent category, as well could be imagined, has the higher percentage of documented immigrants.[20]

The process of settlement for these groups in general follows the following pattern. They enter the country illegally as short-term immigrants to work frequently as day laborers or in temporary farm jobs. These immigrants often remain closer to the border and return to Mexico after they have acquired several hundred dollars. Many of them never return to the U.S., or do so sporadically for similar short-term stays. Some, however, develop a more lasting relationship with their employer and begin to return regularly, leaving their families back in Mexico. These are the cyclical immigrants. Some of these do succeed in legalizing their status by marrying U.S. citizens or through efforts of their employer. In this way they pass over into the permanent category. The home in Mexico is abandoned and the family is brought to the U.S.[21]

An important factor influencing the permanence of immigrants is the shift from agricultural jobs which of their nature are seasonal, to year-round manufacturing and service jobs which encourage permanent residency.

The Rand report also makes the distinction between the primary and secondary immigrants. The secondary immigrants are not the workers themselves but their families. Cyclical immigrants, for example, bring their oldest sons and their relatives north when they are old enough to work. These in turn will either decide to settle permanently or will become cyclical immigrants like their father or other older relative. If the primary immigrant decides to remain permanently, he will bring his wife and children to join him.[22] These family members often enter illegally because the Immigration Act of 1965 did not offer many possibilities for these people to enter the country and remain for any length of time with legal permission.[23] It is not unusual, however, to find legal and illegal immigrants mingled in the same family. A child born to undocumented parents in the U.S., for instance, is a U.S. citizen. It is reasonable to infer from the demographics and the projections made about the undocumented population (between three and five million) that there are thousands of U.S. citizen infants and young children with undocumented parents. Similarly, it can be inferred that a smaller but not insignificant number of U.S. citizen infants and young children have returned to Mexico with their parents and will live there more or less permanently.[24]

In analyzing the differences among the three kinds of immigrants, the Rand report found that the short-term immigrants were almost totally undocumented and spoke only Spanish. The possibility of their integrating with the rest of California society was slight. The cyclical immigrants, however, spoke some English but also were in the majority undocumented. They, too, had little possibility of integrating into the dominant mainstream. The permanent immigrants, on the other hand, showed the greatest possibility of integration since they were well on the way to being bilingual and were in the majority documented.[25]

In an even closer analysis of the data, the Rand report found that motivations, demographic characteristics, and socioeconomic features of each of the three types of immigrant condition the nature and extent of their impact on California society. While the report does not make this point, it may also be suggested that the impact is reciprocal or mutual: namely, the impact of California society and institutions (including the Church) on the immigrants is related to the type of immigrant with whom one is dealing.

Whereas Mexicans have been coming north to California since the eighteenth century (decades before the Anglos), large-scale Mexican immigration is a phenomenon of this century, especially of the last forty years. Consequently, a substantial number of Hispanics, perhaps even the majority, are immigrants or the minor children of immigrants—that is, between two and three million of California's more than five million Hispanics.[26] Efforts to evaluate the situation of California Hispanics, especially how they are integrating or not, are not very successful when based on aggregate numbers that do not distinguish the immigrant from the native-born nor the types within the immigrant category itself. There needs to be more sophistication and differentiation in interpreting the data. The short-term and cyclical immigrants, as noted above, will interact in a more limited way with California institutions, the Church being one of them. Their stay will be impacted mainly by their work. The permanent immigrants will have the possibility of interacting with society and Church to a much greater degree. The native-born Mexican American or Chicano population, it may be noted here, is in the position to interact with society and the Church more than any of the other groups. In chapter five these distinctions and insights will again be surfaced in terms of their relevance to realistic pastoral planning.

Two further studies, both from the Center for U.S.-Mexican Studies at the University of California at San Diego, have shed significant light on the immigrant reality. Like the Rand report, they look at the phenomenon of Mexican immigration from the point of view of its impact on California society. These studies are often framed in the context of controversy regarding the alleged negative impact of immigrants on society—an allegation that owes more to prejudice and ignorance than to knowledge as the studies on this matter attest.[27] This literature, while pointing out some problem areas, verifies the positive impact of immigration on California and southwestern U.S. economies. Both Center for U.S.-Mexican Studies reports point out that permanent Mexican immigrants and their offspring are being integrated successfully into California's economy:

> The first generation improves its income levels and, to a lesser extent, its occupational status, with longer residence in the U.S. Greater economic mobility occurs in the second and third generations. However, both Mexican immigrants and subsequent generations of Mexican-origin people still lag considerably behind the non-Hispanic white population in terms of income levels.[28]

The report goes on to specify in greater detail:

> Culturally and politically, first generation Mexican immigrants, regardless of legal status, are less well integrated, but there is no evidence of separatist tendencies. Retention of Mexican culture and Spanish monolingualism is much less pronounced among the second generation. Fuller integration of Mexican immigrants into the political system will require major efforts to encourage naturalization, which in turn seems to depend upon the expansion of educational opportunities available to adult Mexican immigrants.[29]

Most studies indicate that the English language is being learned by the Mexican immigrant. For instance, the Rand report states:

> The transition to English actually begins among the foreign born. Less than 25 percent of the short-termers have a work-

ing knowledge of English; about 40 percent of them are monolingual Spanish speakers. In contrast, nearly half of the permanent immigrants speak good English, and less than a quarter of them speak only Spanish. However, the most dramatic difference is that between the foreign born and the native born: most of the first generation native born are bilingual, and more than 90 percent are proficient in English; more than half of the second generation are monolingual English speakers. Thus the transition to English begins almost immediately and proceeds very rapidly.[30]

In terms of educational advancement, the Rand report also documents that for the Mexican-born population there is little progress beyond the primary school grades. When subsequent generations are assessed it becomes clear that the Hispanics are doing nearly as well as other Californians educationally. The percentage of second-generation Hispanics still in school at age 20–21, for example, is 27 percent, while it is 33 percent for all Californians.[31]

The Rand report estimates the number of short-term immigrants in the year 1980 (based on the existing pool in Mexico) to have been 2,600,000. The vast majority of these, naturally, were not counted by the U.S. Census. In 1990, the report estimates that the number of short-term immigrants will be 2.5 million to 3.6 million; and in the year 2000, the number will rise to 5.1 million to 7.4 million.[32] If these projections are at all correct, it would appear that there will continue to be a blurring of impressions regarding the impact of Mexican immigration; that is, there will continue to be a tendency to draw conclusions about the nature and meaning of the immigration based on impressions derived from a kind of epiphenomenon and not from a more nuanced interpretation of the entire immigration dynamic. Large numbers of the short-term workers will continue to create the impression of an invasion. Similarly, pastoral agents may ascribe more significance to the epiphenomenon than to the deeper dynamics by not evaluating and distinguishing among responses directed to one or the other of the four typologies—short-termers, cyclical immigrants, permanent immigrants, and the native-born (Mexican American or Chicano) population.

A further analysis of the data shows that California is the preferred place to immigrate for Mexicans. The proportion of legally admitted Mexican immigrants who list California as their state of intended permanent residence has risen continuously since 1968, and a study of immigration to the U.S. from nine communities in Jalisco found that 49 percent of all persons emigrating to the U.S. since 1940 settled in

California. Since 1975, 64 percent of all families leaving Mexico went to California.[33] Another survey of 62,500 Mexican households in 1978–79 found that 50.9 percent of all Mexicans reportedly present in the U.S. at the time of the survey were living in California. The second most important destination was Texas, with 21 percent of the emigrants. Illinois was the third, with 8 percent.[34]

Where in California do the immigrants go? Massively they are going to southern California, especially to Los Angeles County and the four neighboring counties of Orange, San Bernardino, Riverside, and Ventura.[35] A 1984 report of the Southern California Association of Governments (SCAG) points out that 500,000 immigrants came to the five southern California counties in the years 1975–80. This is over half the region's net growth. In fact, one of every eight immigrants (Hispanic or otherwise) coming to the U.S. during those years came to one of these five counties.[36] The report goes on to project more immigration for the following reasons:

(1) the abundance of job opportunities compared to other parts of the country;
(2) the proximity of Mexico and Central America;
(3) the location of this region on the Pacific Rim (source of intense Asian-Pacific immigration);
(4) the similarity (warmth) of this region's climate to Latin America and the Asian-Pacific countries;
(5) the already existing, large ethnic communities and cultural centers in the region (e.g., *barrios*, East Los Angeles, and so forth).

The SCAG report, in fact, projects an Hispanic population of 6,016,000 for just these five counties by the year 2000 if the optimum factors for immigration continue to obtain. The non-Hispanic white population of the region by the year 2000 is projected at 6,149,000.[37] Even if the immigration were to subside (something very unlikely due to continuing economic and political "push" factors in Mexico and Central America), the Hispanic presence in California, especially Southern California, will be massive and in the long run a decisive factor in the region's cultural identity and destiny.

Adaptation of Immigrants to the U.S.: Past Trends and Current Experiences

The intense and ongoing immigration of Hispanics, especially Mexicans, to the United States since 1940 is only a chapter in the long history of U.S. immigration. Legal immigration, in fact, was more intense in the years between 1890 and 1920. Joseph P. Fitzpatrick, S.J. summarizes the historic pattern of immigrant adaptation with the words "contact, conflict and accommodation," stating:

> Conventionally the process of assimilation took a rather consistent pattern. Members of the second generation still had roots in the immigrant community, but their contacts and associations with the host culture increased substantially. In most cases they were educated in the schools of the host culture while they were still living in a home of the cultural background of the parents. As American born citizens they could participate in a political life and institutions of the new society. Occupationally, they frequently found jobs at higher socio-economic levels than their parents. The "second generation" as they were called were the difficult generation. Neither completely members of the old culture, nor yet completely assimilated into the new, they face the classic problems of the children in transition. . . . The "third generation," those born in the U.S. of parents who were born in the U.S., gives evidence of advanced assimilation into the dominant U.S. culture. For the most part they have lost the language of their grandparents.[38]

This pattern, as has already been seen, is holding true for the Hispanics of Mexican origin as well, but it is somewhat obscured by the current ongoing, short-term, and cyclical immigration which was not a feature of the immigration pattern of other historic ethnic groups.[39]

Fitzpatrick goes on to discuss other factors which are also different from those that affected other immigrant groups. He notes that Hispanics, especially Mexicans, are not emigrating across a vast ocean. They therefore are not definitively cut off geographically, socially, or politically from the homeland. Many in fact live symbiotically with the "old country," returning frequently in a kind of "revolving door" pattern. These immigrants are also coming to a land that is not so foreign to them. Geographically this is true if one considers the fact that the vast deserts and mountains and the occasional rivers in the north of Mexico and the southwest United States run north and south, not east and west. There are few *natural* barriers between Mexico and the U.S. More importantly, though, the Mexican immigrant is in the majority of cases coming to a land with which *historically* his Spanish, black, and Indian ancestors had much to do. He is coming to a land where, for instance, Spanish was the first European language spoken and where some of the earliest forms of industry, technology, agriculture, and religion (mining, cattle raising, irrigation, and the Catholic faith) were decidedly Hispanic. The Spanish language and the Catholic faith have been constants in these vast regions of the American southwest since the seventeenth century in the case of New Mexico, Arizona, and Texas, and since the eighteenth century in the case of California.[40]

Hispanic immigrants, Fitzpatrick indicates, are coming at a time of cultural pluralism. The civil rights movements of the 1960s raised the level of awareness in the United States regarding the importance of ethnic identity and pride. New civil rights laws and court decisions defended the rights of minorities such as blacks and Hispanics. United States society appears to have become more tolerant at this time. Horace M. Kallen expressed this new tolerance of diversity in these words:

> The American way is the way of orchestration. As in an orchestra, the different instruments, each with its own characteristic timbre and theme, contribute distinct and recognizable parts of the composition, so in the life and culture of a nation, the different regional, ethnic, occupational, religious and other communities compound their different activities to make up the national spirit. The national spirit is constituted by this union of the different. It is sustained, not by mutual exclusions, nor by the rule of one over others, but by their equality and by the free trade between these different equals in every good thing the community's life and culture produce. . . . The result is a strength and a richness in the arts and sciences which nations of a more homogeneous strain and an imposed culture . . . do not attain.[41]

Cultural pluralism as it is almost euphorically proclaimed by Kallen is to some extent the *initial* experience of many immigrants including the Hispanics. In recent decades that pluralism has been championed more than ever. But historical experience and patterns show something else happening in the long run; namely, the de facto Americanization of ethnic groups. Certainly, the cultural tolerance of the 1960s has made it easier for Hispanics, Asians, and other newcomers to immigrate without experiencing overt conflict. Nevertheless, the data indicates that assimilation continues to be the long-term pattern.[42]

The case of Mexican immigrants has been studied by McLemore and Romo who argue that the traditional pattern of assimilation is being followed by them even though in a slower and less easily apparent manner. They note that the Mexican origin population has become highly urbanized and has moved toward an occupational distribution that is not the same but is approximating that of workers from other groups in the country. The Hispanics are well represented in clerical, craft, service, and transportation occupations. They are also more present in professional, technical, managerial, and administrative occupations than was the case a decade ago. Between 1950 and 1972 the participation of Hispanics in professional occupations rose from 2.1 percent to 5.6 percent.[43]

Another important factor in measuring assimilation is intermarriage between Hispanics of Mexican origin and "outsiders." The studies completed to date reveal that intermarriage is occurring in certain regions faster than in others, but that generally there is an increase. For instance, it is higher in Los Angeles than in South Texas. The rate of exogamous marriage in Los Angeles in 1963 was 40 percent, but in 1971 in Edinburg, Texas, it was 9 percent. A gradual long-term increase in the exogamy rate is verifiable. The rate in San Antonio, Texas, in 1850 was approximately 10 percent; one hundred years later it was 20 percent. In Los Angeles the rate was 17 percent in the period 1924–33 and, as mentioned above, 40 percent in 1963. Studies for California as a whole show that the rate declined from 55 percent in 1962 to 51 percent in 1974. But it is still significantly high. In any case, there is a relatively high rate of intermarriage between Hispanics and other ethnic groups. As one might expect, the literature shows that third generation Hispanics are more likely to marry outside their group than those who were born in Mexico.[44] The traditional three generation pattern of assimilation, then, seems to be verified as well in terms of intermarriage.

There is some departure from the pattern, however, in terms of language retention and political participation. Bilingualism is being fostered by the schools due to pressure from the Hispanic community, federal laws, and more awareness in U.S. society in general regarding the relationship between language and cultural identity and values.[45] Participation by Hispanics in political life, however, is quite low even by the third generation (except in New Mexico).[46] In this the pattern of assimilation is not as clear as in some other historical ethnic groups. In 1950 there were 20 Mexican American legislators in five states; in 1979 there were 82. Since then Mexican Americans have been elected mayors in major cities like San Antonio and Denver, and the influence of Mexican Americans on the presidential elections has been growing.[47] Finally, McLemore and Romo summarize the pattern for Hispanics of Mexican origin indicating that the judgment cannot be made that they are following the *identical* route as previous immigrant groups. Rather, they nuance the interpretation of the data, stating:

Taken altogether, the information presented concerning language use, political success, occupational mobility, and intermarriage may be interpreted as offering general support for the immigrant analogy. To be sure, the continued bilingualism of the Mexican Americans, the probable presence of discrimination against them in employment, the comparative slowness of their political penetration, and the regional variations in their intermarriage rates each depart to some extent from the expected "normal" pattern of assimilation. It seems clear, moreover, that Mexican Americans have chosen not to discard their ethnic heritage. Most of them appear determined to find *a middle way wherein American culture may be added to, rather than substituted for, their own heritage.*[48]

In chapter four McLemore and Romo's understanding of the assimilation pattern of Hispanics of Mexican origin will be discussed in light of its implications for the evangelization of the culture and the liberation that properly flows from that evangelization.

Interpreting the Data

It is important to recognize that there is another approach to the interpretation of the Hispanic presence and the pattern of adaptation and assimilation to the dominant culture. This approach owes much to a Marxist social science perspective. It rejects what is sometimes called the functionalist tendency to stress the interdependence of the patterns and institutions of society and their interaction in maintaining cultural and social unity. Rather, the Marxist concept considers social phenomena in terms of one overarching perspective: namely, an economic perspective—specifically the ownership of the means of production and the class conflict derived from that reality. This approach purports to render a more telling account of the oppressive and conflictual (dialectical) elements of the reality of U.S. Hispanics. It takes for granted the need for change, even radical change, at the structural level. Functionalistic approaches, however, render an account of reality not focused mainly on oppression and conflict. They are congenial to continuity and accept the basic structures of society. At best they contribute to reform, never revolution.

One of the leading U.S. historians of Mexican origin is Rodolfo Acuña. His textbook entitled *Occupied America: The Chicano's Struggle Toward Liberation* is a basic statement of a Marxist historical interpretation of the reality of U.S. Hispanics. Acuña states his thesis in this way:

> As my research progressed, I became convinced that the expe-
> rience of Chicanos in the United States parallels that of other
> Third World peoples who have suffered under the colonialism
> of technologically superior nations. Thus, the thesis of this
> monograph is that Chicanos in the United States are a colo-
> nized people. The conquest of the Mexicans, the occupation
> of their land, and the continued oppression they have faced
> documents this thesis.[49]

Acuña approaches the long history of Hispanics of Mexican origin in terms of the oppression they have experienced under Spain and, more recently, under U.S. hegemony. Some of his concerns and categories are Marxist in a very general way. Undoubtedly he has been influenced by certain Latin American historians who also view the past from a socialist or Marxist perspective. Mixed in with the Marxism is a consid-erable amount of what can be called, for lack of a better expression, "Chicano nationalism," a profound consciousness of the values of Mexi-can American culture and an emphasis on promoting those values and interests against its enemies. Acuña believes that the enemy is Anglo America, and his writings are an effort to demonstrate that thesis.

One of the more systematic efforts to interpret the reality of U.S. Hispanics in terms of Marxist theory is the book *Structures of Depen-dency*, the result of a symposium held at Stanford University in 1971.[50] Dependency theory, as developed by Fernando Henrique Cardoso, Andre Gunder Frank, and other social scientists within a Marxist frame-work, was applied to U.S. Hispanics. The key concepts of dependency as related to U.S. Hispanics are: (1) colonialism, (2) neocolonialism, and (3) internal colonialism. Basically the history and current reality of U.S. Hispanics are viewed in terms of the ongoing history of colonial-ism and capitalist exploitation. The Hispanic people, especially the Mexicans, have provided labor that was and is essential to Spain's and later the United States' voracious need for surplus capital. Both Latin Americans and U.S. minorities are seen as colonized peoples. The Latin Americans are colonized and controlled by the international elites allied to the U.S. power in most of their countries. U.S. Hispanics are colonized by the dominant industrial and technological elites who con-trol politics in the U.S. This latter-day form of economic exploitation is called neocolonialism.[51]

The concept of the internal colony is outlined by Guillermo V. Flores thus:

> We have described internal colonialism as having three essential components: 1.) *economic domination*—which exists as a feature both of (a) the *economic vulnerability* of the individual non-white almost completely dependent on white society and its capitalist social structure for employment and (b) the *structural fragility* of the ghetto or barrio economy which relies totally on white society for its survival; 2.) *racial-cultural domination*—by which the national cultures of these groups have been and are being penetrated and re-shaped to accord with the values and norms of the dominant white society; and 3.) *political and institutional domination* by which racial minorities have been made to *be* and to *feel* powerless within the limits of "legitimate," i.e., socially approved, sources of power such as the electoral system and the government bureaucracy.[52]

One of the main features of the internal colony is racism. It has provided, according to these writers, a justification for the exploitation of nonwhites since the beginning of U.S. history. Analyses of racism in the third world by writers such as Franz Fanon and Albert Memmi are applied to the U.S. Hispanic.[53]

In addition, the classic Marxist understanding of ideology is applied to the Hispanic situation. According to this point of view, the dominant culture promotes "social science" constructs that obscure more than clarify the reality. The schools inculcate an understanding of the world and values that reinforce the status quo. Advertising indoctrinates people with false perceptions and false needs that serve the economic system's need for consumption. And, finally, religion distracts the Hispanics from their true needs and realities, offering salvation in some other world, not this one, and encouraging them to cooperate with their oppressors.[54]

An approach to Hispanic reality from the point of view of Marxist theory emphasizes the ongoing gaps between various income groups, the disparities in access to education, and the lower quality medical care received by U.S. Hispanics and other minorities. It points to the low level of political participation on the part of Hispanics and ongoing instances of discrimination. Tomás Almaguer summarizes the view of Chicano historians and social scientists who share in this Marxist vision:

> . . . Marxism must remain today the most useful and insight-
> ful *method* that can be employed in examining the dynamics of
> oppression in a capitalist society. A materialist interpretation
> of society and the application of the dialectical method, the
> central components of historical materialism, remain unques-
> tionably important tools in analyzing the objective situation of
> oppressed people both inside the United States and through-
> out the Third World.[55]

It is impossible to approach the reality of U.S. Hispanics today
without appreciating the differing points of view taken to that reality.
The vast majority of United States social scientists do not accept Marxist theory. There is a small but significant group of scholars who do.
Some of the scholars in a Marxist tradition are Hispanic themselves and
their interpretation of the reality is very influential on those who seek
sociopolitical and economic change for U.S. Hispanics.

The Marxist approach to the reality of U.S. Hispanics seems to
suffer from the vastness of the data it attempts to explain. While being a
plausible and often compelling interpretation of the negative features of
the Hispanic reality, it frequently draws conclusions that are sweeping
and general. Marxist analysis does not usually deal with the more detailed analyses. It is satisfied with rendering an account of the larger
picture. As a result, it sometimes fails to deal adequately with the
subtleties. For instance, the analyses done in *Structures of Dependency*
deal with the Hispanic in terms of aggregate numbers and fail to distinguish among the various types of Hispanic immigrant. Therefore, it
does not report that the second and third generation are mainstreaming,
are entering into the middle class, and are overcoming some aspects of
socioeconomic and political oppression.

The more functionalistic approach to the reality of the U.S. Hispanic outlined earlier in this chapter stresses the assimilation of Hispanics into U.S. society or mainstreaming, as it is called. This approach
does not highlight the perduring negative features of the Hispanic reality, nor does it posit structural root causes for ongoing discrimination
and injustice that are real features of the reality of Hispanics and other
minorities in the U.S. Many social scientists study discrete phenomena
and show no interest or ability in placing the phenomena in the broader
structural perspective needed to effect change in society. So the Marxists are correct in saying that social science can serve the status quo by
failing to establish causal links between one set of realities and another.
Functionalist social science is suited to the more individualistic, capital-

ist society that tends to absolutize the status quo as the best of all possible worlds.

In 1977 a conference of leading Latin American social scientists was held in Cartagena, Colombia. One of the major concerns was the need to evaluate methodologies used in Latin American social analysis. Considerable dissatisfaction was voiced about limitations in the use of Marxist analysis: (1) the dogmatic tendencies of some investigators; (2) the exclusion of the people being analyzed from the process itself; (3) the failure to recognize the existence of real knowledge among the marginalized and poor who remain more like objects than subjects of the transformative action being promoted.

A more nuanced and sensitive methodology was proposed as a result of this conference. It is called *investigación-acción participativa*. Orlando Fals Borda is one of the leading proponents of this approach. To this writer's knowledge this development in social analysis has yet to be applied to the U.S. Hispanic context. It would seem to be useful for developing a more mature, balanced, and valid interpretation of the Hispanic realities. There seems to be a need to move beyond functionalism and various forms of Marxist analysis in the search for deeper insights.[56]

Respect for the insights of the human sciences and careful analyses of the reality the pastoral agent has at hand, nevertheless, do not automatically lead to appropriate goals and actions. The signs of the times, as the Second Vatican Council puts it, must "be read." Unavoidably that means bringing human intentionality, faith, and ideology to bear on the realities. At some point, then, a vision of God and humanity, an appropriate hermeneutic, a *utopia*, must be applied to even the most "objective" efforts to grasp reality as a first step in the formulation of an effective pastoral praxis.

Both functionalism and Marxist theory are helpful in illuminating features of the reality. Neither approach, however, is totally successful in explaining the data. Preference for one or the other is ultimately determined by one's own ideological convictions. Indeed, that issue— one's ideological convictions—is a recurrent theme among those committed to the service of U.S. Hispanics. It will have to be discussed at greater length in another chapter.

2 | Searching for Roots and Reality

This chapter is an exercise in memory, in searching for the origins of attitudes and interests that today continue to influence Hispanics of Mexican origin in the United States. The synchronic view provided in the first chapter is complemented by a more detailed diachronic view in this one. The importance of taking the time to "remember" the past and to search for the origins of the unique consciousness of a people is stressed by Thomas Groome:

> . . . critical looking back is done as a means toward looking forward. In this sense there is a future interest in the reflection in that the looking back makes way for future action. It is a deliberative and critical asking of—in the light of how and why I am acting—how will I act in the future? Thus the looking back at the genesis and interest is not a contemplative stance toward the past. It is not done out of curiosity. It is a critical looking at the past so that future action *may be freely chosen and be given direction*, rather than allowing the future to be shaped by the ideologies, norms, traditions, etc. of the society that mediates us.[1]

The effective proclamation of the good news and the achievement of the liberation that ensues from that proclamation cannot occur until people are aware of the attitudes, interests, and consciousness that is their historical heritage. Future action will tend to reflect and repeat past action unless people critically appropriate their past and somehow free themselves from it, discerning what the gospel means today. Critical detachment from the past is needed, lest what appears to be new and hopeful in terms of personal and collective options be nothing more than a recycled version of a very old form of inhumanity or oppression.

That is why some time is devoted here to the most important historical periods in the Mexican American past.

An outline of the history of Hispanics of Mexican origin in the United States can be divided into five sections: (1) the pre-Columbian heritage; (2) the Spanish colonial experience; (3) the Spanish border-lands experience; (4) the Mexican national period; (5) the Mexican American period that commenced after the Mexican American War of 1846. Each of these periods is discussed, keeping in mind the attitudes and interests that have flowed from them down to the present.

The World the Spaniards Found:
Pre-Columbian America

The roots of Mexican American culture are found in the indige-nous civilizations that the first Europeans discovered in the New World. At the time of the Spanish conquest there were millions of native Americans in Mesoamerica, the mass of land that unites the North and South American continents. The exact boundaries of the biogeographical unit called Mesoamerica have been disputed by the experts for several decades. In general, however, the southern bound-ary is in Nicaragua and the northern boundary the Pánuco and the Sinaloa rivers in the Mexican state of Sinaloa. This was the home of the Aztec and Mayan civilizations. The majority of Hispanics of Mexican origin in the U.S. today are *mestizos*, racially descended from the union of Spaniards with the indigenous peoples of Mesoamerica.[2]

Who are these indigenous people who have provided a major part of the genetic, racial base and cultural origins of the Mexicans and the Mexican Americans? First of all, they were members of one of the most ancient civilizations that has ever been. Only the civilizations of Egypt, Mesopotamia, the Indus River, and China are as ancient as the Meso-american civilization that the Spaniards found in 1519.

Somewhere around the year 5000 B.C., agriculture made its ap-pearance in Mesoamerica. This made larger and more sophisticated societies possible. From that remote date onward, there is a record of human presence and organization in Mesoamerica. Important foods such as squash, beans, chile, and corn were produced in abundance. Pottery appeared around 2300 B.C. By 1300 B.C., the first great civili-zation of the region emerged—the Olmec—centered in the Gulf of Mexico coast in what today are the states of Veracruz and Tabasco. This civilization is associated with the great archeological sites of Tres Zapotes, La Venta, San Lorenzo, and several others. It was at La

Venta that the first traces of urbanism anywhere in the New World are to be found in the second millennium before Christ. The Olmec civilization continues to be a key civilization for grasping the rich and complex cultures that followed.[3]

Several other cultures succeeded the Olmec in Mesoamerica continuously over a period of more than two thousand years: the Teotihuacan (famous for its ceremonial pyramids), Zapotec, Mayan, Toltec, and finally, the Aztec. Some of these—the Teotihuacan culture, for example—have totally disappeared; others such as the Maya and Zapotec have perdured the harsh centuries of colonization and cultural conflict. Their civilizations were severely diminished by events before, during, and after the Spanish *conquista*. The Aztec was the last indigenous culture to flourish in Mesoamerica.

These mysterious people began to arrive in the Valley of Mexico from the north sometime in the thirteenth century of the current era. They quickly rose to power, showing a remarkable ability to solidify their socio-political, economic, and military hegemony by appropriating the legitimizing cultural and religious symbols of the more ancient peoples they encountered in the central plateau of Mexico, especially in the Valley of Mexico. The Aztecs extended their cultural, commercial, and military ties to remote regions of southern Mexico and Central America. They linked the peoples of the Pacific and Gulf (Atlantic) coasts of the Mexican landmass. The height of Aztec influence in Mesoamerica coincided with the arrival of the Spaniards in the closing decade of the fifteenth and early sixteenth centuries.[4]

This indigenous civilization was complex and manifested the relations toward religion and nature characteristic of more developed societies. Bibliographies on pre-Columbian civilizations are vast. For the purposes of this study, only those features which may have a bearing on the cultural identity of the *mestizos* who find their origins in this civilization can be treated here.

By far the most notable feature of the Mesoamerican world, especially the Aztec or native "Mexican" (from *Mexica*, the name for a particular tribe of Aztecs), was the unequaled importance given religion in every sphere of life. The Aztecs restlessly pursued military and political objectives inspired by their religious ideology. Burr Cartwright Brundage refers specifically to the first Mexicans, the *Mexica* who populated the Valley of México-Tenochtitlan, when he states:

> The history of the *Mexica*—microcosmic of the whole Aztec world—has a lurid quality not often met with in the chronicles of nations. The historian feels that he is looking back

upon a people adrift in a great tempest of their own making. . . . Yet these same *Mexica* were in no sense a heaven-
storming people; they were, on the contrary, most submissive
and melancholy servants of their gods. The perturbations and
egotisms in their political lives were mere enchantments
thrown upon them. In fact they formed a sacred and steadfast
society, disciplined by their belief in the sacrament of human
sacrifice and forever humble under the bans and demands of
gods and demons. The lordship of the heavens was the salient
fact in all their calculations.[5]

The Aztecs lived in ongoing relationship with their gods. They
called themselves the "people of the sun" in honor of the sun god
Huitzilopochtli. Their era was that of the "fifth sun," *quinto sol.* They
believed it their duty to please this god, the Sun, by feeding him human
blood. The Aztecs were convinced that they had been given the divine
task of maintaining the world in existence.

The "people of the Sun" undertook for themselves the mission
of furnishing it with the vital energy found in the precious
liquid that keeps man alive. Sacrifice and ceremonial warfare
to obtain victims for the sacrificial rites were their central
activities, the very core of their personal, social, military, and
national life.[6]

To assure the availability of humans to sacrifice to the sun, the
Aztecs developed a policy of military expansion. They established commercial treaties with the many other tribes of the region and threatened
them with destruction if they did not cooperate by contributing persons
to be sacrificed. They also developed a kind of ritual war called the
"flowery war," the *guerra florida*, whereby the prisoners taken in ritual
combat were to be sacrificed.[7]

The Aztecs were not the only indigenous people in central Mexico.
There were many other groups which did not share the fanatical and
remarkable worldview of the Aztecs. Indeed, the Spaniards took advantage of the hostility the other indigenous peoples felt toward the Aztecs.
Yet characteristic of all the indigenous groups was an orientation toward the worship of many gods and little or no concept of individual
existence apart from the relationship to the powers that brought humanity about and sustained it in being.

There is evidence that the fifteenth century in the Valley of Mexico had been a terrible time of bloodshed and war. The Aztecs of that

period, according to reports available, were overwhelmed with plots, revenges, and violence. The sixteenth century, until the time of the arrival of the Spaniards, was a relatively peaceful period during which a reaction against all the previous violence had set in. Self-control, dignity, compassion for the poor, and a rigid, detailed code of courtesy were being stressed by the *Mexica* elites.

Despite the harshness of human sacrifices, the Aztecs were a profoundly poetic, almost melancholy people. They had exquisite manners. The Aztecs produced a great deal of poetry that revealed a fascination with questions of life and death, the destiny of the human race, and the meaning of life. Their myths were explained in graphic and poetic detail, with ingenious and imaginative efforts to explain the origins of the world and of humanity. They gloried in their elegant language which had developed an abundant literature, both sacred and profane.

The Aztec civilization was brilliant from many points of view. Their art and architecture was highly developed. The cuisine (with the exception of human flesh which they ate!) was considerably more refined than the European cuisine of the period. The mathematical and astronomical discoveries of the Mesoamerican peoples, especially the Mayas, were outstanding. The Aztecs built on those discoveries and developed a sophisticated and accurate calendar of their own—more accurate than the European calendar of the same period.[8]

Efforts to understand Mexico and the Mexican people cannot prescind from the profound cultural bases provided by the indigenous ancestors. The Aztecs and other Mesoamerican peoples enjoyed an advanced civilization, at least in comparison with the nomadic native peoples that the English and French were to encounter more to the north. The Mesoamericans were sedentary and lived in urban centers and small settlements. They also had a great city, even then one of the most populous in the world—México-Tenochtitlan—which the Spaniards correctly likened to the greatest cities of Europe.[9]

The heritage of this ancient civilization was not completely destroyed by the Spaniards even though they attempted to do so. Much of it, in their view, was intimately related to pagan superstition. The central role that human sacrifice had in *Mexica*-Aztec culture itself, as could be expected, tended to turn the Spaniards against the whole culture. The Spaniards quite understandably reacted viscerally and violently against the entire society.[10]

In general, however, it is worth noting that certain traits, both good and bad, in the Mexican character and experience are seen at this early stage in the formation of the *mestizo* people who came about later. Certainly the importance given religion is one of those traits.

In this regard, the great Mexican poet, essayist, and thinker Octavio Paz has provided an insightful interpretation of the underlying presence of Aztec culture in the Mexican. Paz's fascination with Mexican culture has a long history. One of the most influential books ever written on Mexican psychology and culture is his *The Labyrinth of Solitude*, a book inspired by the identity crises of Mexican immigrants of the 1940s in Los Angeles. Since the publication of that book in 1950, Paz continued to reflect on the complex topic of Mexican cultural identity, especially as that identity contrasts and clashes with Anglo American identity. In a dense little book entitled *The Other Mexico*, published in 1970, Paz returned to the theme in *The Labyrinth of Solitude*. In the first book Paz limited himself to the impact of the conquest and subsequent historical eras on "life and thought in Mexico." In the second book he goes into the Aztec experience itself. Therefore it is appropriate to surface Paz's interpretation here since it pertains directly to the question of the relevance of the pre-Columbian period to one's grasp of Mexico, the Mexican, and, by extension, the Mexican American today.[11]

The third chapter in *The Other Mexico* is called "Critique of the Pyramid." The central thesis of this chapter is that underlying the Mexican historical experience and identity is a profound quest for legitimacy and authenticity. The attainment of that legitimacy and authenticity has been repeatedly frustrated. This deep psychic need is rooted in the circumstances that gave rise to the Aztec, specifically the *Mexica*, hegemony in central Mexico from the fourteenth century to the arrival of the Spaniards. The Aztecs built their empire on the *illusion* of being the heirs of the previous Toltec civilization. They consciously appropriated the Toltec myths and rewrote history to make themselves appear to be "civilized" and not the "barbaric" nomads (*Chichimecas*) that up until the thirteenth century they were. It was the gnawing sense of being illegitimate usurpers that promoted the chronic fear they had about Quetzalcóatl's return. Quetzalcóatl was the Toltec god who by a trick played on him by another god, Tezcatlipoca, was exiled "to the East" from where it was prophesied he would return. Many of the Aztecs, especially Emperor Moctezuma, were convinced that Cortés was Quetzalcóatl when the *conquistador* proceeded to march to México-Tenochtitlan from his point of embarkation to the east in Veracruz that fateful year of 1519. The prophecy was that Quetzalcóatl would return in the Aztec year called 1 Acatl—precisely the year of Cortés' arrival! Paz expresses the import of the Spanish arrival and subsequent conquest in this way:

> To Montezuma the arrival of the Spaniards meant, in a way,
> the paying of an old debt, incurred by the Aztecs' sacrilegious

usurpation. Their mingling of religion and politics had served the Aztecs well as a justification of their hegemony, but it became a liability once the Spaniards arrived: the divinity of the latter had the same origin as the purported cosmic mission of the Aztec people. Both were agents of the divine order, representatives and instruments of the fifth sun. The strangest aspect of the situation is that the Spaniards had no inkling of how complex the Indians' attitudes toward them really were. And there was another element that further increased the tragic confusions these errors created: the Spaniards' Indian allies hoped that the fall of México-Tenochtitlán would put an end to the interregnum, the usurpation, and their own vassalage. Perhaps their horrible disillusionment was the cause of their centuries-long passivity: the Spaniards, on making themselves the successors of the Aztecs' rule, also perpetuated their usurpation.[12]

Paz goes on to develop his ideas about the specific contribution of the Aztec experience to subsequent Mexican history. He sees the figure of the Aztec *tlatoani* or sacred leader as archetypical in that history. The Aztec preference for the pyramidal constructions is revelatory of a basic orientation in the culture and society. According to Paz, the *tlatoani* is an impersonal, sacerdotal, and institutional leader. The figures of the viceroy during the colonial period and of the *Señor Presidente* during the republican period are in basic continuity with the Aztec *tlatoani*. The pyramid is the symbol of the fiercely hierarchical orientation of Mexican society that sees in the actions of the *tlatoani*, the leaders, the *jefes*, not only great accomplishments (*hazañas*) but rituals (*ritos*) of an almost sacerdotal and divine character:

> The pyramid is an image of the world; in turn, that image of the world is a projection of human society. . . . To those who inherited the Aztec power, the connection between religious rites and acts of political domination disappears, but . . . the unconscious model of power is still the same: the pyramid and the sacrifice.[13]

The Aztec influence on Mexico, according to Paz, is tellingly demonstrated by the fact that the capital city of that oppressive regime became the name for the entire country. For the other pre-Columbian peoples, the name México-Tenochtitlan evoked the idea of Aztec domination:

> The fact that the whole country was given the name of the city of its oppressors is one of the keys to the history of Mexico, her unwritten, unspoken history. . . . Although the Conquest destroyed the indigenous world and built another and different one on its remains, there is an invisible thread of continuity between the ancient society and the new Spanish order: the thread of domination. That thread has not been broken: the Spanish viceroys and the Mexican presidents are the successors of the Aztec rulers.[14]

Paz believes that there has been a kind of sacred political continuity across the centuries. He analyzes the twentieth century political system of Mexico as a reincarnation of the pyramidal, hierarchical system of domination the Aztecs devised. He sees in the passivity and skepticism regarding political participation the remnant of that initial disillusionment with the Spaniards.

It is possible, then, to discover in the formative pre-Columbian experience, especially the Aztec experience, constitutive elements of Mexican culture. Paz provides a kind of "metahistory," going behind the events to find in the rites and symbols of the Aztec world the seeds of the *mestizo* society that was beginning a long period of gestation.

Specifically, Paz sees in the *tlatoani* a symbol of leadership style that is to perdure in Mexico and among the Mexicans. The Iberian leadership style called *caudillismo* and *caciquismo* will merge in the colonial period with this more ancient root. Given the intimate relationship between this "pyramidal" social and cultural construct and the history of domination among the Mexicans, Paz's metahistory provides a starting point for any historically and culturally grounded discussion of the evangelization and liberation of today's Mexicans and Mexican Americans. Underlying the passing historic ideological enthusiasms—imperialist, democratic, capitalist, Marxist—are deeper currents that reassert themselves like the proverbial snake that sheds its skin. The failure to grasp this dynamic is an important obstacle to liberation.

Paz also points out that the continuity with the Aztec past is seen in religion. He cites the case of the Virgin of Guadalupe, the primary religious *and* national symbol of the Mexicans. The Virgin Mary is believed to have appeared to an Aztec on the site of the ruins of the goddess Tonantzin's temple on the outskirts of México-Tenochtitlan in

1531, not long after the arrival of the Spaniards.[15] This event and powerful myth (in the anthropological sense) is a lasting symbolic expression of Mexican identity over the centuries.

The Spanish Colonial Experience: Forging an Hispanic American Identity

The three hundred years that constitute the colonial experience of Mexico do not generally receive the attention they deserve. The twentieth century has witnessed the dissolution of the once vast colonial world of the European powers. The perspective taken toward the colonial period, whether by some historians or by pastoral agents seeking to acquire a foundation in Mexican American studies, or by Mexicans or Mexican Americans themselves, therefore, generally is quite negative. It emphasizes what was oppressive and unjust in that system.

A consequence of the basically negative understanding of the colonial experience is the tendency to pass it over altogether. Human psychology tends to suppress negative experiences or what are perceived as such. For that reason it is not common to dwell at any great length on the colonial period in assessing the reality and roots of the Mexican and the Mexican American. The failure to do so is the seed of a kind of cultural amnesia whereby the people themselves are deprived of an appreciation of the age-old roots of their attitudes and values and the concrete experiences that gave rise to them. Even worse, the lack of familiarity with the colonial epoch creates a situation whereby the facts can be used in a highly selective manner or even manipulated for political ends. These ends may in themselves be excellent. But manipulation of history by ideology of any sort tends to omit data and complexities required for long-lasting and realistic solutions to the problems.

The long and neglected colonial period provides many important insights into the cultural and religious reality of the people. The *mestizo* not only as a racial type but, more importantly, as a form of humanity, as a culture, literally was forged in this colonial context. Whoever would desire to understand in some small way Mexican society, culture, religion, and values is well advised to dwell at some length on the three centuries of Spanish colonial rule. Whoever is concerned with the fuller life, the evangelization and liberation of Mexicans and Hispanics of Mexican origin in the United States, similarly is well advised to study the salient features of the colonial Mexican experience.

It is impossible, as has been stated before, to do justice to such a rich and varied period as that of colonial New Spain. Once again, the criterion used here is what helps illuminate the reality of the culture and religion of the people today, their attitudes, and lasting interests.[16]

Historians generally have divided the colonial period into three parts: the period of the Conquest from 1519 to 1570; the late sixteenth and seventeenth centuries; and the period of reform and modernization under the Bourbon monarchs in the eighteenth century.

The period of the Conquest was a time of great upheaval. There is no question but that the *mestizo* culture of Mexico finds its origins in a cultural, religious conflict of immense proportions. It was born in physical and spiritual violence. This was the point that Octavio Paz made in his first study of the Mexican character, *El Laberinto de la Soldedad*.[17] The ferocity with which the Spaniards attacked and destroyed the religious bases of indigenous society is well documented. The way of life and values of the native Americans were generally not respected even though from the beginning there were missionaries, bishops, and some public officials who sincerely sought to protect and respect that world which they found so strange and unacceptable. There were outstanding churchmen like Bartolomé de las Casas, Vasco de Quiroga, Pedro de Gante, and Antonio de Valdivieso who fought for the human rights of the indigenous people. They are the originators of a brilliant current of humanistic thinkers, religious leaders, and theologians who in every period of Mexican and, more broadly, Latin American, history have fixed their gaze on the poor and the powerless.[18] The efforts of these men in the field of human rights were complemented by an outstanding school of missionary-ethnographers who were the first to preserve the ancient documents of the indigenous peoples, documents that are the basis for most of today's knowledge of the religion, literature, and customs of these people. The most outstanding of these are Bernardino de Sahagún, Toribio de Benavente (Motolinía), and Alonso de la Veracruz. These devoted missionaries lived in the sixteenth century and are among the first ethnographers of the modern era. Building on the achievement of these missionaries, the eighteenth century Jesuits, especially Francisco Xavier Clavijero, were to contribute to the birth of modern anthropology with their systematic and scientifically oriented view of the indigenous peoples and their languages.[19]

The period of the Conquest, nevertheless, was a negative time in many important respects. Many of the non-Aztec indigenous people were profoundly disillusioned by the failure of the Spaniards to liberate them from the arbitrary, religiously based domination of the *Mexica*. The temples, idols, sacred scriptures, and religious leaders of the native Mexicans were violently suppressed. The people were deeply de-

pressed as the famous, melancholy response of the Aztec elders to the
religious doctrines of the Spanish missionaries dramatically reveals. In
it is seen the extraordinary tactfulness and courtesy of the Aztecs even
in the face of what they considered extermination. The Aztec spokes-
man addresses the Catholic missionaries:

> My Lords, my most esteemed Lords, you have borne many
> hardships to arrive at this land. Here in your presence, we
> contemplate you, we ignorant people.
>
> For the sake of him, our God, we risk our lives. That is
> why we enter dangerous situations. . . . Perhaps it will be to
> our perdition, to our destruction, that we will be taken by all
> this. . . .
>
> You have affirmed that we did not know God, the Lord of
> What is Close and Together, He Who Made Heaven and
> Earth. You affirmed that our gods were not true gods.
>
> What you say is a new (false) concept. Hence we are per-
> turbed, we are deeply distressed. For our forefathers, those
> who have come before us, those who have lived on the earth,
> were not accustomed to speak in such a manner. . . .
>
> It was the doctrine of our ancients that it is precisely for the
> gods that one lives. They made us worthy of life, of living.
> (Through their sacrifice they gave us life.)
>
> And now do you really expect us to destroy this ancient
> standard of life . . . ? Listen, gentlemen, do not do something
> to our people that will lead only to misfortune and will make
> them perish. . . .
>
> Impossible it is for us to be tranquil under these circum-
> stances. Surely we do not believe what you say, we do not
> take it as truth even though we thus offend you.
>
> Now it is enough that we have lost; much has been taken
> from us, and we have been denied our own government.
>
> Do whatever you wish with us. . . . Please let us die. Al-
> low us to perish from the face of the earth. For there is noth-
> ing more to do: our gods are dead.[20]

The first fifty years of the *Conquista* was a bitter time for the
indigenous peoples. The sudden destruction of the gods and the
worldview that rested so solidly on their shoulders led to a malaise
among the first Mexicans. As Franz Fanon and others have documented
in their study of colonialized peoples and slaves, a kind of passive
resistance develops, a slave mentality characterized by outward acquies-

cence and internal resistance. The people learn to maintain two standards of belief and action: that of the oppressors and their own. The civility and respect with which authority is treated is sometimes a defense mechanism. The indigenous people became good at keeping their own counsel. There is good reason to think they became even more reserved after the *Conquista* than had been the case before it.[21]

Virgil Elizondo has studied the initial evangelization of Mexico in *La Morenita: Evangelizer of the Americas*.[22] The central event in this period involved the apparitions of Our Lady of Guadalupe. This event provided an opportunity for the evangelization of the indigenous culture, the inculturation of the Christian faith that the Spanish missionaries themselves had been unable to provide. Unlike the approach taken by the missionaries, the Guadalupe apparitions and the people's reaction represented a positive evolution in religious thought and experience, not a violent rupture. The Guadalupe experience is central, then, to any understanding of Mexican Catholicism today and so it is important to summarize the more salient features of that tradition.

It is said that in December of 1531 an Aztec maiden appeared to a respected Aztec convert to Christianity by the name of Cuauhtlatoatzin, or "he-who-speaks-like-the-eagle" in Nahuatl, the Aztec language. His Christian name was Juan Diego. The maiden appeared on Tepeyac Hill, one of the principal places of sacrifice for the Aztecs and the site of a shrine to Tonantzin, the mother of the gods. This maiden spoke to Juan Diego in Nahuatl. She was dressed in typical Aztec attire. Her conversations with Juan Diego are preserved in a document called the *Nican Mopohua* originally written in Nahuatl and Spanish (two parallel texts) and purporting to be a commentary provided by Juan Diego himself to Antonio Valeriano, an Aztec scribe trained by the Franciscans in both Spanish and Latin.[23]

The conversation between Juan Diego and the Virgin indicates that she identifies herself with the Aztecs and not with the Spaniards. She expresses Christian truths about the redemption in terms palatable to the Aztec. She expresses a deep commitment and concern for the people, especially the poor and powerless. Juan Diego asks for a sign since the bishop is hard pressed to believe that the Virgin is really Mary, the Mother of Jesus. This sign is a *tilma* full of roses that leave the imprint of the Virgin on it. This simple tunic imprinted with the image has been preserved to the present and is currently in the Basilica of Guadalupe in Mexico City—along with Rome, Jerusalem, and Mecca, one of the most visited places of pilgrimage in the world. The image for the indigenous people was an ideogram telling them about a new age inaugurated by the Son that the Virgin brought into the world.

In an otherwise bleak first fifty years of history, the Guadalupe apparitions represent for New Spain a positive and promising development. Many, if not most, of the missionaries, however, resisted the growth of this devotion, identifying it with the former paganism of the native peoples. Slowly over the centuries it was to grow in recognition. Shortly before the Independence period in the eighteenth century, Our Lady of Guadalupe was to emerge as the principal religious and national symbol. The broader implications of this devotion and other expressions of popular religiousness, however, will be treated in chapter four.

One other notable fact about the first fifty years of Spanish rule in New Spain is the decline in the indigenous population. That decline was precipitous. Of the approximately 4.5 million people in central Mexico at the arrival of the Spaniards in 1519, almost 1 million had disappeared by 1570. The decline was to continue into the seventeenth century. Something similar had happened to the native populations of the Caribbean islands first settled by the Spaniards. Disease, epidemics, and mistreatment seem to account for most of this decline.[24]

During the colonial period, especially at the beginning, a serious debate took place between the missionaries and the *conquistadores* regarding the rights of the native peoples. The Laws of Burgos (also known as *Nuevas Leyes*) were enacted in 1542. These laws established the manner in which the indigenous people were to be treated and established the system of taxation that would impact the native people. In general, these laws were an attempt to protect the rights of the people. For instance, it was forbidden that *peninsulares* or native born Spaniards live with the indigenous people. The missionaries realized early on that the contact between the two races was usually harmful to the native peoples who in many respects had customs, habits, and a way of life more in consonance with the gospel than the Spaniards themselves. There were some missionaries, for example, who began to teach that a new and more authentic Christendom, a millennial kingdom, was beginning in the New World due to the relatively wholesome ways of the indigenous people.[25]

Despite the sincere efforts of the missionaries and the good intentions of some of the colonial officials, the first fifty years of Spanish rule was a time of great conflict and hardship. Elizondo has called this the period of the first rejection or *rechazo*—the rejection of the Indian by the Spaniard. The basis for that rejection was the conflict in values seen over a wide range of issues. Elizondo has characterized the conflict schematically as illustrated below.

SPAIN	NATIVE AMERICA

Basis of All Reality

The *individual* soul/spirit One God creates one soul for each individual	The *cosmic community* From the one couple ema- nates everything which is and is sustained in existence through the One spirit/soul

The Person

The individual as an indivisible unity . . . incommunicable	The individual as indivisibly united to the group . . . perfect communi- cability

Knowledge of Reality

The *intellect* knows abstraction-concepts definition-judgments syllogism-conclusions	The *face* sees intuition-symbols inter-relationships emblems-movement hieroglyphic
it is best expressed in the sin- gle concept	it is best expressed through dual symbols "difrasismos"

Truth

Through a process of abstrac- tion, the intellect is capable of obtaining truth and communi- cating it through words.	Only the heart is capable of ob- taining truth. It can never get it through words . . . only through "flower and song: poetry" can it be obtained and communicated.

Time

Not important A logical being . . . only the *now* exists . . . "no hay prisa" we have all the time in the world.	*Most important* It is the "footprints" we have left behind . . . measurable but our actions can stretch it out . . . its measurement is one of the main obsessions.

Space-Earth

Was given to man . . . man has a *right* to claim it for himself . . . to use it for his own good . . . private property of divine right.	Belonged to the gods . . . held as sacred. Man could only use it . . . had to live in harmony with it. Private property sacrilegious and incomprehensible.

All Important Value

"Salvation for my soul" in the hereafter and make a name for oneself	"Salvation of the group" = well-being and preservation of the way of the group in the here and now

Basis for Salvation

One died that all might live	*Many* had to *die* . . . that the *one* might continue to live

Lived-Value

(in America) Missioners: gospel values: poverty charity, great zeal	for all: moderation, respect for others, simplicity, good conduct and continuing the tradition of the ancestors

Greatest Sin

Heresy Apostasy Idolatry	Greed Perversion = turning away from way of elders Disrespect for human life

Death

Time of judgment "eternal rest . . ." "They now sleep . . ." reward and punishment	No concept of judgement . . . Time of *awakening* from the dreamlike existence of this life No reward or punishment, simply a different form of existence.[26]

Elizondo maintains that this experience of cultural conflict is only the first of three. For something similar occurred when the Mexican came into contact with the Anglo American later on. This is the second *rechazo*—the rejection of the Mexican by the Anglo American. The third *rechazo* is the rejection of the Mexican Americans, the children of Mexicans born in the United States, by their Mexican parents. The point is that the first of these negative experiences is found at the very origins of the people. Cultural conflict and rejection are among the principal experiences of the Hispanic of Mexican origin in the United States. That conflict and rejection have a long history.[27]

After 1570 New Spain entered into a relatively quiet time of consolidation. Rigid lines of class distinction solidified with the *peninsulares* or native born Spaniards monopolizing most of the important positions. Then came the *criollos* or the sons and daughters of *peninsulares* born in the New World. Then there were *mestizos* and a baffling number of other racial types who were the product of unions between Indians, blacks, and Spaniards. There were a good number of blacks in Mexico, some of them free, but most were slaves brought to work in the mines. They were at the bottom of these class and racial divisions. The indigenous people were just one notch above them.

During the seventeenth century the rural *hacienda* system took hold of Mexico. This semifeudal system of peonage was to last well into the twentieth century. The Church itself reflected this sharp division based on class and race. Only *peninsulares* and *criollos* were admitted to Orders. The clergy, with few exceptions, were uniformly white and European during the entire colonial period.[28]

The eighteenth century was a time of change for New Spain. The Bourbon dynasty took over in the early part of that century and brought with it certain modernized French notions of government. The rigid ideology of the Hapsburgs as embodied by the austere Philip II went into decline, and modern European ideas and values began to make their presence felt even in the distant colonies. The ideals of the Enlightenment *philosophes* began to filter down to the colonies. It was these ideals that nurtured the class of *criollos* who were to win independence from Spain in 1821. It is this period that gave rise to the more liberal, scientific, modern, and secularistic group of leaders and thinkers that Mexico has had ever since.[29]

It is important to remember that the relationship of the Mexican people to the Church as institution was firmly established during the colonial period. The Church worked hand-in-glove with the state, was actually subservient to the state because of the concessions made by the popes to the Spanish Crown. The *Patronato Real* gave the Spanish government power to name bishops and promulgate ecclesiastical decrees. The Church historically was, for the Mexicans, an institution identified with the status quo, with the prevailing elites and political power system. Even after winning independence from Spain, the Church leadership continued to identify with the European elites and to look with considerable nostalgia upon the old order that had been swept away. It should be noted, however, that important elements of the Church, especially the lower clergy, were sympathetic to emancipation and social change.[30]

Ambivalent attitudes toward the Church as institution, therefore, are part of the historical legacy of Mexicans. For the Church has admitted in the documents of the Puebla Conference in 1979 that it needs to ask forgiveness of the people for certain sins of commission and omission.[31] Mexicans who study the history of their nation at depth begin to find examples of what appears to be a negative role on the part of the Church in their history. Some of that negativity is exaggerated using today's moral standards and awareness to condemn people and institutions of very different periods. Some of it, as the pope suggests, is justified. Nevertheless, the events of the past can be manipulated to make the institutional Church a scapegoat. Protestants, for example, took advantage of the ambiguity of the Church's historical role in Mexico to win converts. Since the Independence period onward, liberals, progressives, and revolutionaries have also used this ambiguity in the Church's record to galvanize sectors of the population on behalf of social change. Anticlericalism coexists in Mexican culture along with a strong, traditional Catholicism. The roots of these seemingly antithetical currents are to be found in Mexico's colonial experience.

Insight into the colonial period can also be gained by contrasting that period with the comparable period in Anglo American history. In this writer's view, not enough has been written about the dramatically diverse starting points of the two cultures. Hispanic America was already well into a period of cultural consolidation when the Anglo American colonies were just beginning. The Spaniards were alone as a colonial power for one century in North America. England was to begin its colonial enterprise in that area a century after Spain. When a great university already existed in Mexico City, for example, the English were establishing relatively small towns on the Atlantic Coast. The intervening century, moreover, was a watershed. The Spaniards were still a feudal and medieval people when they began their colonial labors. The English, in contrast, were well on their way to the development of the more individualistic and democratic ways that were to characterize their North American colonies.[32]

Another important difference between the English and the Spanish colonies is the literacy of the English versus the orality of the Spanish. By the seventeenth century the printing press had made a profound impact on Europe, especially Northern Europe and England. The English settlers were by and large a literate group. This was not the case for the Spanish who never succeeded in making Mexico a predominantly literate country. That has hardly been accomplished even in this century. The North American colonies, on the other hand, were predominantly literate *from the very beginning*.[33] The consequences of that are enormous.

Walter Ong, Milman Parry, and others have developed a school of cultural and literary analysis based on the differences between orality and literacy. The roots of Mexican culture are found in the pre-Columbian and colonial experiences both of which were characterized by orality, the predominance of oral communication over print. Anglo American society was the first in history to be founded by a group of predominantly literate and burgher class persons. Mexican culture continues to this day to be what Ong calls "residually oral," that is, perhaps the majority can read but the peculiar kind of consciousness appropriate to oral society continues to powerfully influence at least the popular, majority culture of the *campesino* and urban working classes. These are precisely the classes which constitute the majority of Mexican immigrants to the United States.[34]

Oral consciousness or orality is characterized by a strong sense of tradition and solidarity. Knowledge in an oral or residually oral culture is communicated through memory, especially through myths, stories, and legends. Oral cultures relate to knowledge as something to be preserved and faithfully passed on to new generations, not as something to be controlled and multiplied. Knowledge does not exist "out there," but rather it is within, inside the person of the respected leader, community person, priest, or elder who speaks it. Knowledge is not communicated through impersonal words that exist coldly on a page. Rather, it is communicated personally from an "interior" to another human "interior." Science and technology cannot flourish in an oral culture because information cannot be retrieved easily. Knowledge cannot be treated with a great deal of objectivity in an oral culture because it is inextricably related to the person who proclaims it. It is always personal and more subjective than objective. Individualism is not enhanced by orality since knowledge in the oral culture is a collective patrimony, never the exclusive confine of a few who can recall it, control it, and use it for their own specialized interests.[35]

Mexican culture from colonial times to the present has exhibited the major characteristics of a residually oral culture. The ongoing popularity of the *corrido*, an ancient ballad form that preserves the important historic moments in the life of the people, is an example of orality. The importance of rhetoric or oratory whereby verbal dexterity is prized and cultivated is another aspect of orality. The popularity of plays on words in Mexican Spanish and the peculiar type of verbal sparring called *albur* which is cultivated by Mexican comedians and by the people themselves is another interesting example of the perdurance of oral communication skills among the Mexicans. The popular music of Mexico, especially the *ranchera* music which preserves traditional attitudes toward life, love, human joys, struggles, and death, is a reflection of an oral culture for which traditional verbal formulas are essential.

The discussion regarding orality also bears directly on a more complex discussion about modernization and secularization. One of the great differences between Mexican culture and North American culture is precisely the degree of modernization undergone by each. Mexico is a much less modernized and secularized country. The reasons for that are found, more than anywhere else, in the historical circumstances of the colonial period. Modernity comes with literacy, and literacy was much less extensive in colonial Mexico than in colonial North America.

The high degree of literacy among the first Anglo Americans led to a situation in which science and technology could flourish. It also contributed to the rise of individualism since literacy frees one from dependence on others in regard to knowledge. Hence democracy becomes more possible.[36]

A careful comparison of the two colonial experiences—the Mexican and the Anglo American—reveals, then, two drastically different starting points that shed light on the cultural, sociopolitical, and religious differences of today's Mexicans, Mexican Americans, and Anglos.

A further aspect of the Mexican colonial period that emerges by comparison with its Anglo American counterpart is the different attitude toward the indigenous peoples. At the root of the Anglo American experience is a marked prejudice against peoples of color. This prejudice led practically to the extermination of the Indians. There never was any significant miscegenation between the English and the Indians of North America, while the Spaniards, in contrast, quickly went about begetting a new *mestizo* race. The Indians of central Mexico were sedentary, whereas those to the north were nomadic hunters. It was easier, consequently, to mingle with sedentary Indians than with the more warlike nomads. But prejudice grounded in racial theories played an important role in the Anglo-Saxon attitude toward peoples of color. Reginald Horsman in *Race and Manifest Destiny* states:

Although the concept of a distinct, superior Anglo-Saxon race, with innate endowments enabling it to achieve a perfection of governmental institutions and world dominance, was a product of the first half of the nineteenth century, the roots of these ideas stretch back at least to the sixteenth and seventeenth centuries. Those Englishmen who settled in America at the beginning of the seventeenth century brought as part of their historical and religious heritage a clearly delineated religious myth of a pure English Anglo-Saxon church, and in the seventeenth and eighteenth centuries they shared with their fellow Englishmen an elaborately developed secular myth of the free nature of Anglo-Saxon political institutions.[37]

In a rather telling summary on historic Anglo-Saxon attitudes toward persons of other races, Senator Benjamin Leigh of Virginia, remarking in 1836 on the impact that emancipation of the black slaves would have on society, states:

It is peculiar to the character of the Anglo-Saxon race of men to which we belong, that it has never been contented to live in the same country with any other distinct race, upon terms of equality; it has, invariably, when placed in that situation, proceeded to exterminate or enslave the other race in some form or other, or, failing in that, to abandon the country.[38]

Hispanic culture never developed a strong and defined racism. Surely it exists in Latin America. Anglo American culture, however, was born and nurtured in it. A comparable racist phenomenon in the Hispanic world was the policy of *pureza de sangre* (purity of blood) that the Hapsburg monarchs pursued. This racism was directed principally against Jews and Moors. It had little impact on Spain's distant colonies. Nor did it interfere in the least with the Spaniards' mingling with the indigenous peoples. *Pureza de sangre* was never raised to the level of an absorbing ideology in the New World as it was in peninsular Spain. The contrast, then, between the Hispanic notion of race and the historic Anglo American one is a fact rooted in the colonial experiences. It is relevant to the understanding of the contemporary relationship between the two cultures, especially the ongoing forms of conflict and misunderstanding that the Mexican American and other Hispanics experience.

The Spanish Borderlands Experience

A third area of special importance is the unique society that developed on the periphery of both the Hispanic and the Anglo American centers of colonial power. In 1921 Herbert Eugene Bolton published a small volume called *The Spanish Borderlands* in which the famous University of California historian attempted to show how the history of Hispanic immigration north from Mexico is one of the most important dynamics in the settlement of what is now the United States. Efforts to understand the origins and destiny of the North American peoples cannot leave out the centuries-old movement of civilization north from Mexico. Bolton argued that it is that movement, together with the dramatic movement westward by Anglo American immigrants, that constitutes the underlying dynamic of U.S. history. He conceived of his borderlands thesis as complementary to the frontier thesis of Frederick Jackson Turner which depicted U.S. history almost exclusively in terms of the movement of Anglo Americans west from the eastern seaboard.[39]

Bolton's pioneering work and that of his students provide a solid basis for historical studies of the first Mexican Americans. However, an important clarification should be made; namely, that most Hispanics of Mexican origin in the U.S. today can trace their history back to Mexico itself, while some can trace it back one, two, or even three centuries to Hispanic outposts in Texas, New Mexico, and California. These are the original Mexican Americans. In Texas they are called *Tejanos*, in New Mexico *Hispanos*, and in California *Californios*. All of them were subjects of New Spain, people of Spanish, Indian, and/or black descent who first settled in the northern outposts of Spain's American empire.

The majority of Hispanics of Mexican origin in the United States today do not trace their ancestry back to these borderlands. Rather, their cultural and historical backgrounds are quite similar to those of Mexicans in Mexico for whom the culture of the central plateau, not that of the northern hinterlands, is normative. Histories of the Mexican American people, nevertheless, sometimes give the impression that the borderlands experience is proper to all Mexican Americans. That is not so due to the ongoing migration north from Mexico that began again in earnest after 1900. These newcomers do not share directly in the background of the *Tejanos*, *Hispanos*, and *Californios* who have deeper roots in what is today U.S. territory than their Mexican distant cousins.[40]

Nevertheless, the discussion of the borderlands theme is important personally for many Mexican Americans as well as for an understanding of the evolution of Mexican American issues. It was on the Spanish borderlands that Anglo Americans and Hispanics first came into sustained contact with each other. This occurred after the Louisiana Purchase of 1803 when, for the first time, the United States acquired a border with the Viceroyalty of New Spain.[41]

The rich history of the borderlands goes back to the sixteenth century, to the Spanish foundation of San Agustín in Florida in 1565, the oldest city in the United States. In the seventeenth and early eighteenth centuries peninsular Spaniards and *criollos* (sons and daughters of Spaniards born in Mexico) settled in Texas and New Mexico. The great cities of Santa Fe, El Paso, and San Antonio find their origins here. In the eighteenth century Spain began its final colonial effort in North America with the foundation of the California missions by the intrepid Mallorcan Fray Junípero Serra.

Carey McWilliams has described the borderlands as "a fan thrust north from Mexico with its tip resting on Santa Fe. Gradually the fan unfolds—eastward to Texas, westward to California—with the ribs . . . of the fan extending northward from the base in Mexico."[42]

What is important to note is the isolation of each settlement. They were separated by vast, uninviting stretches of desert and mountain. Politically they were governed from the interior of Mexico and had little or no contact with each other. This fact is important to note, for it helps explain the special identity that *Tejanos, Hispanos,* and *Californios* have with respect to other Hispanics of Mexican origin whose ancestors migrated more recently. This is only one of several distinctions that must be made in the effort to grasp the differences in identity and attitudes among the various Mexican American groups.

The history of the Spanish borderlands reveals that the Hispanic presence in what is now the United States is not a recent phenomenon. Rather, it confirms Bolton's insight into the specifically Hispanic element that is constitutive of United States history, not an appendage. Unlike other immigrants, Hispanics of Mexican origin are not coming to some "foreign" land; rather, they are continuing the historic movement of people northward, a movement that in many respects can be compared to the similar movement of Anglo Americans eastward. The notion, therefore, that persons of Mexican origin are "aliens" in the American southwest is not justified by the facts. A self-serving, partial, and discriminatory view of U.S. history contributes to the perception of the movement north from Mexico as something foreign, an "invasion," while in point of fact it is one of the central socioeconomic and cultural dynamics of southwestern and western United States history.[43]

An appreciation of the Spanish borderlands view of history is important. It helps explain why the Hispanic of Mexican origin, whether recently immigrated or rooted in the area for centuries, *is unlike any other immigrant in the United States.* In every respect except the strictly juridical, the movement of Hispanics northward is more an internal migration than an immigration. The failure to acknowledge this reality has led to policies that treat Hispanics of Mexican origin as "aliens" and as some kind of unique threat to the integrity of the Anglo American society. Such a view is short-sighted.

The foundations of the society Anglo Americans enjoy in the southwest and west were laid specifically by Hispanics before the Anglo Americans started their migration westward. While the population of these Hispanic hinterlands was relatively small (except in the case of New Mexico), the Hispanic presence was clearly defined by the time the Anglo Americans arrived in Texas, New Mexico, California, and parts of Arizona and Colorado. The current U.S. policy of portraying Mexican immigrants as "aliens" is a self-serving exercise in historical amnesia.

The Mexican National Period

The history of the Mexican nation since it won independence from Spain in 1821 has been exceptionally dramatic and tragic. In the decades that followed independence, the integrity of the nation was repeatedly threatened by factionalism and internal conflicts among federalists, regionalists, centralists, and neomonarchists, as well as by external threats from Spain, England, and France who were plotting to reintroduce colonial rule. The greatest threat to the integrity of the Mexican nation, however, came from the United States which, in what many today believe was an unjust and unwarranted war, took control of almost half of Mexico's national territory as the result of the Treaty of Guadalupe Hidalgo ending the Mexican American War in 1848.[44]

The Mexican people have not forgotten the disaster of the Mexican American War. There is a deep ambiguity among the Mexican people regarding the United States and Anglo American society. That ambiguity has been exacerbated over the decades by repeated intrusions by the United States into Mexican affairs. Mexican immigrants to the U.S., while admiring the economic and social advantages of life in the United States, do not generally have the view of the U.S. as a land of generosity and democratic benevolence. They know enough about history to realize that their nation and people have suffered great losses at the hands of a nation imbued with the ideology of manifest destiny whereby the United States declared itself sovereign over the Americas.

Mexican immigrants have also borne the brunt of considerable abuse by unscrupulous U.S. employers who have desired to have an abundant supply of excellent and inexpensive workers (especially in agriculture) without providing them adequate salaries, living conditions, and human and civil rights. Mexican immigrants have experienced as well various forms of racism and discrimination at the hands of their U.S. neighbors. Consequently, Mexican immigrants do not have as idealistic a concept of the United States as some other immigrant groups may. They have experienced in their own flesh some of the darker and more sinister aspects of United States history. As the people become middle class and assimilate the prevalent worldview, they begin to participate more actively in civic and political affairs. They also begin to experience positive aspects of U.S. society such as equality under law and due process.

One of the more positive experiences of the early period of the Mexican nation was the rise of Benito Juárez, a Zapotec Indian, to the highest office of the land. His life and policies gave expression to a democratic and compassionate current in Mexican political life which the subsequent history of abuse and corruption has not totally erased.

For several decades during the nineteenth century the Mexican state and the Church were involved in conflicts on several fronts. It should not be lost on anyone that the "Father of Mexican Independence," Miguel Hidalgo y Costilla, was a priest defrocked and excommunicated precisely for leading a revolt against the ancient order. When independence was finally won the new Mexican state, like many of the other newly independent Latin American nations, desired to retain the special privileges of the *Patronato Real*. The Holy See desired to take back many of the privileges it had conceded to the Spanish crown. Therein ensued a controversy that resulted in no new bishops being appointed by Rome for a decade.[45] Especially significant was the identification of the Church's hierarchy with Spain and other European monarchies. Some Church leaders were actively involved in bringing the Archduke Maximilian of Austria to establish an empire in Mexico in the 1860s, under the patronage of Napoleon III of France who invaded Mexico. This was one especially dramatic instance of a negative role played by the institutional Church in Mexican history.[46] These negative experiences served well the purposes of intensely anticlerical Mexican political leaders of a liberal, democratic orientation. The image of the Mexican Catholic Church as uniquely identified with the more conservative, classicist, traditionalist, and antimodern forces has not been totally overcome today. The Church's opposition to the Mexican Revolution, especially to the Constitution of 1917, which is the current constitution of the country, for example, has placed the Mexican

Church in a role of opposition to the government. Even though that opposition has been greatly reduced by mutual agreements between Church and state worked out over the years, the more progressive elements of Mexico have used that opposition to feed the now traditional anticlericalism of Mexico's political elites and of many of its intellectuals. They allege that the Church is opposed to the ideals of social justice of the Mexican Revolution of 1910.[47]

The gradual disillusionment of the Mexican people with the Mexican Revolution, and especially with the oligarchic political system under the patronage of the Party of Revolutionary Institutions (PRI), ironically makes the Church's opposition to the Constitution of 1917 and its other difficulties with the state now appear progressive, even prophetic. Moreover, the development of Catholic social doctrine since the late nineteenth century and especially since the Second Vatican Council has significantly impacted the Church in Mexico.[48] Nevertheless, the Church's image as a force in favor of social justice is new and relatively untested in Mexico.

It should not be forgotten that many Mexican Catholics—intensely loyal to the Church and the clergy—engaged the Revolutionary government of Mexico in a partially successful guerrilla war called the *Cristero* uprising. The "soldiers of Christ the King," as they were called, laid down their weapons only when the Vatican and the Mexican bishops asked them to. Many subsequently lost their lives when the central government failed to observe the promised amnesty. The history, therefore, of the institutional Church's involvement in important political events in Mexico is long and ambiguous.[49]

There is reason to think, therefore, that unlike other Hispanic peoples, the Mexicans have a less sanguine view of both revolutionary projects and official Church-sponsored efforts promoting sociopolitical participation and change. That reluctance is the result of the unique historical experiences of the Mexican people throughout their national period. On the one hand, political change within a socialist or Marxist framework has been attempted and found wanting, that is, the fairly radical promises of the Revolution of 1910 formulated in terms of Marxist ideology were systematically broken.[50] On the other hand, the Church's credibility in offering a critique or encouraging some other sociopolitical and economic path has been compromised by the social and political ambiguity of the Church's historic role in Mexican society.

One of the consequences of this broad disillusionment with ideology motivated either by religious or by revolutionary ideals is a deep skepticism by Hispanics of Mexican origin regarding the usefulness and practicality of political participation in general. The historical experience of political abuse, hypocrisy, and corruption by both Church and state in Mexico has made the people cautious about appeals based on what appear to be official ideologies. Moreover, the modern, liberal ideal of separation of Church and state has deeply influenced Mexican Catholics. Luis del Valle describes this concept of privatized religion thus:

> It is not only a matter of the Church having no power with respect to the state, but that religion remains purely an individual matter. Nothing that is religious ought to be involved in what is public. Religion pertains to one's private life. This is the total separation of religious awareness from other domains of life . . . frequently leading to a morally negative judgment about politics. Whoever gets involved in politics necessarily dirties him or herself.[51]

Perhaps the most important aspect of the national period are the economic policies pursued by the Mexican government after World War II. Those policies led to the industrialization and rapid urbanization of the country. During this time Mexico ceased being a primarily rural and agriculturally-based nation to become predominantly urban and industrialized. One of the side-effects of this dramatic change was the depopulation of the countryside and the decline of agricultural productivity. The policy that led to the concentration of huge numbers of migrants in the cities, especially Mexico City, also led to the emigration of millions of Mexicans to the north, to the border cities of Tijuana, Mexicali, and Juarez, and, more importantly, to the United States. The Mexican government's economic development plan and the policies of the transnational corporations did not give priority to labor intensive development but preferred capital intensive approaches. That, combined with the high birth rate, created a situation in which not enough jobs were available for the large number of youthful workers. This was the "push" factor that has made emigration to the United States an important kind of escape valve for domestic tensions due to unemployment and underemployment.[52]

One of the consequences of this rapid change in the Mexican economy in the last forty years is the modernization and secularization of significant sectors of the *campesino* and urban working classes. Not only have they undergone a rapid process of urbanization, but frequently they have moved from a town or *rancho* to a large U.S. city. The change from rural life to urban life is drastic enough in Mexico; it is even more disorienting when the change is from the Mexican countryside to the

U.S. megalopolis. The consequences of that kind of change on a people are profound; in chapter three they will be discussed in terms of their significance for pastoral ministry.

The Mexican American Period: 1848 to the Present

The period immediately after the Mexican American War, the second half of the nineteenth century, was a period of decline for the Mexican presence in the southwestern United States. Millions of Anglo Americans migrated west and quickly became the majority in the entire region except in New Mexico. The history of the contacts between the Anglo settlers and the Hispanic minority is not pleasant. There was considerable abuse, violence, prejudice, and racism exhibited by the Anglo newcomers.[53]

The Spanish language was being spoken less and less. Toward the end of the century there was a fear that it would disappear altogether. Gradually, however, the trend began to reverse itself.[54] After 1910, due to the turmoil of the Mexican Revolution, significant numbers of Mexicans began to move northward once again. The period of the 1920s saw the arrival of tens of thousands of Mexicans, especially to California and Texas. When the Great Depression of the 1930s began, the latent racism of Anglo American society was to show itself again and thousands of Mexican immigrants were rounded up and deported, among them some U.S. citizens.[55]

During World War II, however, the need for agricultural field-workers issued in another period of Mexican migration northward. At this time the *bracero* program began whereby the Mexican and U.S. governments agreed to allow thousands of workers to reside in the U.S. for specified amounts of time and under mutually agreed upon terms. The *bracero* program lasted until 1964. The failure of the agricultural interests to live up to their agreements in terms of salaries, living conditions, and benefits for these workers led to the decision of the Mexican government not to push for the renewal of the programs after 1962.[56]

The workers began to organize under César Chávez who founded the United Farm Workers (UFW) and affiliated it to the powerful American Federation of Labor–Congress of Industrial Organizations (AFL–CIO). The UFW was the first and most successful union of agricultural workers in the U.S. Chávez was successful in winning recognition for the union and in bringing about in California the most comprehensive agricultural labor law in any state of the United States.

The struggle of the union for the rights of farmworkers received national notoriety and Chávez became the most well known and respected Hispanic leader in the country.[57]

Another important development in the history of Mexican immigrants in the U.S. was the outstanding participation of Mexican Americans in World War II. Thousands of Mexican Americans fought for the U.S. in that war with considerable distinction. When they returned home they qualified for veterans' benefits, especially for studies at the college level. These veterans became the first prominent generation of Mexican American leaders and professionals. They founded organizations that are still active, such as the League of United Latin American Citizens (LULAC) and the GI Forum. This generation of leaders was inspired by Chávez' courageous struggle for the farmworkers as well as by the black civil rights movement under the leadership of Martin Luther King, Jr.[58]

In the mid-1960s the Chicano movement arose. The word "Chicano" had been used among the Mexican American people to refer to one of their own. It had almost a pejorative connotation along the lines of "poor, downtrodden Mexican in the U.S." This ambiguous term was selected to be a term of pride just as the word "black" was selected to express pride among people previously known as "Negroes." The Chicano movement lasted to the end of the 1970s when the use of the term began to decline, although it still is used by some. This movement had many features. One was the promotion of pride in the Mexican heritage; another was the promotion of political awareness and participation among the Mexican Americans. This movement coincided with similar ones among blacks, women, Filipinos, Asians, and homosexuals within U.S. society. The Chicano movement was undoubtedly part of a broader liberation and ethnic awareness period in U.S. history. This was the period that saw the rise of affirmative action programs and a more equitable presence of blacks, Hispanics, and other minorities in the professions and in politics.

3 | The Pastoral Reality of Hispanics in California

The previous two chapters provide a broad introduction to the human reality and roots of Hispanics of Mexican origin in California. This chapter now turns specifically to the pastoral reality of these people. This chapter highlights the services and ministries available to Hispanics within the context of Church as Catholic Christians. In the past ten years the expression Hispanic ministry has become the accepted term for the whole range of pastoral services and care provided by the Church. The pastoral care of Hispanics and Hispanic ministry are more or less two ways of referring to the same reality.[1]

In assessing the phenomenon of Hispanic ministry, several areas of Church life need to be considered: (1) the parish; (2) apostolic movements; (3) the basic ecclesial communities (BECs); (4) catechesis and adult education; (5) urban ministries; (6) the care of undocumented immigrants; (7) rural (especially migrant) ministry. It is useful to consider the organizational structures and processes established by the U.S. bishops for the planning, coordination, and networking at the regional and local levels. Finally, the role of the mass media in reaching out with the gospel message to Hispanics is another important aspect of the pastoral reality treated here.

The Meaning of "Pastoral" in the Hispanic Context

The previous chapter, devoted to the historical roots of California's Hispanics, will be helpful here for making a distinction regarding pastoral care. The notion of pastoral care as commonly understood by U.S. Catholics is quite different from the popular notion of pastoral care among Hispanics of Mexican origin. That difference is a consequence of historical and cultural factors. Mexican Catholicism is the result of the clash and gradual assimilation of the medieval and baroque sensibilities of the Spaniards and indigenous religious beliefs and practices. This Catholicism is markedly different from the Catholicism of the United States that was powerfully influenced by Irish Catholicism, French Jansenism, and the Protestant milieu in which it eventually flourished.[2]

Virgilio Elizondo has spoken of the clash of Nordic Catholicism from the eastern seaboard with the vastly different Hispanic Catholicism rising up from the south.[3] José Oscar Beozzo, a Church historian, has pointed out the peculiar characteristics of the evangelization of Latin America that help explain diverse notions of pastoral care between Hispanic and Anglo American Catholics.[4] One especially notable difference is that the Catholicism of Latin America including Mexico was set in place *before* the decrees of the Council of Trent were promulgated. The sense of Catholicism and Church order that was transplanted onto the Latin American continent was fundamentally medieval, although features of the dramatic baroque period were soon to manifest themselves in the preaching, architecture, and religious pageantry promoted by the missioners. These approaches reflected a less centralized and standardized kind of Catholicism than that which the Council of Trent was to embrace and promote in Europe.

The *Patronato Real* gave the Spanish kings the right to promulgate Church decrees or not. Even though the Council of Trent was an event of the mid-sixteenth century, its decrees were not promulgated in Latin America until well into the seventeenth century. Those decrees were important and influenced Hispanic Catholicism, especially the official religious orientation of the bishops and priests in the nineteenth century when the *patronato* began to decline and a persistent process of Romanization commenced. By the nineteenth century the masses of indigenous peoples had been evangelized for two centuries.[5]

The implications of the pre-Tridentine origins of Mexican Catholicism and post-Tridentine orientation of American Catholicism are many. One of them is that the popular devotions of the Mexican people are a curious blend of medieval, baroque, and indigenous practices. The popular religious orientation of North American Catholicism, in contrast, owes much to nineteenth century efforts by Rome to standardize and centralize Church practice and doctrine, especially in the period after Pio Nono and the First Vatican Council. One may recall, for instance, the fact that Rome did not directly appoint bishops in Latin America for three centuries and was able to do so only with difficulty as late as the mid-1850s. The centralizing and standardizing influence of Rome was present in the foundations of Anglo American Catholicism through the Propaganda Fidei, the Roman congregation entrusted with the supervision of Church matters in mission countries. Consequently the original Anglo American ideas of pastoral care and Church practice reflect the more coherent, standard, and centralized norms of nineteenth century Catholicism.[6]

It was only in the nineteenth century, especially through the efforts of the Jesuits and other European-based religious orders, that Rome began to exert steady and direct influence on Church life in Latin America. Upon the ancient, more pluralistic pre-Tridentine Catholicism of the popular masses a more standardized and monolithic version of Catholicism was being impressed. This process made an impact especially on the urban middle class. Its influence on the great rural masses was much less.[7] And it is the great rural masses who have and are immigrating to the United States.

Mexican Catholicism, therefore, has a rootedness and popular character that Anglo American Catholicism is lacking. The absence of such a pronounced popular dimension is the result of a more effective clerical presence in the United States and hence more effective control. The Mexican popular masses remained rural well into the twentieth century. They remained isolated from the great ecclesiastical centers and developed a Catholic faith and practice that was, de facto, less dependent on the priest.

This popular Catholicism has been called by Elizondo and others *religión casera*, "homespun religion."[8] It was inculcated by grandmother and mother and concretized in a whole gamut of popular devotions. This religion merged with civic and social celebrations such as the annual celebration of the town's patron saint.[9] The standard norms for measuring the religious commitment of Catholics in post-Tridentine Catholicism—attendance at Sunday Mass, frequent communion, and involvement in the life of the parish—were not exactly relevant to the majority of Mexican Catholics for most of their history. Not that those things were considered inappropriate or bad; rather, those expressions of Catholicism were simply not available or not valued to the same degree they were in the U.S. Clerical presence was more likely in the urbanized context of the U.S. than in isolated rural settings typical of Mexico until the 1950s.[10]

The nature of this primary form of popular religion among the Mexican people has been expressed by Luis Leñero Otero and Manuel Zubillaga V. in this way:

When we speak of primary religiousness we refer to that kind of belief and sensibility in "what is beyond." This sensibility is transmitted down through history from fathers to children in a way that is, as it were, spontaneous and natural. It is done not so much articulately through words but by the very communication of the parents' attitudes, fears and beliefs about matters that cannot be explained except in terms of a somewhat intuitive faith. These sensibilities are expressed for the most part in the magical and mythic thought about God and whatever is divine—the efficient cause of the mystery of life.

This primary religiousness reveals itself as well in a ritualism and symbolism which lies just under the surface of every liturgical expression of worship toward the divine whether religious, expiatory, contemplative, festive or charismatic.

Finally, there is a manifestation of primary religiousness in human attitudes and behavior regarding the origins and development of the life cycle shared in common by a people. There is a similar manifestation of primary religiousness with regard to the eschatological mystery of life and death and what comes after death—the world of the dead.

In these three dimensions of primary religiousness an unquestionable force appears moving and giving meaning to the everyday life of Mexicans. It does so at a level which is almost always semiconscious or unconscious. This aspect of primary religiousness is frequently ignored or combatted precisely by the priests and by the formal agents of the institutionalized religion. They see in these primitive manifestations the persistence of atavisms, superstitions and trickery that is contrary to a rationalized, dogmatic religion regulated in an organic and institutionalized manner.[11]

Pastoral care for the majority of Mexican Catholics is whatever sustains, nourishes, and promotes their popular Catholicism which is the only Catholicism they know. Leñero and Zubillaga note that historically the clergy *in Mexico* have clashed with the people in the effort to put more order and reason into this mythic, symbolic, and instinctive religiousness. The result, after centuries, seems to be a standoff.[12] A fortiori, the clash between this primary religiousness and the standard norms and procedures of North American Catholicism is greater. It is present in every aspect of the pastoral care of Mexican immigrants and their children in California. The failure to understand it is manifested in the tendency to dismiss the popular religion as "primitive, superstitious," or "alienating." This tendency is the source of great misunderstanding and ineffectiveness in ministering to and with the people.

Popular religious expressions or primary religion as Leñero and Zubillaga call it will be discussed at greater length in chapter four, especially in connection with the phenomenon of secularization. Nevertheless, it is important to mention it here since the failure to understand and value this popular form of religion is a circumstance that helps explain the ineffectiveness of some of the Church's pastoral activity among Hispanics. [13]

The Parish

Any adequate treatment of the pastoral reality of Hispanics in California must begin with a detailed analysis of the parish. Many have noted the peculiar strength and vitality of the parish in the United States. That strength is the result of the special circumstances of Catholics in the U.S. Cardinal Luis Martínez Aponte of San Juan observes:

> The immense vitality of the Church in the U.S. has depended largely on the strength of its parish life. Indeed, the parish is the heart of American Catholicism. The tradition of Latin America has not been the same due largely to the fact that Catholicism is not a minority religion. In the U.S. it has been the parishes that traditionally held together, educated, and sustained the Catholic identity in a non-Catholic environment. Not having this particular concern, Latin Americans are generally less attached to the parish structure. [14]

The parish became a supportive environment for the traditional Catholic immigrant groups. The national parish was an effort, largely successful, to serve the newcomers. It received wide support from the people for more than a century, until after 1945 when many of these groups assimilated and moved away from the narrower ethnic communities in which they had originally huddled. [15] The experience of assimilation was confirmed during World War II in the camaraderie and cooperation of the ethnic groups that fought together on their country's behalf.

Just as the national parish as an instrument of U.S. Catholic Church policy was declining after 1945, the country was experiencing increased immigration from Mexico. Parishes devoted exclusively to the care of these immigrants have continued because the neighborhoods or *barrios* in which they exist are predominantly Hispanic. These are *de facto* national parishes. But the official policy of the bishops after World War II was to discourage the national parish in favor of either the assimilated/Americanized parish or the multiethnic parish where all the groups of whatever culture or language group would ostensibly be served.

Little or nothing has been written on the abandonment of the national parish just when the Hispanic presence was becoming strong in the U.S. Catholic Church. There are undoubtedly pros and cons to the discussion regarding the usefulness of national parishes. One thing seems clear, namely, that the Hispanic community was to some extent deprived of the strong local institutional base that national parishes provided for generations of Catholic ethnics. The policy of trying to integrate the people of whatever ethnic background and language in a territorial parish promoted unity when it succeeded, but also deprived the less assimilated, less influential group (in this case, Hispanics) of the security and clarity that comes from having one's own turf. The question may legitimately be made: Why did the bishops abandon the national parish when they did, and has not the de facto result possibly been the weakening of the Hispanic community's base in the Church?[16]

The rise of the civil rights movement created a situation whereby the maintenance of "separate but equal" ethnic congregations appeared discriminatory and created if nothing else public relations problems for pastors and bishops. In some cases, of course, the maintenance of national parishes was probably due to racial and social class antagonisms. What was lost in this discussion was the practical need of the national parish for the first wave of immigrants.

The revised Code of Canon Law has incorporated the notion of national parish in the broader category of "personal parish" based upon rite, language, nationality, or some other determining factor. Previously it was necessary to petition Rome in order to establish a national parish. Canon 518 of the revised Code now gives the diocesan bishop power to do so. It is ironic that in the case of Hispanics this option, now rendered easier to authorize, has been obscured to some extent by the policy of encouraging all national, language, and ethnic groups to use the territorial parish.[17]

One important factor in regard to the evolution of parish ministry among Hispanics has been the notable absence of Hispanic priests accompanying the immigrants. That absence is the result of the historic shortage of clergy in Mexico and Hispanic American countries after Spain lost its colonies. There simply were not enough priests in Mexico (nor are there even today) to adequately serve the millions who have immigrated over the past five decades.[18] Something similar occurred with the Italian immigrants. At the beginning of their immigration in the second half of the nineteenth century, they had very few priests.

The Holy See, however, became aware of this problem and succeeded in convincing the U.S. bishops of the need to serve the people in their native language and with pastors familiar with the culture.[19]

A factor influencing the ability to find priests adequately prepared to minister to the people was the unpleasant experience some U.S. churchmen had had with the immigrant priests. The image of the Italian priest as problematic, as not a good priest, etc., created ongoing tensions for decades.[20] Gradually, however, the Italians strengthened their position in the Church vis-à-vis the Irish who were the most influential and the first to Americanize. Having priests from the culture itself was very important—some would say essential—in achieving a sufficiently firm base for the particular immigrant group within the total U.S. Church. It is the priest who by reason of his authority in the Church can advocate for the people. Without their priests the people are at a great disadvantage in getting their portion of attention, cooperation, and assistance within the institution.

Difficulties in creating stronger parish communities among Hispanics are due in part to the absence of Hispanic priests who would champion the needs and causes of their people. That absence is due to the lack of priestly vocations among the people whether here in the U.S. or in Mexico. It is also due to ongoing tensions between the local North American clergy and the Hispanic clergy due to different cultural norms and attitudes.[21] The history of Hispanic priests in the U.S. has sometimes not been a happy one. Emblematic of the difficulty is the fate of the first Mexican priests who were serving the Hispanic communities of the southwest and California when this area passed to U.S. control in 1848. They experienced terrible difficulties partly due to the diverse priestly spiritualities and cultures among the Irish and French (rather Jansenistic) clergy of the U.S., on the one hand, and Mexico's nineteenth century diocesan clergy on the other.[22] The Mexican priests did not live in rectories. They were active in social matters and not monastic spiritually. Tensions of this sort have perdured and various efforts to recruit and orient Mexican and Hispanic American clergy for pastoral service in the U.S. continue not without difficulty.[23]

The consequence of the scarcity of Hispanic priests for service in U.S. parishes is that the institutional base for service of the people and continuity from their Mexican experience to their U.S. experience is weakened. And those there are frequently lack influence. This is due largely to their status as newcomers who are unincardinated (do not have all the rights and security of the local clergy), do not speak English well, and are unfamiliar with how the local ecclesial and social systems work. It is estimated that there are nearly 2,000 Hispanic priests in the

U.S. out of a total of 57,000. That means that less than four percent of the clergy is Hispanic, while more than 35 percent of the U.S. Catholic faithful are.

Despite the difficulties in providing priests for the service of Hispanic people, parishes are the main point of contact between the people and the Church as institution. There is considerable diversity among the parishes. That diversity needs to be spelled out in order to realistically grasp the pastoral reality of California Hispanics. Frank Colborn has provided some models of the actual parishes that exist in California and that relate to the Hispanic communities. He calls them (1) the Americanizing parish; (2) the ethnic or national parish; (3) the missionary parish; (4) the divided parish; (5) the integrated parish.[24] No systematic effort has been made to determine the percentages of each type of parish in California. It would be reasonable to assume, however, that sizable numbers could be found for each category except, perhaps, the integrated.

The Americanizing parish is one in which the clergy and frequently the lay leaders have decided that newcomers will have to adapt themselves to the way things have always been done. The usual reason given for this policy is that the newcomers will not advance economically and socially until they learn English and assimilate. The result of such an approach, nevertheless, is that the newcomers do not feel welcome. Another result is that the promotion of assimilation or Americanization is put before evangelization. That does not conform to the Church's stated goals.[25] It sometimes can happen that large, significant numbers of Hispanics are simply ignored. Pastors and others will express surprise when they hear how many Hispanic people live in their parish. Because everything is done in English and there are no other signs of reaching out to the new cultures, the Hispanics draw the obvious conclusion that the parish is not for them.

The lack of service to Hispanics is often due to the lack of appropriate Spanish-speaking ministers. But it is also the result of a semiconscious or conscious policy of Americanization. This leads to situations in which a few parishes equipped to deal with Hispanics become the centers of sacramental services for large numbers of people who do not live in the parish but are forced to go there because their own territorial parish is not offering them anything. For instance, in the diocese of Orange, the second most populous diocese of California, three Hispanic parishes out of a total of fifty-two accounted for almost 20 percent of all the baptisms and weddings in the diocese in the early 1980s.[26] These parishes were functioning like ethnic or national parishes, the second model that Colborn describes.

The ethnic or national parishes of today are not the de jure ones of the last century. They exist de facto especially in rural situations where it would be especially difficult to bring the various ethnic groups together because of cultural and social class disparities. But these ethnic parishes exist in the urban centers as well. Since there are relatively few priests able to speak Spanish and perform the range of pastoral and sacramental services, certain parishes are designated or simply become the centers for Hispanic ministry.[27] These parishes are sometimes characterized by a kind of unspoken policy of doing things as closely as possible to how they were done in Mexico. These parishes become a recognizable haven especially for immigrants, but as could be expected, their children who rapidly Americanize are increasingly uncomfortable in this traditional milieu.[28]

Colborn identifies a third kind of parish at which Hispanic ministry is being provided. He calls it the missionary parish:

> In this parish the staff wishes to serve the needs of the people "where they're at" but has difficulty in doing so because of the cultural differences. For example, everyone on the staff may be Anglo or Mexican American while the majority of the parishioners are Mexican by birth and culture.[29]

The strictly national parishes are frequently entrusted to native Mexican or Hispanic clergy. The missionary parish is often staffed by Anglos or Mexican Americans. Consequently the staff relates to the people in a way similar to missionaries in foreign lands. It takes a long time before the two groups are really comfortable with each other since their perceptions of pastoral care and Church, as well as their cultures, are quite different. In the missionary parish the staff frequently is striving to implement the approaches of Vatican II. The national parish is often unable to introduce much novelty since the sheer numbers of parishioners and sacramental services take up most of the energy.[30]

The fourth type of parish is the divided one. It is divided in the sense that the cultural groups are served in isolation one from the other. A kind of track system is maintained. Sometimes, for instance, for a Thanksgiving Day liturgy or the Mass of Holy Thursday, the people are brought together for bilingual services. By and large, though, two almost parallel parishes are maintained. Indeed, in California it is possible to have three or more parallel parishes functioning physically at the same place—Anglo, Hispanic, Vietnamese, black, Korean, Filipino, Portuguese, and so forth.

The fifth type of parish is the integrated one. This is very difficult to achieve, though not impossible. The presence of large numbers of bilingual Mexican Americans and other Hispanics in many California parishes helps overcome the language barrier. As can be imagined, integrating two groups who do not speak each other's language is a challenge. A great deal of patience is required as the people, clergy, and staff get used to occasional bilingual liturgies, for instance. Communicating with parishioners is complicated by the linguistic and cultural differences. In this situation bilingual persons become important bridge-builders. Unfortunately, there are not as many integrated parishes as one would hope for. The presence of millions of recently arrived immigrants with little knowledge of English tends to reinforce the national and the divided parish models.[31]

The Apostolic Movements

Another influential form of pastoral service and Church organization among Hispanics is the apostolic movement. These movements have at times rivaled the parish as the basic unit or organizational force among Hispanic peoples in Mexico and the United States. Perhaps the most elementary form of apostolic association—the one with the longest history in the Hispanic world—is the *cofradía*. Church historian Jay P. Dolan, speaking about Hispanic Catholics in the American southwest and the lack of priests to serve them, explains that

> . . . religion remained a very central part of the lives of the people. For them the most important religious organization was not the parish, but the religious confraternity, the *cofradía*. Rooted in medieval Spain, *cofradías* were quickly established in the New World. The vital center of religion, they could be found in every *pueblo* in New Mexico and throughout the Southwest. Together with the celebration of religious festivals, they nurtured the religion of the people and helped them to maintain their identity as a people once they became part of the United States.[32]

It should be recalled that the *cofradías* were lay organizations. In the period after the Council of Trent a protracted battle ensued between the *confradías* and parish priests and bishops for effective control of the local Church.[33] The juridical claims of parish and pastor were used to bring the *cofradías* under control. With the exception of New Mexico, *cofradías* in the United States never attained the status they possessed in Mexico and other Latin American countries.[34] The special power of the parish in the United States meant that such organizational units as the *cofradía* would become largely subservient to the parish.

Nevertheless, apostolic movements under the direction of laity continue to hold the second place in terms of the Church involvement with Hispanics in the United States.[35] They do so in a manner somewhat analogous to the *cofradías*. These movements continued to give the laity a forum and a base for influencing the faithful. Relating their energies to the fundamental juridical unit of the parish has continued to be somewhat problematic. By and large, however, the many apostolic movements have been cooperative with the local pastors and submitted themselves to the supervision of the bishops.

Among the Hispanics of Mexican origin there are several apostolic movements that historically have played a prominent role in their Catholic history. The reason for speaking of them here is mainly historical. One is *Acción Católica*. This movement flourished in Mexico in the 1920s and 1930s. Many strong lay leaders emerged from *Acción Católica* during the harsh period of official persecution after the Mexican Revolution of 1910. This laity was inspired by European lay movements that championed the social doctrines of the Church.[36]

Even more influential than *Acción Católica* on the lives of those who participated in it was the *Cristero* movement of the 1920s. This movement was already mentioned in chapter two. It was concentrated in the intensely Catholic heartland of Mexico—the central plateau states of Jalisco, Michoacán, Guanajuato, and Zacatecas. The Cristeros received their name from their devotion to Christ the King to whom they dedicated Mexico by erecting a large statue on a mountaintop called the Cerro del Cubilete in the geographic center of Mexico.

The Cristeros were nothing less than a large guerrilla force organized to protect the clergy who were being exiled, imprisoned, and in some cases killed by the governments of Presidents Alvaro Obregón and Plutarco Elías Calles. Thousands of *campesinos* were killed in defense of the Church. The Cristeros fought the central government to a standstill. Only the decision of the Mexican bishops under pressure from Rome prevented the Cristeros from keeping effective control of significant sections of central Mexico.[37]

The *Cristero* movement is one of the more curious events in the twentieth century history of lay Catholic participation. It antedates other Latin American guerrilla movements by several decades. It was rather successful—militarily speaking. The movement had no sophisticated ideology behind it other than the pursuit of freedom to express one's Catholic faith. There were also social justice concerns underlying their resistance to the Revolution. The people behind it were by and large practicing Catholics, many of them *campesinos*. Unlike most other popular movements in twentieth century Latin America, the Cristeros had no interest whatsoever in Marxist ideology. On the contrary, they viewed the Mexican Revolution's anticlericalism as a byproduct of the Marxist leanings of some of its ideologues. [38]

Even though the movement ceased to exist in the early 1930s after Rome and the Mexican bishops asked the Cristeros to lay down their arms, the memory of the trauma that touched the lives of so many families in central Mexico continues to live among the grandparents of many Mexican immigrants to California. As this is being written the Holy See is planning to beatify Jesuit Father Miguel Agustín Pro who was involved with the Cristeros. Father Pro was executed during the period of the Cristero rebellion by President Calles. Pro can be considered one of many martyrs, most of them, unlike Pro, Mexican *campesinos* who gave their life for what they believed was the love of Christ and the defense of the clergy.

The *Cristero* movement is an example of the seriousness with which the laity took their faith at one crucial moment in history. It is one important chapter in the history of lay participation that needs more study and reflection. Its memory and harsh lessons live on in the mind of a whole generation of Mexican Catholics in California.

The *Adoración Nocturna* is another lay movement that is loosely organized and continues to exist at the parish level. The nocturnal adoration of the Blessed Sacrament is a devotion that has a peculiar appeal to many Mexican Catholics, especially the men. Once a week or once a month, people volunteer to spend time before the Blessed Sacrament. The women do so at hours during the day, and the men during the late and early morning hours. This devotion combines a sense of doing penance or making a sacrifice for God with a deep, eucharistic devotion. In the calm atmosphere of the small village this custom seems to thrive even now in Mexico. The conditions of city life, whether in Mexico or California, make this devotion more problematic. It is mentioned here because it is usually organized and carried out by the laity—usually with men—with only a minimum of presence by the priest. It provides a focus for the community and can contribute to building a mystique of prayer and sacrifice among the people. This devotion counterbalances the negative effects of *machismo*, for it is a noble, almost chivalrous custom that promotes the notion that a serious relationship with God and the external expression of it is not just for

women and the elderly. The potential of *Adoración Nocturna* for providing a much needed mystique appropriate to men may be overlooked
and it deserves more attention by pastoralists.[39]

Another influential lay association at the parish level is the *Asociación Guadalupana*. These associations exist almost everywhere Mexicans are found. In California they are among the oldest parish-based
associations of Hispanics. They usually do not have a central organization beyond the parish. These associations are similar, nevertheless,
from parish to parish in the sense that they all tend to function along the
same lines. The main purpose of the Guadalupanos is to give honor to
Our Lady of Guadalupe. The first responsibility, then, is to prepare for
the appropriate celebration of her day, December 12. At a special Mass
once a month the Guadalupanos march into church wearing a distinctive medal or ribbon and carrying a banner displaying the Guadalupe
image. The special medal is a sign of the commitment the person has
made to serve Our Lady. Only those who have shown a willingness to
work at the service of the parish are normally admitted to the association. Being a Guadalupano is taken very seriously and considered a
great honor and duty.[40]

The Guadalupe associations frequently become exclusively fe-
male, although there are some that are mixed and others that are
exclusively male. Sometimes the Guadalupe association assumes the
character of an elite core. The members can become rather protective
of their influence. In a system that gives much power to the pastor,
the Guadalupe association can become a countervailing force. Intrigue
and cronyism sometimes insinuate themselves into this setting. The
influence of the Guadalupanos can sometimes appear to rival that of
the priests or be used to favor the interests and points of view of the
Guadalupano leaders. In such a situation, pastors feel the need to
exert strong control over the association. This association and others
in the parish milieu can become rather authoritarian. A certain kind of
personalism and ready acceptance of charismatic leaders can make
associations like the Guadalupanos centers of power and influence that
compete with the clergy in a manner reminiscent of the ancient squab-
bles between the *cofradías* and the local priests.

The tendency of lay associations to become centers of lay power
over against that of the clergy in the context of parish is exacerbated in
the Hispanic milieu by the relative lack of democratic experience by the
people. The experience of participation and mutual accountability is
relatively low in the Hispanic context. Consequently there is a certain
amount of pressure on the pastor to assert his authority rather vigor-

ously. Otherwise there may be confusion and personalistic rivalry among the various lay groups.

Cursillos de Cristiandad

The *Cursillo de Cristiandad* has had a profound influence on Hispanic Catholics of Mexican origin ever since its introduction from Spain in the early 1960s. The principal goal of the intense weekend experience is to promote a conversion experience. It frequently succeeds in giving the men and women who participate in it an experience of their faith, of God, of the Church, and of their fellow Christians qualitatively different from their previous experience. The *cursillo* sets in motion a kind of dynamic whereby the person is moved to be more generous in service and more open to further opportunities to serve in the Church and the broader civic community.[41]

The *Cursillos de Cristiandad* continue to take place in Spanish in almost every diocese of California as well as throughout the country. Their success was noted in the English-speaking community and *cursillos* in English are also popular.

In assessing the popularity of *cursillos* the following observations can be made. First, the *cursillos* provide an experience of one's faith that is more personal and relational. It goes beyond the culturally conditioned, ritualistic, habitual faith into which most Hispanics are born. It helps the *cursillista* realize that he or she truly has a personal relationship with God that is verified in one's past, in the manifold ways that God is experienced in his providence, mercy, love, and justice in one's own life. Second, the *cursillo* creates a context in which ordinary people can give testimony to their faith. This testimony does not come exclusively or even mainly from the priest or religious. Rather, it comes from the lay men and women themselves. The power of such testimony to move hearts is incalculable since, unlike the testimony that comes from those who are publicly and permanently consecrated, it has a relevance and appeal grounded on life as it is lived by the laity in the world. Third, the *cursillos* and the follow-up meetings which are called *ultreyas* promote a kind of community, a sense of family, beyond one's own family. This sense of community and family is frequently missing in the parish. In the case of immigrants, this sense of community is even more valuable since they find themselves in a relatively hostile environment most of the time. The parish and especially a *cursillo* group can be a powerful support in such an otherwise hostile milieu. The *cursillo* community, moreover, goes beyond the parish and links the *cursillista* with a broader and humanly richer community than the family parish.

Another consideration that enters into the discussion of the *cursillo* is the role assigned to feelings and devotions by the movement. The style of the *cursillo* is unabashedly affective. Songs and sharing of emotions such as joy, laughter, tears, and sorrow are much in order. In this, the *cursillo* seems to provide a continuity with the religious past of the Mexican people. That religious past is not cerebral, rational, or reflective. It is spontaneous, affective, and demonstrative. It seems that the *cursillo* provides a counterbalance to a more somber, even cold, kind of Catholicism of northern origins that has dominated North American Catholicism. The *cursillo's* appeal, as mentioned before, has not been limited to Hispanics but has been well received by Anglo American Catholics as well.

A critique of the *cursillo* can be made in terms of its alleged failure to take people beyond the stage of emotional conversion. Using Bernard Lonergan's concept of conversion, it can be said that the *cursillos* provide an excellent *beginning* for a deep and lasting Christian conversion by helping the person feel differently about himself or herself and God. But that conversion remains merely affective and is truncated if it does not go beyond feeling to the deeper levels of intellectual, moral, and religious conversion.[42] There appears to be a pattern in this movement as well as in others whereby affective conversion remains the primary focus of the effort. A kind of dependency develops in which those who have undergone the pleasant experience of affective conversion seek to repeat it continually in their *cursillo* activities. In such a situation the less attractive, less emotionally satisfying work of ministry and the hard-headed planning it requires is put off if not prescinded from altogether.

A second criticism of the *cursillo* is similar to that made of almost all apostolic movements, namely, that it does not relate well with the parish needs, that it functions independently without regard for the needs of the parish. The *cursillo* can sometimes set up a dynamic in which the parish with its mundane functions is ignored in favor of the more stimulating and gratifying *cursillo* activities.

A third criticism is that the *cursillistas* sometimes act like an elite. They can give the impression that they alone have truly experienced their faith, that they alone have the secret to a deep relationship with God, to joy, peace, and happiness. Their enthusiasm leads them to sometimes not respect the many spiritualities and spiritual traditions that exist in the Church and the manifold ways that God can work in one's life. While creating an admirable *esprit de corps* they can fall into exclusivism and elitism.

The appeal of the *Cursillos de Cristiandad* has declined somewhat in the 1980s. The plethora of movements such as marriage encounter and the charismatic renewal compete with it to some extent. Similarly, some of the leaders of the Hispanic community in the Church have tended to view the *cursillo* and the other movements as less in tune with the spirit of the Second Vatican Council and the conferences of Medellín and Puebla. There are other, perhaps more appropriate approaches that emphasize not so much individual conversion as solidarity and sociopolitical conversion.

The Charismatic Renewal

Another highly successful movement is the charismatic renewal. In the archdiocese of Los Angeles alone an estimated 60,000 Hispanics, most of Mexican origin, are involved in charismatic prayer groups. The success of the charismatics is due largely to the prominence of affectivity in its style of worship and prayer. Despite the fact that it finds its origins in evangelical Protestantism, the Hispanic people find its warmth and conviviality familiar—familiar to the popular religion they have left behind in Mexico. But now the devotion is no longer focused on the saints, novenas, rosaries, pilgrimages, or other forms of mediation. It is squarely focused on the person of Christ and on the scriptures. It stresses the existential presence of the Holy Spirit in the life of the Christian and communicates for the first time the role of the Holy Spirit in Christian tradition. Without destroying the affectivity of the Hispanic religion, the charismatic renewal focuses practice and belief on essentials. It simplifies and Christianizes the myriad customs and beliefs inherited from the Mexican past by stressing the person of Jesus and the Bible as the norm of Christian life. To some extent, the appeal of fundamentalism to Hispanic Catholics, so much discussed today, is the same appeal as the charismatic renewal.[43]

Like the *cursillo*, the charismatic renewal has always encountered a certain amount of opposition or at least benign neglect from the clergy. The opposition in the case of the charismatics is due to the following factors:

(1) the Protestant-evangelical origins of the movement;
(2) the suspicion that the movement fails to link emotional conversion with the more important intellectual, moral, and religious kinds;

(3) the fact that many clergy and religious are simply not comfortable with a religious style that is unabashedly affective;
(4) the tendency of some groups to function outside the parish context, sometimes in opposition to it;
(5) the fact that some Catholic charismatic groups (and clergy) have converted to Pentecostalism.

The relative absence of priests at charismatic functions provides opportunities for gifted laypersons to assume leadership roles within the charismatic renewal. The style of prayer and the personal sharing that goes on in the prayer meeting provides a context for the giving of testimony about God's presence in ordinary life and the "miraculous," the extraordinary, the grace-filled moments, that are daily occurrences. This testimony is given by the people themselves, not by the clergy and the religious.

The atmosphere of the charismatic prayer group is one of great tolerance and openness in the sense that usually the group is interested in the marginal, the weak, the "little people" who are struggling with great vices, perplexities, and needs. Indeed, it is precisely this openness that sometimes makes the charismatic groups resemble some kind of group therapy. This circumstance contrasts with the frequently closed atmosphere of the parish churches where the impression is conveyed that church is for the strong and the saved, not the weak and the sinners.

The charismatic group, like the fundamentalist sect, offers the people the possibility of finding real fellowship. In the hostile world of urban Anglo America the Hispanic immigrant or the second generation Mexican American or Chicano finds support and hope in a simple, faith-filled interpretation of the gospel.

The leaders of the Catholic charismatic renewal have generally been aware of the critiques that clergy and others can and do make about their activities. Consequently, there is usually considerable attention given to the proper celebration of the eucharist and the other sacraments. Obedience to the decisions of legitimate ecclesial authority is inculcated. Devotion to the Blessed Virgin Mary is promoted as an important way of distinguishing the Catholic charismatic renewal from evangelical sects.

The Basic Ecclesial Community

So far this discussion regarding apostolic movements has considered three types of movements or lay associations. One, the *cofradía*, goes back centuries; others such as *Acción Católica* can be traced to the early decades of this century in Mexico; still others such as the *Cursillo de Cristiandad* and the charismatic renewal sprung up in the period immediately prior to or after the Second Vatican Council.

There is another development in the pastoral care of Hispanics in California, however, the basic ecclesial community (BEC), which merits considerable discussion. The BEC first came into prominence in the 1960s in Brazil. Since that time it has continued to generate a great deal of interest not only in Latin America but in every part of the world. The BEC was singled out by the U.S. bishops in their 1984 pastoral letter on Hispanic ministry:

> Hispanics in the Americas have made few contributions to the church more significant than the *comunidades eclesiales de base*. The small community has appeared on the scene as a ray of hope in dealing with dehumanizing situations that can destroy people and weaken faith. . . . Since these communities are of proven benefit to the church, we highly encourage their development.[44]

The Hispanic Catholic communities of the United States in the wide-ranging national pastoral planning process called the Tercer Encuentro have also singled out the BEC as an especially effective instrument of evangelization.[45] The BEC has been described in several ways. For this discussion the description proposed by the National Federation of Priests' Councils will be used: a process of liberation of persons who in the light of the gospel unite as a community to confront their reality in order to give a creative response.[46]

Interest and enthusiasm about the BEC generally has served as a catalyst for reorienting Hispanic ministry in California and the entire United States. There is a general conviction that the effective pastoral service of Hispanics must give priority to whatever process leads to the creation of viable small communities. This goal, along with the goal of *conscientización* or the raising of socio-political and economic awareness, is happily wedded in the BEC as it is understood and implemented in Latin America.

It should not be forgotten, either, that the BEC has become an approved instrument of evangelization in a relatively short period of time. Pope Paul VI spoke positively of it in *Evangelii Nuntiandi* (1975) as did the Document of Puebla (1979).[47]

Despite the high hopes shared by many pastoral agents regarding the BECs, it is not clear to what extent they have been successfully introduced and sustained as instruments of evangelization among Hispanics in the United States. There is no reliable study available regarding their number and location, their successes, or their limitations.

The literature that is available suggests that the impact of the BEC on the Hispanic communities of California and other places in the U.S. is less than what some may have expected. There is considerable evidence that the charismatic renewal and the *Cursillo de Cristiandad* appeal to the people, reach the people, and are sustained by the people to a much greater degree than the BEC.[48] This is not to say that the BEC is an instrument of evangelization comparable to the charismatic renewal or the *cursillo*. It is a different kind of instrument and therefore cannot be fully compared to other approaches that may have a greater impact quantitatively but may be less effective qualitatively. The BEC is truly promoting a new way of being Church—a rather ambitious project.

There have been several attempts to implant the BEC among Hispanics in California. The most sustained and coherent effort was in the diocese of San Bernardino where in 1981 there existed ninety-nine BECs spread throughout the vast desert expanses of that diocese.[49] Similarly there have been efforts to implant and sustain BECs in other parts of California, notably in the Redwood City area of the archdiocese of San Francisco in the 1970s and in parts of East Los Angeles in the early 1970s. With the exception of the San Bernardino experience, there has not been any report or evaluation of these efforts. A 1987 telephone survey directed to the diocesan directors of Hispanic ministry in California by the present writer indicates that there are very few BECs in California. Information on this question for the rest of the United States in not available, but it does not seem that there are as many ongoing BECs in the U.S. as the commentary on them would indicate.

It is curious, then, that despite the lack of firm data in support of the BECs as an instrument of evangelization in the U.S., they continue to receive the enthusiastic support of Hispanic leaders who participated in the Tercer Encuentro in August of 1985. The U.S. bishops' National Pastoral Plan for Hispanic Ministry gives to the BEC a central place in the carrying out of its goals. Perhaps the continued interest in BECs is due to the general aspiration of the Hispanic leadership that strong units of Christian community be initiated and that those units have as one of their distinctive marks an orientation toward social justice. To some extent, however, it appears that the discourse about BECs reveals a considerable amount of "wishful thinking," that is, hard data demonstrating the existence, development, and spread of such BECs is simply lacking in the U.S. context. Ample evidence of the ongoing success of the BECs is available, however, in many third world situations.

One obvious reason for the limited success of BECs in the U.S. is the highly urban and mobile character of U.S. Hispanics. The stability of rural settings is undoubtedly an important factor in their success in Brazil and other Latin American countries.[50]

However, there is another explanation for the discrepancy between the stated goal of promoting BECs and the relative lack of success in doing so over the past ten to fifteen years in the U.S. The underlying issue is ecclesiological, the existence of diverse and sometimes conflicting models of Church.[51] The institutional strength of the parish in most pastoral contexts in the U.S. makes it extremely difficult to introduce and sustain models of Church that do not clearly reaffirm the parish structure. Unless a great deal of time is devoted to explaining the BEC and showing how it relates to specific parish needs, it remains somewhat alien and even threatening to those committed to building up the parish structure. Even movements with a more subdued or even nonexistent social justice orientation are perceived at times as a threat to the parish structure. A fortiori the BECs are perceived as removing the focus from the parish to small groups meeting in homes and to issues clearly related to the temporal or sociopolitical order. The center of attention is refocused, moreover, on the small community as the basic unit and, in a sense, the justification for the parish, not vice versa.

Parish Renewal: The Case of RENEW

In addition to the efforts to promote the BEC more or less as it has come to the United States from Latin America, there have been several parish renewal programs. These parish renewal programs usually do not focus on the Hispanic community and sometimes have not been actively promoted by the Hispanic leadership at the national, regional, or diocesan levels. One such program is RENEW, developed in the archdiocese of Newark, New Jersey, in the late 1970s.[52] One of the central goals of RENEW is the promotion of small faith-sharing communities within the parish. These small groups that often develop into more serious, lasting communities are formed over the three years that the RENEW program formally functions in a diocese and parish. RENEW is a very ambitious renewal program that attempts to implant a model of Church in the spirit of Vatican II.

Different methods for achieving conversion and renewal have been tried over the years immediately prior to and after Vatican II. RENEW has combined them into a coherent process. There are elements of the *cursillo*, for instance, in the program as well as the reflection and study techniques of the Christian Family Movement (CFM). The emphasis on forming small communities is great and there is a notable emphasis on Catholic social doctrine as well. RENEW appears to be a nuanced and balanced effort to promote renewal gradually, with a balanced pedagogy. The highly developed organizational aspects of the program—the committee structure proposed and the techniques for involving people—seem inspired on a very North American sense of what is practical, efficient, and orderly. A strenuous effort is made to win the explicit backing of the bishops and the local pastors. In this way RENEW avoids the suspicion and fear that all movements coming from outside the parish and diocese can often generate. RENEW constantly tries to relate the renewal to the parish and diocesan structures and thus ameliorates the underlying conflict in models of Church that the promotion of the BEC by itself can sometimes cause.

It must be recognized that the Newark RENEW program has been responsible for the creation of thousands of small faith-sharing groups among Hispanics thoughout the U.S. It can be disputed whether these small groups which meet for the most part in homes are BECs or not. For one thing, they do not usually meet throughout the year, but rather during strong seasons such as Advent and Lent. The emphasis of these small group sessions is given to reflection on life in the light of the scriptures. Programmatically, the RENEW faith-sharing group does not deal with social justice issues initially, nor does it introduce a critique of sociopolitical and economic structures at the outset. Rather, it addresses issues of a more strictly personal and spiritual nature in a manner somewhat reminiscent of the *cursillo* or a spiritual retreat. While emphasis to social justice and structural sin issues is eventually given, it is programmed over the three years, especially in one of the last seasons. The themes being developed in the small group reflection materials are reinforced by similar materials for the Sunday homily and for other devotional and learning experiences within the home and parish. Almost all the materials of the RENEW program have been developed in Spanish.

RENEW has taken place or is taking place in more than seventy dioceses in the United States. Several of these dioceses have significant numbers of Hispanics. In California alone, RENEW has been introduced in two dioceses, Orange and San Diego, where it succeeded in forming scores of small faith-sharing groups. In addition, several parishes throughout California have gone through the RENEW process even without their dioceses doing so. Other dioceses in California are seriously considering entering the process.[53]

The case of RENEW in the diocese of Orange may be illustrative. Before the initiation of RENEW there were no small faith-sharing groups in the diocese. The first season of the three year program saw the creation of one hundred such groups in Spanish. By the end of the program there were more than four hundred and fifty such groups, many of them intending to continue by developing their own materials or using materials furnished by the diocesan office of evangelization.

These results have been repeated in several other dioceses throughout the U.S. In this sense something like the BEC appears to be taking root among U.S. Hispanics even though it has not been recognized as such by some of the Hispanic leaders. In chapter five the BEC and other pastoral approaches will be discussed in terms of their relationship to the concepts of evangelization and liberation as these are understood in the documents of the magisterium today.

Catechesis and Adult Education

One of the more developed aspects of Hispanic ministry are the catechetical programs available in Spanish in every diocese of California. These programs are usually focused on the preparation of children for their first communion in the parishes. A significant number of Hispanic laity, especially women, have volunteered to be catechists. No survey exists giving the number of certified Hispanic catechists in the twelve dioceses of California, but it is conservatively estimated to be in excess of two thousand. Among Hispanics of Mexican origin the reception of first holy communion by children at the age of seven or eight is a matter of high priority. After baptism, providing for the reception of first holy communion is an important reason for contacting their local parish. Many parishes, therefore, have seen the need to train catechists and organize a religious education program in Spanish. The dioceses, through offices of catechetical ministry, provide training and supportive services for the parishes. In addition, there are catechetical congresses in almost every diocese once a year. Workshops in Spanish serve to update the catechists. One of these congresses, the bilingual Religious Education Congress in Anaheim, California, is the largest such event in the United States. Every year it attracts thousands of Hispanic catechists and youth.[54]

The bishops of California have issued guidelines for the certification of catechists and master catechists. This aspect of the pastoral care of Hispanics was one of the first to be organized.[55]

Catechetical ministry is undoubtedly one of the first opportunities many Hispanic laity have to participate at a deeper level in the life of the Church. Training in catechetical ministry has become the first step for many in the formation of a religiously educated Hispanic laity. Some catechists have gone on to become permanent deacons. Others have enrolled in schools of ministry where they can acquire more education in theology. In some cases the catechists have seen the need to obtain a more formal education and have returned to studies to complete high school or college.

One of the limitations of the catechetical programs is the narrow focus on the preparation for the reception of first holy communion. Classes beyond that level are offered, but the size of the classes generally drops off quickly. The incentive to stay in religious education through the years of primary and secondary education is low among the Hispanic people. While the percentage of Hispanics in Catholic elementary and secondary schools has steadily increased through the 1970s and 1980s, to the point where more than 20 percent of Catholic school students in the U.S. are of Hispanic origin, the vast majority of young people, especially the children of recent immigrants, are attending the public schools.[56] Consequently, the majority are receiving only the religious formation that their parents can provide without the aid of catechists, the parish personnel, and so forth.

Over the years there have been many calls for adult education programs. Parish bible study programs in Spanish are quite common throughout California. Less common are classes in other areas of theology. Undoubtedly the emphasis across the state is given to the religious education of children. There are those who maintain that such emphasis is ineffective, since whatever good is done with the children in the parish religious education program is undone back at home or at school.[57] There is also the conviction, especially strong in the Anglo American milieu, that the emphasis on the formation of adults is essential if the traditional, customary faith of Catholics is to be lived intelligently and responsibly in the world today. Given the importance that Mexican and other forms of Hispanic Catholicism give to certain customary celebrations of the sacraments such as first communion, it is possible to "capture" a large number of children if attendance at religious education classes is made compulsory in order to receive the sacrament.

Other teachable moments for catechesis are the *quinceañera* and the marriage preparation. Certain times of the year such as Advent and Lent (with its "missions"), the period before and after Christmas (with the Posadas), the *acostando* (laying the infant Jesus down in his manger), or the *levantando* (picking him up from his manger), the Feast of Epiphany, the Feast of Our Lady of Guadalupe, and Holy Week are special occasions that can be seized to do some ongoing religious formation.[58]

Opportunities for systematic formation of Hispanic adults in their faith are difficult to find. Much can be done, however, within the context of parish by appealing to the popular religious devotions, feasts, and customs of the people. In the period after Vatican II there has been a marked decline in devotions in the mainstream U.S. Church. The celebration of the eucharist has tended to monopolize the prayer of the parish community. While in no way denigrating the centrality of the eucharist in the Church's life of prayer, more recognition must be given, especially in the case of traditional cultures such as the Hispanic, to the role of extraeucharistic ritual, color, custom, and celebration (*fiesta*) in nurturing the faith.

Catechetical programs for children and formation programs for catechists have tried to build on the popular religious orientations of the Hispanics. More thought needs to be given, however, to the content of instruction and learning situations that can be generated in the context of popular religious celebrations. The failure to take advantage of these situations contributes to little or no movement in the renewal of the Hispanic community. For instance, the majority of Hispanics in the U.S. (55 percent), according to the study of González and LaVelle in 1985, *had never heard of the Second Vatican Council!*[59] That fact alone indicates how limited the opportunities have been to reach the people with even the most basic messages, let alone engage them in any prolonged religious formation.

In addition to the formation of catechists and catechesis of children, there has been some formation of evangelizers. Guidelines for the certification of evangelizers have been issued by the bishops of California.[60] The evangelizer is understood as the person involved in outreach especially to marginal groups, the unchurched, and the forgotten. The exact relationship between the function of the evangelizer and the catechist has not been spelled out clearly. Specific ongoing activities for the evangelizers being trained are in the process of development. In some dioceses there is a move to carry out the formation of catechists and evangelizers in schools of ministry. There is also the possibility of doing the formation of permanent deacons in Spanish within these schools of ministry.

The permanent diaconate has attracted scores of Hispanic men since its restoration after Vatican II. Sixty percent of all permanent deacons in the world are found in the United States. Approximately 13 percent of them in the U.S. are Hispanic, a much higher percentage than that for priests which is less than four percent.[61] There has been some difficulty with the permanent diaconate in that the clergy are not always ready to work with the deacon. The deacons continue to struggle with their identity within the Church.

Ministering to Urban Immigrants

As the analysis in chapter one indicates, the vast majority of Hispanics in California and throughout the United States live in urban centers. Since the early part of this century the number of Mexican immigrants has steadily increased. In recent years due to war and economic hardship, Central Americans have begun to arrive by the tens of thousands. Consequently the local churches have felt the need to provide services in Spanish more than ever before. The number of pastoral services such as Mass and confessions offered in Spanish has risen dramatically. For instance, in 1975 there were nine parishes offering Mass in Spanish in Orange County; in 1986 there were twenty-four.[62] These services are sometimes offered in parishes that are more or less entirely Hispanic, but more frequently they are found in mixed parishes.

The fact that Hispanic immigrants frequently do not have their own Hispanic priests and that the national parish is not the preferred type of parish for them today are circumstances that point to the difference between the Hispanic experience of the U.S. Church and that of earlier Catholic national/ethnic groups. These facts perhaps are the most relevant for an understanding of the ongoing tensions and conflicts experienced in Hispanic ministry today.

There are several tension-filled issues that arise in the context of urban ministry to Hispanics. One is the question regarding popular religious practices of the Hispanics—the contrast between the customs and pastoral norms of the U.S. Church and those of Mexico. In several areas the approaches are quite distinct and can be the source of considerable misunderstanding and/or conflict between the priests, pastoral agents, and the laity. One of the principal differences has already been alluded to, namely, the fact that the popular Catholicism of Mexico is centered on the performance of certain customs, the celebration of certain feasts, and the adherence to a certain culturally defined value system. The Catholicism of the U.S. parish is quite different. Generally it revolves around the parish church and stresses personal preparation of the laity for the reception of the sacraments. Participation in the life of the parish is based on meeting certain requirements such as providing financial support in the form of donations made directly to the church in weekly envelopes assigned to the family or parishioner, attendance at classes that prepare parents and godparents to baptize their infants, attendance at classes that prepare a couple for Christian marriage, and commitment to send the children to catechetical instructions, etc. The underlying concern of this approach is that the faith be personally appropriated and, insofar as possible, rationally understood. To some extent, middle-class Hispanics will have little or no difficulty with this orientation since Catholicism in the more affluent urban centers of Mexico has something in common with U.S. Catholicism. The rurally based Catholicism of the working class or *campesino* Mexican finds most of the criteria of the urban, middle-class Anglo American Catholic Church quite foreign. Mexican Catholicism is popular and "cultural," embedded in attitudes and customs that are of a pattern with their rural past.[63]

There are several customs that continue to cause difficulty since they reflect social patterns and values distinct from those of the North American Church. One is the *quinceañera* or fifteenth birthday celebration for young ladies. It is given an importance that often appears exaggerated in the eyes of Anglo Americans. The fiesta and other preparations for it are given the same or more importance than the sacrament of confirmation or perhaps even the first communion. The *quinceañera* can sometimes resemble an elegant wedding. In a Church where the distribution of the sacraments takes the major portion of time, many priests are reluctant to add another one. Sometimes when the young lady is found not to have been confirmed, the condition is put that first she receive confirmation—a process that in most U.S. parishes takes two years. This is disturbing to the young lady and her parents who have difficulty understanding how something as important as the fifteenth birthday celebration should not be celebrated with a special Mass, party, and dinner. Mexican society is still nonmodern in certain respects. One of the manifestations of that is the importance given to rites of passage, to a puberty rite like the *quinceañera* that reaffirms the family affiliation.

In the criteria for each of the sacraments there arise differences between the U.S. manner and the more traditional Mexican approach. Sometimes the people are unaware that requirements and approaches have changed even in Mexico, since they have not had direct contact with the Church there for years, or they come from parts of Mexico that are still quite traditional, where certain Vatican II reforms have barely been implemented. An example would be the insistence on maintaining the *compadrazco* or godfather system. In selecting the godfather of one's child, one makes an important alliance and literally extends one's family. The priests of the U.S. are not generally concerned about that. They insist, rather, on the parents' preparation to assume the responsibility of being a Catholic for their child and the responsibility of the godparents to aid the parents. Similarly, the priest will insist that the basic conditions for raising the child as a Catholic be verified—for instance, that the couple be married in the Church since that is a sign of their commitment to be good Catholics. This requirement clashes with the people's deeply felt conviction that baptism is a humanizing rite whereby the infant becomes a person in a way he or she was not before.

For a priest to deny baptism to a child because of something the parents did or did not do (e.g., marry in the Church) seems punitive and uncalled for. In the circumstances of poverty and migration it seems unrealistic to be insisting on certain things that in themselves are good but which are increasingly less possible. Instead of being happy that the people have come to the Church, the priests are perceived as punishing parents for doing what they think is their duty. Large numbers of Mexican Catholics continue to believe that something bad will happen to infants who die without baptism. They simply continue to affirm a belief that was instilled in them centuries ago by the missioners.[64] Many U.S. priests, however, have little or no background in the people's popular Catholicism. Consequently they appear to belittle it, misunderstand it, or simply ignore it.

In the area of marriage there are many tensions. For one thing, the U.S. idea of marriage conceives of what is happening in terms of two independent persons coming together to form a lifelong union. The notion of independent persons is foreign to many Mexicans. Marriage occurs in the context of families. They are part of it from the beginning and are expected to be part of it to the end. The roles and values of married life are not discovered. Rather, they are already determined. They are known. The question is putting them into practice. For instance, the husband should be hard-working; the woman a strong support, dependent on her husband, centered on her children. The vows of marriage psychologically exclude the possibility of divorce. What it is to be married is somehow known; it is embedded in the ideals and images of life that have been passed on from generation to generation.[65] Marriage in the U.S. Catholic Church, on the other hand, is influenced by contemporary theology, especially the notion that the end of marriage is the happiness of the spouses as much as the procreation of children and the fulfillment of the traditional roles. It is also influenced by new insights and discoveries regarding human psychology.[66]

The difference in attitude toward marriage is also seen in the way marriage problems are handled. The sense of marriage in the Church being a lifelong commitment is very strong among the Mexican people. It is difficult for them to admit that psychological factors have much to do with maintaining the marriage bond. Whatever be the circumstances that led to a Catholic marriage, once that marriage is properly performed there is really little or nothing that can be done to undo it. The notion of psychological development and maturation is not viewed as particularly relevant. Consequently, when marriage difficulties do arise, the couple—especially the woman—seems to have no real option other than to bear with the difficulty.

The priest trained in the United States frequently will approach the marriage problem in terms of interpersonal dynamics and psychological factors—freedom, maturity—and in terms of the impact of the problem on the individual, while the Mexican couple will approach it as a matter intimately impacting their identity as human beings and Catholics. The couple's main concern is the effect which separation and divorce will have on family and friends. Being separated or divorced from one's spouse is a *disaster*, a failure of monumental proportions. For these reasons the pastoral approach commonly used in the United States in dealing with marriage problems, separation, divorce, and annulment frequently clashes with the mindset of the people. For instance, it appears at times that the North American priest is less concerned with the preservation of the marriage bond and that the idea of a lifelong commitment is somehow taken less seriously. This perhaps is due to the priest's awareness of developmental psychology and the tendency to view the person as a unique individual somehow apart from family and culture.

A consequence of this distinctive understanding of marriage is the fact that marriage tribunals in California receive relatively few annulment petitions from Hispanic couples. There are dioceses where a large percentage of all Church weddings are among Hispanics—perhaps 30 to 40 percent. This has been the case for many years and the number continues to rise. Yet the number of annulment petitions among Hispanics remains quite low.[67] Naturally, one explanation is the general unfamiliarity of the Hispanic people with the new annulment procedures and the fact that the divorce rate among Hispanics is less than that for the general population. Another is their reluctance to get involved in any processes at all since a good percentage of the population consists of undocumented immigrants who are afraid of being detected. Frequently the priests who work with the Hispanic community are less inclined to explain the possibility of annulling a marriage precisely because they sense that the concept is foreign to the people and not as viable an option as it might be in the case of Anglo Americans. They also sometimes think that the red tape would be prohibitive for Hispanics, too time consuming, or the financial cost too great.

The Catholic Church in California, despite all the differences mentioned, does represent a familiar institution for the first generation of immigrants. It is one of the few with which they can identify in an otherwise inhospitable land. Consequently the U.S. Catholic Church once again has a special role to play in the ongoing and often conflictual process of cultural adaptation. The Hispanic peoples who come to the Church for assistance, for spiritual and religious inspiration, are in need of support and understanding. The effort to impose Church rules and maintain pastoral norms regarding sacraments can interfere with the basic need to project an inviting image. It is the failure to do so that explains in great part the success that fundamentalist sects are having in proselytizing the people. The joyful, accepting environment of fellowship promoted by these sects stands in sharp contrast to the colder and complicated religion seemingly being projected by the Catholics.

Efforts to promote conformity in requirements for the reception of the sacraments without providing a deeper conversion experience are very ineffective. The norms and expectations regarding the sacraments and participation in Church life in the United States are different from those of Mexico. To some extent explanation and education can be helpful. This must be done in Spanish. Even more necessary, however, are conversion experiences. Many of the Hispanics of Mexican origin in California have never undergone a conversion experience whereby the faith they have received from their ancestors, from their culture, becomes self-appropriated and personal. The imposition of norms for membership and participation in the Church without this kind of self-appropriation does violence to the people. Consequently, it seems fitting that the norms be gently applied or perhaps applied in a different manner or, in some cases, not followed at all.[68]

What has been said so far may explain the fact that sometimes the norms for baptism, the requirements for first holy communion and for marriage, are sometimes applied in the Hispanic parish in a more lenient manner than in the Anglo parish. In those cases where the Hispanic people have experienced a deeper conversion experience through a *cursillo*, in a prayer group or small faith-sharing community, then it becomes more possible to apply consistent norms based on a solid theological understanding of the Church, the sacraments, and the lay person's role in the world and the Church. What appears to be lacking in the pastoral approach of some pastoral agents is a sound pedagogy that takes as its point of departure the people *as they are*, rather than norms based on how they *ought to be*.

The inability or failure on the part of pastoral agents to make these distinctions is the source of the feeling of rejection and/or misunderstanding that the Hispanic people sometimes experience as they approach the Church in the United States.

Undocumented Immigrants

One important theme relevant to the question of the pastoral care of Hispanics in the urban context is the situation of undocumented immigrants. In chapter one it was learned that approximately half of the Hispanics in California are native-born Mexicans or their minor children. This group is estimated to number between two and three million.[69] The majority of these are undocumented. Consequently, the Church's pastoral mission is seriously affected by this circumstance. For one thing, the undocumented experience ongoing anxiety and fear. They can be deported at any time. Since the 1960s when the phenomenon of illegal immigration first became a major political issue in the United States, government has followed a policy of sporadic enforcement of the law. This enforcement has taken the form of raids in factories and on agricultural fields. There are also highway checkpoints and occasional inspections of train depots and airports. In order to find work, people must provide social security cards. Since the mid-1970s it has been impossible to obtain a social security card without proving that one is in the country legally. Consequently the production of false social security cards is a lucrative business. Since the people have to work in order to live, they sometimes are forced to obtain false documents and lie to their employers. The Immigration and Naturalization Service (INS) and the Border Patrol also engage in other enforcement activities such as stopping people at bus stops and on the street. They have been known to raid restaurants and places of business.[70]

As can well be imagined, life in such an insecure milieu is characterized by ongoing anxiety and fear. It creates a situation in which the immigrants do not participate in society at all. They live a kind of underground existence. They sometimes will not give their name or address; they will not go out at night; they will not join associations at their child's school or at church. When they are ill they even avoid getting medical care for as long as possible, especially if they do not have medical insurance and may have to apply for some form of financial assistance from the state. Generally they use public services less than other groups. They pay more in taxes than they use in public services. The main exception to this would be the service of the public schools where they do have many children enrolled.

For twenty years the undocumented have lived under these conditions. They have become a kind of sub-class living in fear and unable to plan ahead with any degree of confidence. If they have to leave the United States and return to Mexico for some reason—a family emergency, for example—or if they are picked up in an INS raid, they face the expensive, dangerous, and humiliating prospect of having to return through the services of a smuggler called a *coyote*. For a fee of $300 to $450 or more, they are led across the international border and through the desert or mountains where someone is waiting to pick them up at a rendezvous point. They may be caught again and deported again. After a second or third attempt they may finally get back to their spouse, children, and friends in California. For the past twenty years the INS has maintained a bus system from Los Angeles to the Mexican border. Daily it deports hundreds of Mexicans across the border. Those who are caught two or three times are sometimes punished by being placed for a week or two in one of the detention centers or prisons. Usually the people avoid this by never carrying real identity papers on them and by using a fictitious name if they are caught. In this way there will not be a record against them should they get caught again.[71]

As one can well imagine, the cumulative effect of this underworld existence over such a long period of time is very negative. There are young people who arrived in the United States as infants and are now completing high school or already in college who have never obtained legalization. They and their families have had to live with the weight of this clandestine status for years; some lies have had to be told, and chronic fear and worry has been their lot for decades.

In 1986 the U.S. Congress passed the Immigration Reform Act, signed into law by President Reagan. Many are involved in legalization through the services of Church agencies. It remains unclear how many of the approximately two million undocumented immigrants in California will eventually be legalized. The excessively harsh requirements of the new law and inflexible ways of interpreting other requirements casts doubt on whether this new law will truly legalize even a half of those who supposedly were to qualify. In any event, more immigrants continue to arrive. So the prospect of eliminating the problem of illegal immigration is nonexistent, given the ongoing economic crisis of Mexico and other Latin American countries.

The illegal status of so many Hispanics of Mexican origin in California has a negative effect on their participation in the Church. As already mentioned, they are afraid of being detected by immigration officials and so they avoid giving their names and addresses—sometimes even when they are asked for them at the church. The uncertainty about their status—how long they will continue to live in the U.S.—militates against the people making long-term commitments. Their economic precariousness means that they are quite mobile. For instance, a study undertaken at one *barrio* church in Santa Ana, California, revealed that one half of the congregation of that parish moved away in one year, that is, a 50 percent turnover.[72] Pastoral planning based on the notion of long-range goals and objectives is seriously impaired by the people's mobility and the pressures placed on them. Difficulties experienced by parishes and pastoral agents in organizing and forming the people are explained in great part by the immigrants' condition—the socioeconomic and political marginalization and mobility that characterize their situation.

In regard to the pastoral service of undocumented immigrants, the Church has shown considerable sensitivity and concern. The bishops of the United States have maintained an Office of Immigration and Refugee Services at their headquarters at the United States Catholic Conference (USCC) in Washington, D.C. There is also a very active Committee on Migration supported by the National Conference of Catholic Bishops. The Scalabrini Missionaries on Staten Island in New York have the most productive center on migration studies under Catholic auspices in the U.S. They publish *Migration World*, a scholarly journal that systematically and sympathetically exposes the facts about worldwide migrations. Every diocese of California is providing immigration and naturalization services and is one of the major agencies if not *the* major agency, involved in the massive legalization of those who have resided in the U.S. since January of 1982, in accordance with the new immigration law. This activity is bringing the Church agencies into closer contact with the Hispanic community.[73]

Not all the facts are yet available regarding the efforts of Catholic agencies to provide legalization services. Such assistance seemed logical and appropriate given the high level of confidence Hispanics have in the Church. The record, however, seems to be indicating that the agencies were sometimes ill-prepared to do this work and consequently may have disappointed some people. More perplexing is the perception—correct or incorrect—that the Church was functioning as an agent of the Immigration and Naturalization Service. This perception may reduce the credibility of the Church among Hispanics. It was risky for Church leadership to get involved in the application of a law that increasingly is being viewed as prejudicial to the majority of U.S. Hispanics even though it did provide legal status for a minority of them.

One major issue, then, related to the question of the pastoral care of Hispanics within an urban environment is the need for an accepting, affirming community to receive the people. The parish environment, especially when the parish is predominantly concerned with serving Anglo American Catholics, can be less than inviting. The austere, sometimes even somber, spirit of the Roman liturgy as it is celebrated in North American churches can leave the people cold. Even more, the parish can at times project the image of being a place for the saved, for the well-washed, for those who are "in control." The Hispanic people who are largely poor and frequently beset with difficulties of all sorts may find it difficult to relate to a North American church which has transcended its immigrant origins. Even physically, the Hispanic people sometimes find the Anglo American church cold and uninviting.[74]

The clergy found in many North American parishes are more educated than ever before, but their education frequently reflects the demythologizing and rationalistic currents characteristic of a modern, secularized, urban society. A considerable amount of tension exists, then, between the mentality of the Hispanic peoples, especially the first generation immigrants, and the clergy who serve them in urban centers. The people's "wavelength" is simply different from that of many clergymen and pastoral agents they will find at their local parish.[75]

Rural Hispanic Ministry

California has the single largest population of migrant workers in the United States. There is a perceptible pattern of migration of these families which, according to the California Department of Education (Migrant Education Program) involves at least 150,000 Hispanics. Their movement in search of work takes them from the Imperial Valley on the Mexican border north to the San Joaquin and Salinas Valleys. Many also move farther north, as far as Oregon, Washington, and even Alaska in their search for work. Many but certainly not all of these migrants are undocumented. Their children, however, are frequently U.S. citizens.[76]

Over the years some discussions have taken place regarding the need to develop a coherent ministry among this significant population. But little has been done to evolve the regional, interdiocesan program which the reality requires.

In addition to the difficulty inherent in organizing a regional pastoral program, there is another circumstance that helps explain the lack of a rural, migrant worker ministry. It has to do with the energies that have been invested in recent years in the struggle for the social and political rights of farm laborers. For many years there has been a "migrant labor ministry." This ministry has been closely allied with the labor union itself and has had the primary task of obtaining and maintaining the support of Catholic, Protestant, and ecumenical groups for the workers' human rights struggle. It has been difficult to move beyond this goal in order to address the admittedly less urgent but still important needs of a pastoral nature. Due to constant pressure from well-financed agricultural interests, the social and political situation of the workers continues to be fragile despite the historic gains made by César Chávez and the United Farm Workers. Similarly, a considerable amount of energy has been expended by the bishops and various Church agencies and leaders in defending the rights of undocumented immigrants who are found predominantly in urban centers but also in rural areas. For these reasons, perhaps, the development of a well-rounded pastoral plan for rural Hispanics has tended to be a low priority.

Another factor that directly impacts rural ministry is the inability of many of the Church's main pastoral agents—priests, permanent deacons, men and women religious—to effectively immerse themselves in the life of the migrant workers. If the stability and tranquility of the rectory or convent is stressed, it becomes almost impossible to identify with the instability of the migrant's life style. The constant mobility in search of work and the serious material poverty of the people mitigates against the maintenance of the support system that most priests and religious require.

In the past decade some efforts have been made to address the issue of "going where the people really are" by means of mobile evangelization teams and mobile pastoral centers. While these projects were designed to reach out to Hispanics generally, especially to the huge urban concentrations of Hispanics, there has been an effect on rural Hispanics as well. The results of these attempts unfortunately have been less than hoped for due probably to the difficulty of articulating the evangelization outreach with local parish and diocesan programs and approaches. Nevertheless, these efforts need to be supported and ways found to overcome the difficulties. The concept behind them appears to be sound. The difficulty is to be found in the inability of parishes and dioceses to develop a sense of pastoral planning and cooperation on a scale vast enough to impact the reality of rural Hispanic populations. As long as the dioceses concerned and the region do not make a sufficiently serious effort to plan in unison, energies will be scattered, follow-up rendered difficult if not impossible, and the material, economic, and moral support needed for such an ambitious project rendered unattainable.[77]

Ecclesial Structures: Diocesan, Regional, and National

In addition to the pastoral ministry being carried out at the level of parish, faith-sharing community, and apostolic movement, there exists an Hispanic ministry network at the official levels of diocese, region, and nation. Briefly each level will be described.

Within the past fifteen years offices of Hispanic ministry have come into existence in every diocese of California and in scores of other dioceses throughout the nation. Generally these offices are entrusted by the diocesan bishop with the task of providing resources for the local parishes in meeting the needs of the growing Hispanic presence. These resources and services can take the form of formation of catechists, and evangelizers, of lay ministers of various kinds such as eucharistic ministers, lectors, and youth ministers. In some areas where the parishes are barely able to provide services, the Hispanic office functions as a pastoral center. It provides certain direct services that normally would be provided at the parish. These offices relate to the other diocesan offices in different ways. It varies considerably from diocese to diocese.

An issue that emerges here is whether the Hispanic office is to provide the whole range of services such as youth ministry formation, catechetical formation, animation of basic ecclesial communities, etc., or whether it is to work with already existing diocesan departments that perform those tasks in English for the Anglo American communities. There is no easy solution to this structural problem. It seems to depend on local circumstances, although in an ideal world it would seem proper that the department of a diocese take responsibility for as many people as they can—that they learn to do their ministry in an inculturated manner. Sometimes that is not possible. In that case the Hispanic ministry office may fill the need.[78]

At the regional level there exists an Office of Hispanic Affairs in Sacramento, California. This office is part of the California Catholic Conference. The director of this office has the task of promoting Hispanic ministry throughout the twelve dioceses of California. This person is a resource for the diocesan offices in terms of planning and coordination of projects impacting Hispanics across diocesan boundaries. For instance, the Office of Hispanic Affairs supervised the development of a radio program in Spanish that is carried on stations throughout California. Franciscan Communications produces the program. The audience targeted by this fifteen-minute weekly radio program, "Voces de Peregrinos," is the rural Hispanic migrant who may have little or no contact with a parish. Similarly, the Office of Hispanic Affairs developed an evangelization project that had as its goal reaching out to marginalized Hispanics in California. A mobile team was organized and scores of laity were trained in various methods of evangelization and religious formation. As a result of this project a proposal was made to the U.S. bishops to assist in the funding of a regional pastoral, cultural center called the Catholic Hispanic Institute of California (CHIC). The purpose of this institute is to provide lay ministry formation wherever it is most needed. Many other needs such as the orientation of Hispanic priests coming into the region and other forms of theological and cultural reflection on the Hispanic reality are part of its mandate. Unfortunately this project has been put on hold and it is not clear how the needs that CHIC proposes to meet will be met in the future.[79]

The Office of Hispanic Affairs is only one of seven such offices that have been established in various regions of the United States. These offices relate, in turn, to the Secretariat for Hispanic Affairs established by the U.S. bishops in 1971 as a department of the USCC. The Secretariat has organized three national meetings called *encuentros* in which the Hispanic Catholic communities of the entire nation have sent representatives to prioritize needs, share experiences, and make proposals for better service of their communities. The first *encuentro* took place in 1971, the second in 1977, and the third in 1985. The *Tercer Encuentro* was a grassroots process that involved more than 200,000 Hispanic Catholics in a prolonged reflection process on their realities and needs. At the *Tercer Encuentro* the general outline of a pastoral plan for U.S. Hispanics was devised.[80]

The diocesan and regional offices as well as the Secretariat have been the source of considerable renewal and movement within the U.S. Church in the service of Hispanics. There continues to be difficulty in translating into action the initiatives that derive from the people and are taken to the higher organizational level and then brought back to the local churches. The mobility of the Hispanic communities and the difficulties experienced in trying to involve the local priests in these processes has been considerable. For that reason, the initiative, concerns, and resources of these higher offices frequently do not reach the people "in the pew." Nevertheless, the *Tercer Encuentro* process encouraged more coordinated planning—pastoral plans at the regional and diocesan levels. One example of this trend is the ambitious pastoral plan for Hispanics developed in the archdiocese of Los Angeles, by far the largest Hispanic diocese in the United States.[81]

The leadership of the Hispanic Catholic communities of California and the rest of the nation has been powerfully influenced by developments in other Spanish-speaking regions, especially Latin America.

The concepts of *pastoral de conjunto* (coordinated ministry), *opción pre-ferencial por el pobre* (preferential option for the poor), *educación integral* (integral education), analysis of reality in its socioeconomic, political, and cultural coordinates as a starting point for theological reflection and pastoral planning have all become standard points of reference for Hispanic ministry in the United States. All of these seminal concepts as well as the emphasis on the BEC as a preferred instrument of evangelization have been systematically promoted by the diocesan, regional, and national Hispanic ministry agencies. Thereby they are providing new and exciting ideas relevant to the effective evangelization and pastoral care of U.S. Hispanics.[82]

Mass Media and the Hispanic

The formidable presence of evangelical Protestant sects on radio and television in English and Spanish has brought to the forefront the question of Catholic use of mass media as a tool of evangelization. Much of what is said regarding the media is conjectural and impressionistic. Serious studies of the short- or long-range effects of mass media on evangelization in English or Spanish do not exist. Why do they not exist? A fundamental reason seems to be that the concept of evangelization, or a foundational notion of what the Church's mission is, is lacking. Generally the Church's task is conceived of as simply "reaching out" or arriving with a message. If that is the case, then getting Catholic speakers on radio and television is a logical objective, since radio and television are by far the most effective ways to reach the masses with one's message. Lacking in this perspective are the following:

(1) a sense of whom one is communicating with (an analysis of their reality, context, etc.);
(2) a sense of the organic relationship between outreach and the rest of the Church's mission.

What is supposed to happen after they hear the message? How are the existential units of the Church integrated into this outreach?

It is clear that an outreach to others in the name of evangelization ought not to consist only in announcing the gospel message. There must also be an invitation to participate in community, for community is the essence of the Church. The history of religious mass media and "electronic" religion reveals that it has not found a means to relate to viable communities. Stated another way, the function of mass media outreach has not been clearly articulated in reference to the life of the

Christian community or parish. Perhaps that is why the mass media have not been cultivated nearly as much by Catholics as by certain sects who apparently use the mass media quite effectively to create nothing more than a *listening* audience and to bring in significant sums of money.

Radio, television, and other media such as print, movies, slides, and videos are especially effective when used in conjunction with a process of outreach or evangelization that is *planned* and reflects the more complex view of evangelization that is Catholic. The relatively few efforts that there have been to use mass media in the evangelization of U.S. Hispanics have frequently prescinded from the question of how concretely the interest raised by the outreach can be translated into Christian commitment beyond the sending in of contributions and an improvement in personal morals. This in turn reflects the fact that real pastoral planning, *pastoral de conjunto*, is frequently lacking in the efforts of diocese and regions to reach out to the Hispanics. Until there is such coordination based on a comprehensive view of evangelization as understood in the magisterium, efforts to use the media effectively will be seriously hampered. The impression of truly having reached the people may be achieved, but the prospect of any long-term *commitment* is doubtful indeed. For long-range commitment to the following of Christ, seeking his kingdom in community, is achieved through identification with Christ, through exposure to his word and sacrament and through loving service to others in the world. The privatized world of living room or automobile is not the context within which evangelization as understood in the Church can take root. Mass media can be supportive and complement more fundamental efforts that take as their point of departure real communities of faith, worship, and service. But media approaches cannot substitute for the building of viable, concrete communities.[83]

This rather long phenomenology of Hispanic pastoral realities invites one to step back and view the panorama from different and perhaps complementary perspectives. The following chapter proposes to raise issues that contribute to deeper insight into what the evangelization of Hispanic culture in the U.S. is all about.

4 | Major Issues In Hispanic Ministry

This chapter begins a second, more challenging part of the present work. Keeping in mind the many contexts for the pastoral care of U.S. Hispanics, these pages will be a reflection on those contexts in terms of four key issues linked in ways that will become clearer. Those issues are:

(1) inculturation or evangelization of culture;
(2) the promotion of social justice or structural transformation;
(3) modernity and secularization;
(4) popular Catholicism/religiousness.

Much has been written about these issues—the bibliography is extensive indeed. The focus here will be narrow. After trying to synthesize the most general notions regarding each theme, the implications for Hispanic ministry will be set forth.

What Does It Mean To Evangelize?

Before entering into each theme, a few words are in order regarding the overarching issue, implicit and explicit in everything that follows, namely, the Church's understanding of its mission in the world—the Church's understanding of what it means to evangelize.

It would be helpful if the concept of evangelization were a simple one. It would then be an easier matter to assess the effectiveness of evangelization as it is pursued among the growing numbers of U.S. Hispanics. But that is not as easy as it might seem for the simple reason that there is considerable room for debate about the meaning of evangelization. The pluralism characteristic of theology today is also characteristic of the various outlooks on this one central issue—evangelization.[1]

92

Serious discussions about the Church's mission in the world today reflect two perspectives. One gives priority to the evangelization of culture and the other to structural change or social justice. The documents of the magisterium, especially Pope Paul VI's *Evangelii Nuntiandi*, actually define evangelization in such a way that both the personal-cultural and the social-structural aspects are respected:

> . . . the Church evangelizes when she seeks to convert, solely through the divine power of the Message she proclaims, both the personal and collective consciences of people, the activities in which they engage, and the lives and concrete milieux which are theirs.[2]

There are two poles, then, within evangelization—one focused on the person, the human heart; the other focused on the milieu, the material structures that influence both the individual and society. The term inculturation or the evangelization of culture is conceived of as impacting personal values, feelings, customs, and thought, while liberation is conceived of as relating more to the transformation of the social order, the achievement of a more just society.[3] In the thought of *Evangelii Nuntiandi* there is, nevertheless, a social and personal dimension to both the evangelization of culture and to liberation. But subsequent reflection on the meaning of these terms has tended to reveal a dichotomy that fails to respect the proper balance which *Evangelii Nuntiandi* maintains between personal conversion and social transformation of structures. It is true, however, that this apostolic exhortation gives a certain priority to personal conversion as the product of evangelization:

> The Church considers it to be important to build up structures which are more human, more just, more respectful of the rights of the person and less oppressive and less enslaving, but she is conscious that the best structures and the most idealized system soon become inhuman if the inhuman inclinations of the human heart are not made wholesome, if those who live in these structures or who rule them do not undergo a conversion of heart and outlook.[4]

It appears, then, that there has been a bifurcation among pastoral agents, a division that reflects a preference for understanding evangelization as focused primarily on a change of heart, on the one hand, or a view of it as structural change, on the other. The first preference tends to emphasize spirituality, prayer, morality, and personal ethics, while the second emphasizes sociopolitical commitment and action for justice.[5] Fidelity to the magisterium, however, seems to demand that *both* polarities be respected. What that means is that the evangelization of culture has much to do with structural change, and structural change has much to do with cultural transformation.

That is why the first two issues to be discussed here are inculturation and structural transformation. The proper evangelization of the Hispanic communities of the United States cannot occur until and unless the gospel message is proclaimed in such a way that changes take place in *both* the personal and the social/structural dimensions of the Hispanic people and the larger North American society of which they are only a part.

Evangelization of Culture

The magisterium seems to give a certain priority to personal and cultural conversion, over against social conversion. That priority appears to be grounded on Christian humanism and personalism that prefer to make the human person in his or her incalculable worth and dignity as a child of God and brother or sister of Jesus Christ the starting point of all moral reflection. This option for the person, however, is subject to misinterpretation. For it may appear at times to obscure the structural, collective aspect of sin by interiorizing, "spiritualizing," and privatizing discourse about the meaning of the gospel. Persons sensitive to Marx's rich theory of alienation and the role of religion in the alienation process are especially suspicious of Christian humanism and personalism. It seems to them to be a way of avoiding the central reality of structural injustice that holds in place many of the evils that beset humanity collectively *and* individually.[6] This humanism can also be confused and implicated with the individualism characteristic of the capitalist world and market economies. Thus it appears biased in favor of one ideology and to that extent a betrayal of the gospel. Gregory Baum speaks of this in *Religion and Alienation:*

> . . . a major distortion of the Christian religion in the West has been the "privatization" of the gospel, i.e., the excessively individualistic interpretation of the Christian message, and since this privatized religion has legitimated and promoted the atomization of the social order and an economic system of each man for himself, it is the task of critical theology to deprivatize the inherited religion.[7]

Giving priority to personal and cultural conversion can be taken as contributing to this harmful distortion of the gospel. Nevertheless, fidelity to the magisterium requires a "both/and" rather than an "either/or" mentality.[8] Keeping this in mind, then, the first key issue in the evangelization of Hispanics is inculturation.

For the Church the centrality of the question of culture in its deepest anthropological sense was clearly affirmed by Pope Paul VI in *Evangelii Nuntiandi*. The pope characterized the split between faith and culture as "the drama of our times." There are many definitions of culture. But for the purposes of this discussion it can be defined as "the meanings, values, thoughts, and feelings mutually shared by a people." Or another definition, even broader than the first, is "the specific, concrete ways in which a person is human."[9]

The word that most adequately designates the relationship between faith and culture is inculturation. The proclamation of the gospel message in an effective way requires in the evangelizer a high degree of knowledge, respect, and sensitivity to the culture and context in which the gospel is to be proclaimed. Pope Paul VI expressed the nature of the challenge of effective evangelization in these words:

> . . . what matters is to evangelize man's culture and cultures [not in a purely decorative way as it were by applying a thin veneer, but in a vital way, in depth and right to the very roots], in the wide and rich sense which these terms have in *Gaudium et spes*, always taking the person as one's starting-point and always coming back to the relationships of people among themselves and with God.[10]

The meteoric rise of the term "inculturation" in the documents of the magisterium dramatizes the powerful influence that sensitivity to the issue of culture has had on the Church's understanding of its mission in the post-Vatican II period.[11] The issue of how to evangelize in a contextualized way, of how to evangelize culture and develop methods and instruments of evangelization that are truly inculturated, has been central to the Church's reflection especially with regard to missionary activity in the third world.

This development is explained by the fact that for the first time in the history of the Church the worldwide hierarchy is in the majority non-European. This was reflected already in Vatican II, an ecumenical council in which African, Asian, and Latin American bishops actively participated for the first time in significant numbers. Since then the extraordinary synods have reflected this irreversible trend. The next ecumenical council will be the first one in which non-European bishops will be in the majority. The point here is that the very meaning of the term universal or "catholic" has taken on a more concrete and real meaning than ever before in the history of the Church. This is the result of the historical fact that many non-European local churches began to thrive on their own only in the twentieth century with the decline of colonialism.[12]

The demise of colonialism encouraged reflection on the relative importance of European culture versus the autochthonous ones. This decline relativized the norms, values, customs, and worldviews of European as well as Anglo American culture. The newfound sensitivity to the question of culture has had immense practical repercussions on the Church in liturgy, pastoral care, missions, preaching, and life style. Inculturation is one of the major themes, if not the most important, in missiology today. Nor is the impact of inculturation felt only in these practical areas and in the field of missiology. All of theology has been shaken to the foundations in the sense that a new, long, and arduous journey has begun. This journey consists precisely in discovering the interplay between faith and culture at work in every aspect of the Church's life and thought over the centuries.[13]

Pope Paul VI expressed the concept that today is being pursued to its logical consequences in many areas of the Church's life and praxis, namely:

> The Gospel, and therefore evangelization, are certainly not identical with culture, and they are independent in regard to all cultures. . . . Though independent of cultures, the Gospel and evangelization are not necessarily incompatible with them; rather they are capable of permeating them all without becoming subject to any one of them.[14]

This insight into the relationship between faith and culture was present before in the Church, for instance, in the heated controversy between Peter and Paul regarding the Judaizers as recorded in Acts. The theme of faith's encounter with culture is implicit and often explicit in patristic writings. This theme was present at the time of the evangelization of the Americas in the great theological discussions of those exciting and tumultuous times when, once again, the Church experienced the opportunity to evangelize entirely unknown cultures in the North and South American continents. Nevertheless, only in this century have advances in anthropology, history, sociology, economics, and politics shed light on the process of evangelization and made Christians more conscious of the supracultural aspects of the gospel faith that they formerly often confused with their cultures. Karl Rahner articulated the meaning and import of this development in his conference, "Toward a Fundamental Theological Interpretation of Vatican II." Reflecting on Rahner's understanding of that great ecclesial event, Louis J. Luzbetak writes:

> Rahner regards Vatican II as the most significant event in Church history since the Council of Jerusalem. It was then, in 49 A.D., that the infant Church inaugurated a theologically new era passing from being a Jewish community to something that was Gentile, Graeco-Roman and European, abandoning such sacred Judaic practices as circumcision, the sabbath, and laws regarding unclean food, not mere externals but traditions with deep theological consequences. The Second Vatican Council was the official beginning of a no less theologically radical understanding of the Church, an understanding that Rahner sums up under "*world* Church," that is to say, a Church whose *life* is *supra*-cultural, no longer Western, but a Church at home equally everywhere, as Asian and African in its *self-understanding* as it is European, and not only potentially as before but actually (even if at the moment still imperfectly and rudimentarily so).[15]

Luzbetak articulates the impact of the change in this way:

> At Vatican II, the Church for the first time officially thought, judged, decided, spoke and acted as a true world entity, as a single People of God, with the bishops acting in a truly worldwide collegiality. This new direction was not a contradictory change, an aberration of some kind, but the result of growth and precedent, the result of previous insight and hope, an actualization of an existing potential. It nevertheless took a Vatican II to steer Peter's bark in this radically new direction.[16]

The condition for the possibility of a truly world Church are the supra- or transcultural elements of the good news it proclaims. Separating that gospel experience—its inner spirit and heart—from the myriad culturally conditioned mediations it has assimilated from the beginning is perhaps the great task that will occupy the Church at every level in decades to come. That task is no less relevant to Hispanic ministry in the United States than to Catholic pastoral agents in Asia or Africa.

Yet the evangelization of culture in the United States is made more problematic by the fact that the U.S. is a leader in the production of culture on a global basis. Through the accelerating transfer of technology, liberal capitalist ideology, and the mass media, United States culture has become in many significant ways the trend-setting if not the normative culture of the West. It has considerable influence in the East as well. Modernity understood as culture, moreover, is largely indistinguishable from Americanization. [17]

The cultural hegemony of the United States in the world makes it especially difficult for the Church and pastoral agents to develop the cultural critique needed if the evangelization of this powerful culture is to advance. While it is relatively easy to discover differences between the dominant European/North American culture (first world) and third world cultures, there is considerably less interest in and awareness of the differences between first world cultures (often called "Christian") and the gospel message. Indeed, the Church's understanding of that gospel message continues to be mediated by first world culture and ideology. Consequently there is a lack of objectivity when it comes to self-analysis. This in turn creates a situation where culturally specific norms and attitudes are confused with the gospel message itself. [18]

Another difficulty is that the symbiosis of faith and culture is present in the Bible itself, in the very formulations of revelation. Hence it is problematic to speak of a "core gospel message." [19]

There is another more obvious reason why the critique of culture in the light of the gospel message does not come about. It has to do with the nature of evangelization *as a form of communication*. St. Augustine in *De Doctrina Christiana* lucidly explained what is needed if the gospel proclamation is to be effectively communicated so as to lead to action:

> . . . if what you promise him is what he really likes, if the danger of which you speak appears real, if your censures are directed against something he hates, if your recommendations are in harmony with what he embraces, if he regrets what you say is regrettable, if he rejoices over what you claim is a reason for joy, if his heart is sympathetic toward those whose misery you describe, if he avoids those who you advise should be avoided . . . not merely imparting knowledge about things that ought to be done but rather moving them to do that which they know must be done. [20]

Luzbetak summarizes the import of St. Augustine's observations: "Before we can understand a message, it must somehow be compatible with our psychological frame of mind and *our particular cultural experience*." [21]

These elementary principles of effective communication create a dilemma for the evangelization of culture: on the one hand, evangelization demands that the evangelizer accommodate himself or herself to the culture in question, know it well, and show deep sympathy for it; on the other hand, the evangelizer must remain at a distance, critical of the culture, because the gospel is, in important respects, always transcultural and countercultural.

In the North American milieu there does not appear to be a great deal of interest in introspection. Yet that interest and ability is necessary for North American pastoral agents desiring to evangelize their culture. They must somehow break away from the comfortable truths, the prevailing attitudes, expectations, values, and feelings characteristic of their society if any kind of significant evangelization is to take place. Yet ironically they must be experts in their culture, know its values in a reflective manner, grasp the symbols that express its deepest understanding of itself, and know how to effectively communicate them, nuance them, and even transform them at the service of the gospel to be proclaimed.

Hence there is an inherent tension in all evangelization. In the case of the evangelization of Hispanics in California those tensions are surely exacerbated. First, North Americans in general and even many Hispanics tend to take for granted that North American culture is somehow superior to Hispanic American cultures. The racism, prejudice, diverse historical starting points, and experiences alluded to in chapter two help explain this difference in attitude. Second, the immigrant origins of the United States have led to a strong emphasis on assimilation to the prevailing cultural norms, to cultural conformity in everything but the most superficial.

While being pluralistic in a sense, United States culture was and is profoundly influenced by its Protestant origins as Max Weber implied in *The Protestant Ethic and the Spirit of Capitalism*. Robert Bellah and others have more recently traced the evolution of the North American character and culture in the much commented *Habits of the Heart*.[22]

Briefly put, Bellah's understanding of the dominant North American value system highlights the meaning of individualism and provides a framework for assessing the points of contact with and divergencies from gospel norms including the norms proposed by Catholic social doctrine. North American individualism is

> a belief that the individual has a primary reality whereas society is a second-order, derived or artificial construct, a view we can call *ontological individualism*. . . . It is opposed to the idea

that society is as real as individuals, a view we call *social realism*, which is common to the biblical and republican traditions.[23]

One of the more serious consequences of this "ontological individualism" is the diminution of community including family within North American culture. North Americans, according to Bellah, have become less interested in community and tend to substitute "lifestyle enclaves" for it. By "lifestyle enclave" Bellah means an association

> . . . formed by people who share some feature of private life. Members of a lifestyle enclave express their identity through shared patterns of appearance, consumption, and leisure activities, which often serve to differentiate them sharply from those with other lifestyles. They are not interdependent, do not act together politically, and do not share a history. If these things begin to appear, the enclave is on its way to becoming a community.[24]

The end result of North America's ontological individualism is an inability to live in solidarity. Indeed, the absence of the word solidarity in the socio-political and economic discourse of the U.S. is very telling. Its strong presence in the discourse of Catholic social doctrine is equally revealing. The Protestant notion that human happiness is the end result of independent agents pursuing their self-interest has never been embraced by Catholic social/ethical discourse. The corporatist idea harkening back to the middle ages has perdured despite the onslaught of bourgeois and capitalist ideology. Catholic social doctrine, then, is countercultural in that it makes the common good as much a norm of social morality as the individual good.[25]

John Francis Kavanaugh provides another cogent example of a critique of North American culture in his *Following Christ in a Consumer Society: The Spirituality of Cultural Resistance.* He analyzes Christian life as essentially countercultural. It is opposed to consumerism that reduces the human person to the status of an object; it promotes life styles such as Christian marriage, celibacy, and religious life which go contrary to the prevailing cultural norms.

Dean Brackley discusses some prevailing Anglo American ideals as expressions of "the spirit of the world" as understood in the early Christian literature and spirituality. He cogently demonstrates how the "upward mobility" orientation of U.S. society is contrary to the way of Christ in *Downward Mobility: Social Implications of St. Ignatius's Two Standards.*[26]

These and other studies like them are necessary if the evangelization of culture is to occur in the United States. They provide a coherent analysis of the underlying value system of a people tracing the evolution of those values over the centuries. The effective proclamation of the gospel occurs when the prevailing cultural values are critiqued and new, more radical gospel values are proposed in place of them. To fail in this critical function is perhaps what is meant by the gospel message: "Salt is good, but if salt loses its flavor what good is it for seasoning?" (Lk 14:34). The failure to maintain the critical function of the gospel message renders it insipid, manipulated in the name of ideologies and cultural values foreign to the message of Jesus.[27]

The failure to articulate the transcultural and countercultural elements of the gospel in the North American milieu makes it impossible to effectively evangelize that culture. It also makes it impossible to address the question of Hispanic ministry. For the evangelization of Hispanics is only part of the larger question which is *the evangelization of United States culture.* The effort to evangelize the Hispanic community apart from strategies to evangelize North American culture is counterproductive, reminiscent of Penelope's spinning her loom by day only to undo her weaving by night. In chapter one the data on assimilation of Hispanics indicated that, by the second generation, Hispanics are usually well along in the process of Americanization. The effort to provide pastoral agents imbued with a knowledge of the immigrants' language and sensitivity to their values must be matched by the formation of pastoral agents critically sensitive to North American culture. The Hispanic immigrants served by the Church today will within a generation be more North American than Hispanic. The central question, therefore, is how to impact the core of North American culture on behalf of the gospel.

A kind of romanticism may have influenced the approach being taken by some in the field of Hispanic ministry—the notion that somehow the language, values, customs, and traditions of Hispanics can be preserved from the inexorable forces of Americanization. The data does not substantiate such a view. Rather, the influences pushing the Hispanic communities toward assimilation to U.S. values are very considerable. The crucial issue is not only how to provide an affirming, receptive environment for the recently arrived immigrant, but also how to promote in some programmatic fashion the acquisition of an awareness about the serious differences between Christian values and some values promoted by U.S. society. An adequate pastoral plan cannot be focused on Hispanics alone or on assimilated North Americans alone. Rather, there needs to be an underlying cultural critique of both the

Hispanic and the North American cultures that responds to the changing language needs and levels of assimilation achieved by Hispanics over the many positions they will assume on the continuum of cultural adaptation. This kind of coordinated, organic pastoral planning has generally not occurred.[28]

The first elements of an explicit gospel-based critique of North American culture are available in two outstanding pastoral letters issued by the U.S. bishops, one on war and peace, the other on the U.S. economy in 1983 and 1986 respectively. For the proper evangelization of U.S. culture such a direction is essential. These pastoral letters, however, have not been communicated or engaged to any considerable extent by the leadership in Hispanic ministry throughout the country. Pastoral planning based on an awareness of the interrelationship between the dominant, North American Catholic milieu and the Hispanic Catholic milieu has not been pursued. The end result is a fragmented, confused, and ultimately ineffective evangelization of culture.[29]

Assessments of Hispanic cultures and critiques of them from a gospel perspective are equally important. The understandable sensitivity to Hispanic culture as often misunderstood and disdained and the need to respect and accept the people's culture do not exonerate pastoral agents from the responsibility to promote a critical gospel-based attitude toward Hispanic cultures as well.

Resources similar to Bellah's and Kavanaugh's are also available with regard to Hispanic culture, specifically in regard to Mexican culture. Rogelio Díaz-Guerrero's *Psychology of the Mexican: Culture and Personality* is an example in point. Similarly, Santiago Ramírez analyzes many disvalues within Mexican culture in his *El Mexicano: Psicología de sus motivaciones*. The prolific anthropological studies of *campesinos* and urban poor produced by Oscar Lewis provide powerful elements of a critique of Mexican culture. The same could be said of Octavio Paz in his classic study of the Mexican character discussed in chapter two, *Labyrinth of Solitude* and its sequel, *The Other Mexico*. The brilliant novels of Carlos Fuentes also provide a deep insight into the foibles and limitations of Mexican culture in history. Joaquín Antonio Peñalosa gives a humorous and telling account of the more common defects of Mexicans in *El Mexicano y los 7 Pecados Capitales*.[30]

The dependence of Mexican and other Hispanic cultures on the United States make it difficult to critique them. The reason is that in a very real sense these cultures have never been allowed to develop "on their own." The persistence of colonialism, neocolonialism, and North American sociopolitical, economic, and cultural hegemony have made it very difficult and somewhat dubious to engage in critiques of these cultures. There is truth to the contention that many of the negative aspects of Hispanic culture are the direct or indirect product of age-old oppression. Eliminating North American hegemonic presence is logically seen as a remedy to these disvalues.[31]

This point of view seems to confer an excessive influence on Spain, and later on the United States, in shaping the profile of Hispanic American culture. The larger-than-life presence of U.S. culture in Latin America through films, books, fashions, commerce, industry, technology, and militarism creates the perception of Hispanic culture as being more derivative than original and as being a victim. Consequently, a critique of Hispanic culture can often revert to a critique of the dominant cultures to which the Latin American peoples have always been subservient.[32]

While there is truth to this view, it fails to do justice to the complex and deeply rooted cultural reality of the Hispanic people in terms of both the values and the disvalues of their cultures. Keeping in mind that in important ways it is a culture of oppression, it would seem possible to analyze that culture on its own, bringing gospel criteria to bear upon it. The evangelization of Mexican culture in the United States requires that such an analysis take place. The failure to do so is possibly the result of a facile anti-Americanism or a nationalism that can blind a people and promote a kind of scapegoating.

The evangelization of U.S. Hispanics is, therefore, an especially challenging proposition. It involves the attainment of a critical cultural consciousness seldom found in human beings. This consciousness gravitates between the dominant Anglo American culture and the dependent Hispanic culture. North Americans generally are not critically conscious of their culture. Rather, they take it for granted and frequently presume that it is superior to that of others. Hispanics, in contrast, frequently have stereotypical ideas about Anglo American culture, while entertaining notions of inferiority with regard to their own.[33] When some Hispanics become more positive about their own culture through study and reflection, they sometimes develop a stereotypically negative concept of U.S. culture, assigning to it all the woes and limitations afflicting their oppressed, autochtonous culture. All of these postures militate against the critical consciousness required if the evangelization of culture is to occur.

The evangelization of culture also demands more than a little clarity about the gospel of Jesus Christ. Sometimes that clarity can be obscured by personal interests and ideologies of one kind or another.

Finally, the very serious problem of discerning the core message of the gospel from the relative, historically and culturally determined expressions of that core is formidable indeed.[34]

Evangelization as Transformative Action

The second aspect of evangelization is structural change. The transformation of the social order (socioeconomic and political structures) is an integral dimension of evangelization. In this connection, the 1971 Extraordinary Synod of Bishops is famous for the following statement:

> Action on behalf of justice and participation in the transformation of the world fully appear to us as a constitutive dimension of the preaching of the Gospel, or, in other words, of the Church's mission for the redemption of the human race and its liberation from every oppressive situation.[35]

The implications of this view of evangelization are very serious. One of them is that the Church's mission is inextricably involved in political action, not in a narrow, partisan sense but in the sense of participation in the processes by which public policy is formulated and carried out. This dimension of evangelization must be taken together with the first, the evangelization of culture, discussed above. It requires a healthy respect for the temporal order and a conviction that the mission of the Church is not that of a ship sailing calmly through history, oblivious to the disasters that surround it, but a Church, in the words of *Gaudium et Spes*, sensitive to the "joy and hope, the grief and anguish of the men of our time, especially of those who are poor or afflicted in any way."[36]

Just as the emphasis on inculturation, on the conversion of the human heart, on the proclamation of gospel values, as practiced by some can unwittingly contribute to a privatized, middle-class view of Christian faith, so an emphasis on social justice or structural transformation can contribute to the confusing of faith with ideology and the manipulation of a people's faith for purposes unrelated to or in opposition to the gospel.[37]

How does the structural or political dimension of evangelization in general as proposed by the magisterium relate to the evangelization of Hispanics in the United States? A review of the most authoritative documents on Hispanic ministry reveals a great deal of awareness on the part of the bishops, clergy, and laity regarding the structural aspects of evangelization. That awareness is reflected in the documents.

Many social justice issues are raised in the U.S. bishops' pastoral letter on *The Hispanic Presence: Challenge and Commitment* (1984), and in the documents of the second and third *Ecuentro Nacional Hispano de Pastoral*. Several local, diocesan pastoral letters have been produced. They too exemplify the Church's contemporary concept of evangelization leading to both personal and social conversion.[38]

It appears, nevertheless, that neither the evangelization of culture nor action on behalf of justice has become the characteristic mark of the Church's pastoral activity with Hispanics in the U.S. Rather, the predominant pastoral approach reflects the priorities of the period before Vatican II, namely, the maintenance of the people's traditional Catholicism through the dispensation of the sacraments. The fact that there does not yet exist a critical cultural consciousness of either the Anglo American or the Hispanic cultures nor a mutually agreed upon perception of the core values of the Gospel means that the condition of the possibility of evangelization in its fullest sense does not yet exist. There are some hopeful movements in that direction, for example, the bishops' recent pastorals on war and peace and on the U.S. economy, as well as the peace, ecological, feminist, and black human rights movements.[39] But the cultural and structural critiques implicit or explicit to these movements have seldom been related to the Hispanic communities. No attempt has been made to articulate the issues as they impact the present and future of the large Hispanic population of the U.S. Nor has a coherent critique of Hispanic culture been developed, a critique as untainted as possible by the very considerable prejudices of Anglo American culture with regard to the Hispanic.[40]

Action on behalf of justice, moreover, and interest in sociopolitical and economic structures as constitutive elements of evangelization frequently are not promoted in Hispanic ministry. Issues of a more purely religious, sacramental, and spiritual character are given emphasis. There are many reasons for this. One of them, as we have seen, is that the Hispanic peoples in the U.S., especially those of Mexican origin, have inherited a deeply religious view of life, a view rooted in the pre-Columbian past and mingled with Spain's medieval and baroque spiritualities. Underlying this religiosity is a pre-Columbian cyclic view of history. This view of history stands in sharp contrast to a biblical, Judeo-Christian view which is linear. The concept that the world can be transformed, that there is real and not just apparent change, is foreign to pre-Columbian culture and to much of the *mestizo*, rurally-based culture of Mexico.

Consequently, the Christian concept of ongoing conversion or change at either the personal or collective/structural levels is quite foreign. Rather, the notion persists that everything remains the same and will be repeated. The task of humans is to shield themselves as best they can from fate. The *mestizo* peoples of Mexico seldom have experienced "progress," that is, substantial change in the socioeconomic and political conditions of oppression that have been their lot from time immemorial.

The Church's concern for structural change, therefore, can only sound chimerical and foreign to many Hispanics whose historical experience has confirmed repeatedly a cyclical pattern of domination.

Insofar as ideology of either capitalist or socialist origins has influenced the popular masses, it has done so by overcoming a profound state of apathy or anomie with respect to schemes and projects that propose anything more than survival.[41]

Another obstacle to evangelization understood as action on behalf of justice is the residue of negative experiences of sociopolitical action which the Church as institution may have promoted. In chapter two reference was made to the Church's involvement in the oppressive, colonial order of Latin America for three centuries. In the independence period many Church leaders in Mexico and other Latin American nations persisted in plotting a return to the *ancien regime*. In the case of Mexico, the institutional Church's role in the Cristero uprisings and the relatively sudden abandonment of the cause by Church leadership left some thoughtful Catholics with doubts regarding the credibility of Church leaders. This in turn reinforced some of the anticlericalism that has characterized many Mexican thinkers since the nineteenth century. The promotion of evangelization as liberation in the socioeconomic sense, in the structural sense, may be crippled among U.S. Hispanics by these historical antecedents. For the Church and its ministers have been tainted by the errors and sins of the past related to their role in defending the status quo, the rich and the powerful, the autocrats and *caudillos* of which Latin American history is full.[42]

Among Mexicans, especially the working class and *campesinos*, there is a suspicion about politics in general. There is a cynicism about politics and political involvement. This cynicism is the result of centuries of abuse and manipulation.[43] Mexico, it should be recalled, *had* a revolution. The Revolution of 1910 was no insignificant *coup d'etat*. It was a major upheaval in which more than a million Mexicans died. Very significant, if not radical, changes of a sociopolitical and economic nature took place over the decade of struggle that issued on the fall of Porfirio Díaz in 1910. By the 1940s it became clear that the revolution had failed. Perhaps no other people in Latin America have had such a bitter and disillusioning experience of revolution. Hence it stands to reason that the Mexicans should be cautious, if not skeptical, about revolutionary plans. The use of revolutionary jargon and rhetoric inspired on Marxist visions of social change makes those who use such rhetoric suspect within many popular social settings. Demagoguery of a leftist orientation is a standard feature of the ruling party's policy. Similarly, calls to violent resistance to the official oppression are met with skepticism. The path of revolutionary politics and violence was tried and found wanting in Mexico.[44]

Calls to pursue a sociopolitical and economic path more in conformity with United States ideology and interests are met with similar skepticism. For there is considerable awareness in Mexico about the very serious harm, the injustices, violence, disregard of human rights, discrimination, prejudice, and arbitrariness that has characterized U.S.-Mexican relations since the beginning. As was stated in chapter two, the United States is truly the principal foreign enemy Mexico has had in this century. This truism is expressed somewhat jokingly by the Mexican saying, *Pobre Mexico—tan lejos de Dios y tan cerca de los Estados Unidos!* "Poor Mexico—so far from God and so close to the United States!"[45]

The political skepticism of many Mexicans, then, in Mexico or living in the United States makes their evangelization difficult since, as has been seen, commitment to the struggle for justice *is* an essential aspect of evangelization. Mexicans for the reasons given are reluctant to make commitments with sociopolitical implications. In this regard, a notable contrast is seen between Mexicans and Central Americans and other Latin Americans who may be more optimistic about revolutionary plans. This difference is reflected, for instance, in the relative paucity of writings in the area of the theology of liberation emanating from Mexico in comparison with other Latin American countries. The relatively more cautious stance of the Mexican bishops is also a case in point. Another factor is the notable absence of foreign missionaries in Mexico, the fact that the clergy is overwhelmingly Mexican and hence more cautious in pursuing the social justice component of evangelization. Foreigners can count on the support of their embassies and their influential contacts in their country of origin if they should experience difficulties with the local government. Local clergy are in more danger if they choose to oppose oppression.[46]

In addition to these factors which work against the development of evangelization as social transformation and liberation, there is another that also deserves mention here. Catholic social teaching, as the area of the magisterium most relevant to structural change, generally does not provide a *positive* critique of the social order. That is, it dwells on the negative abuses in the area of human rights and equality. Historically, it has been critical of both socialism and liberal capitalism. For some time there was discussion about "a third way," that is, a socioeconomic system different from socialism and capitalism and somehow independent of the competing East-West superpower rivalries. Such a third way has not materialized. Consequently, the thrust toward structural change as a content of evangelization has remained vague and elusive in the context of injustice in Mexico and other Latin American nations.[47]

In the context of the United States, the historical discomfort of the magisterium with features of socialism and liberal capitalism has been muted. On the one hand, clergy and other Church workers have paid little or no attention to the historic difficulties of the magisterium with liberal capitalism since the time of Leo XIII, whereas the magisterium's serious difficulties with communism, especially its philosophical atheism and materialism, have, on the other hand, been communicated by the Church in the United States. The result is a partial and inadequate view, one that hardly promotes structural change but reinforces the prevailing view that North American society is basically just and needs only a few superficial reforms. Even worse, such an omission reinforces the perception—not justified by the documents—that anticommunism is a higher priority for the magisterium than the transformation of the global economic order. The result of all this is that there is little or no interest in the development of a critical consciousness regarding social, political, and economic structures among North American Catholics *including Hispanics*.

The notable opposition and/or indifference experienced by the U.S. bishops in the wake of their pastoral letters on war and peace and on the U.S. economy—opposition organized by prominent Catholic laity—may reasonably be interpreted as the logical consequence of not having communicated the social teachings of the Church in an adequate manner. This omission makes it extremely difficult for the average U.S. Catholic, whether Anglo American or Hispanic, to grasp the rich and complex vision of social order implicit in Catholic social thought.[48]

The lack of familiarity on the part of U.S. Catholics, including Hispanics, with the principles of Catholic social teaching creates a situation in which the vacuum can be filled by ideologies of left or right. It is not that the formulations of the magisterium are not in themselves ideological; they necessarily are. Rather, the ideology espoused there ostensibly reflects values and views consistent with the Church's current understanding of revelation. In its effort to apply those Gospel-centered values to this age it must partake, to some degree, of ideology. That ideology, however, is consciously filtered through the lens of the gospel which contributes something new and altogether unexpected to the often fixed, absolutized, and sinful perspectives provided by the prevailing ideologies of left or right. The perspective of the magisterium is that of faith. Hence it is critical of systemic visions rooted in either the *philosophical* materialism of collectivism and certain forms of socialism or of the *practical* materialism characteristic of capitalism.[49]

Evangelization in the context of structural change or liberation is impossible for Hispanics or any other group as long as the originality of the gospel message, its relevance to the daily struggles of the poor and powerless, is systematically manipulated by interests not grounded on the gospel message itself. While it is possible to cooperate with all persons of good will, whether leftist or rightist, the Church's critical role cannot be maintained without a certain independence. Hence the importance of the people of God seeing themselves as a universal community rooted in local contexts and historical moments but never totally identified with one people, race, economic system, ideology, or nation. Such a position undoubtedly leads to tension. Popular movements rooted in powerful ideologies and nationalisms tend to demand a total allegiance. While promoting concrete social, political, and economic changes, the gospel message invites men and women of good will to relativize their ideological commitments in the light of their commitment to God and neighbor.

The lack of critical sensitivity to the issue of ideology renders efforts to evangelize Hispanics counterproductive. For the effort can become fixed either on the other world and thus accept the status quo, or it can fix its gaze squarely on injustice and the transformation of a given historical situation. In doing so, this effort may lead to "gaining the world, but losing a soul."[50]

Modernization and Secularization: Implications for Ministry

The literature devoted to the topics of modernity and secularization is vast. It is impossible to summarize this rich discussion here. What can be indicated, however, is merely the relevance of the topic to the question of the evangelization of U.S. Hispanics.[51]

U.S. Hispanics—certainly this is the case of Hispanics of Mexican origin—come from cultures that are premodern in many important respects. Basically that means these people were born into a culture that was organically integrated and in which religion and myth provide an explanation for the origin of things. A premodern or nonmodern society is experienced as a totalizing presence in which the interests and perceptions of the group, not of the individual, are paramount. There is a clear-cut pattern of behavior and social organization, an holistic attitude toward life in its physical-material and spiritual dimensions. This society is hierarchically structured and characterized by continuity and permanence. It is closer to nature and has developed less control over it. There is a tendency toward authoritarianism, a heavy emphasis on vertical relationship, hierarchy, in the premodern societies.

Modern society of which the United States is the paragon is just the opposite. It is basically fragmented and egalitarian. It is distanced from nature and ecology by science and technology. There is a preference for democratic approaches in modern culture. In the modern society, science—not religion and myth—provides the majority of answers, and there is a movement away from transcendent views of God and humanity toward more immanence.[52]

The contrast between the nonmodern, traditional world and the modern one is extremely relevant to the question of the evangelization of U.S. Hispanics. While Mexico itself, for example, is undergoing a rapid process of modernization, a process that began many decades ago and has been accelerated by mounting U.S. influence, the fact of immigration has exacerbated that process for many millions of Mexicans and their children in the United States. Part of the clash between North American pastoral workers and the Hispanic immigrants alluded to in chapter three is directly related to the more traditional values and perspectives of the immigrants versus the modernity of the pastoral workers.

The clash of values and perspectives often described as a clash of cultures can be described as a clash between traditional and modern worldviews as well. It is helpful to dwell somewhat on this clash because not only does it characterize the main areas of conflict between the Hispanic and the Anglo American or dominant worldviews, but it also sheds light on the serious intracultural differences between Hispanic parents and their U.S.-born children. Marcello de Carvalho Azevedo has provided an outline of these conflicting values for his classes at the Pontifical Gregorian University, as illustrated below. From the point of view of evangelization several observations can be made in regard to this sketch.

Nonmodern Cultures	Modern Cultures
Social system organically integrated	Fragmented social system, each element follows its dynamic
Exchange among persons and institutions leads to homogeneity and stability	Pluralism
Religion explains the origins, cements, and legitimizes	Ideologization: systems organized and legitimized in separate camps
Totalizing idea of family, group, person	Primacy of the individual, emphasis on microcosm. Person as center of decision-making. Rights at individual level
Meanings, values, and behaviors are determined and agreed upon, e.g., marriage, sexual roles	Social, economic, and geographical *mobility*
Holistic (physical, mental, and spiritual health are interrelated)	Spiritual, mental, and physical aspects of person compartmentalized
Order is preestablished and permanent	Individualism and pluralism lead to destruction of the internal order of society, to conflict
History is cyclical and static	Change, development, process, linear conception of history
The person is an object, not a subject of history	Order does not derive from culture, but from consent, consensus, or negotiation
The idea of transforming world is foreign	
Basic context for life: person-to-person person-to-family person-to-group	Basic context for life: person-to-things[53]

There are undeniably positive features in both worldviews. It would be a mistake to identify one or the other with the gospel. For instance, the teachings of Jesus appear to be a challenge to traditional ways of thinking about the role of elders, about the place of religious practices, about prejudice and discrimination toward persons of other ethnic or national origins, and about women. Jesus' use of the parable emphasized the people's need to make up their own mind and not blindly follow the precepts of clan, tribe, or official religion. His teachings about justice and his promise to return at the end of time, the eschatological promise, seem to show preference for a linear and not a cyclic view of human existence. A real change can take place, ought to take place, in the world as a result of Christ's saving action. All of these are features that relate positively to modernity.[54]

Nevertheless, there are features of the Gospel which show a preference for traditional values. For instance, there is a strong sense of the interdependence among all persons. This is revealed especially in the institution of the eucharist. Person-to-person relations are preferred to person-to-things relations. Jesus' life is a powerful example of a unifying ideal, a faith, centered on the Father and his will, that motivates everything he does. Jesus also expresses a sense of continuity with history and the past. Atheism as either a philosophical or a practical denial of God and his claims is rejected. Solidarity with others, especially the poor and marginated, is advanced instead of individualism. Materialism as a form of idolatry is condemned, and an ideal of simplicity and generosity is clearly advanced by Jesus' words and actions.[55]

The issue of modernization and secularization, then, is directly related to the changes—personal, structural, and collective—that evangelization as defined by the magisterium promotes. There are aspects of that modernization process which are in conformity with the gospel message and others that are not. In this regard it is important to note that a change has been taking place in the way modernity and secularization are understood. There is increasing discussion about a postmodern era.[56]

Langdon Gilkey has tried to identify the nature of this postmodern period at least as far as theology is concerned. He describes the historical evolution of the secular ideal that finally has entered into crisis. The crisis of modernity has to do with the failure of science and technology to live up to the myth of progress, to answer all the questions, to liberate humanity from all forms of bondage as had been proposed since the age of the Enlightenment. The traditional religious world had long ago entered into crisis. Modernity's emphasis on science and technology had gradually replaced religion as the "cement" of western civilization. But now, according to Gilkey and many others, modernity is also in decline.[57]

The point here is that efforts to evangelize U.S. Hispanics must be grounded on an awareness that the world is entering or has entered a postmodern period. Much of the tension with regard to Hispanics in pastoral settings and in contact with the dominant Anglo American culture is precisely its premodern orientation or qualities. Hispanic culture is not imbued with that awe for science and technology, that enthusiasm for progress, egalitarianism, and independence so typical of the Anglo American.

The point of departure for the evangelizer, then, must be a critical reading of the gospel and the magisterium, not the uncritical, cultural assumptions of the dominant group, especially when those assumptions and values are entering into a period of decay and decline.

By the same token, the evangelizer must go beyond a romanticized concept of premodern, unsecularized cultures. The goal of evangelization cannot be turning back the clock to a purportedly more blissful past. Rather, evangelization must be grounded in a careful, critical view of where the human race is going as it turns the corner into the twenty-first century. Hispanic ministry ought not be a way of assimilating Hispanics into an American Catholic mainstream that is inexorably drying up. Rather, it must be a process whereby persons and communities of Hispanic origin are provided a gospel message that is understandable and accessible yet challenging and relevant to the postmodern period coming into view. The failure to discover this new way of being Catholic and North American is the result of a dichotomous approach to evangelization in which the Anglo Church goes its way and the Hispanic Church goes its. The timely evangelization of U.S. culture depends upon there being a prolonged, serious dialogue between the two. That dialogue, however, has not yet occurred to the extent justified by the reality of the massive Hispanic presence.

Popular Religiousness/Popular Catholicism

Juan Carlos Scannone provides a helpful synthesis of the relevance of popular religiousness or popular Catholicism for evangelization. In a talk at Notre Dame University in 1983, he characterized the discussion in terms of three positions which he believes to be complementary, while personally giving the greatest amount of importance to the third.[58]

The first was initially treated and critiqued by Gustavo Gutiérrez and is called the "distinction of planes" approach. It posits a distinction between the salvific and the temporal within the unity of God's plan. Inspired by Vatican II's thought regarding the autonomy and integrity of the temporal order, on the one hand, and the Church's clearly religious mission on the other, this approach ultimately favors the education of persons and the formation of individual consciences. Because it conceives of the Church's role as more strictly spiritual and remains at a distance from earthly concerns, this approach tends to neglect the formation of the collective conscience and does not attempt to do systemic structural critiques. It focuses more on the individual echoing or mirroring certain values rooted in humanism and the Enlightenment mindset.

With regard to popular religiosity this option tilts toward the more modern aspects of Latin American culture—the culture of the elites—for it views the traditional popular religiosity as needing to adapt to modernity or simply disappear. It proposes to promote this change away from a popular Catholicism that is outdated by forming leaders imbued with the more relevant view of Church and world.[59]

This option is quite prevalent in the United States as well. It is implicit in the pastoral approach which views popular Catholicism as simply something to be programmatically eliminated even if temporarily tolerated. Persons of a strong progressive orientation frequently find this approach congenial.[60]

The second approach to popular religiousness sees it as an essential dimension of evangelization understood in the context of sociohistorical liberation. The understanding of culture here, according to Scannone, is based on an understanding of labor as the most humanizing of experiences. The labor context—access to work, meaningful occupation, and adequate remuneration—is viewed as the main conditioning element in the production of values, meaning, and culture in general. Class conflict as it is understood in the Marxist tradition is an important element in the analysis of the reality of labor and hence of culture. The task of evangelization consequently must be focused on social relations, on structures and conduct that is antisocial, the product of the conditions of labor which need to be changed.

This option, then, stresses the need for all inculturation or evangelization to pass through the liberation from oppressive material conditions. This change is viewed in relation to socialist movements throughout Latin America.[61]

Popular religiosity has a very important instrumental role to play in promoting this fundamental liberation. For popular religiosity is one of the more powerful forms of *cultural resistance* that exists in Latin America. Despite the many "invasions" and forms of colonialism and neocolonialism to which the popular masses have been exposed, popular religion has remained a special sphere of power that thrives and prospers even in persecution or especially in persecution. This perspective is sympathetic to Antonio Gramsci's critique of the traditional Marxist position regarding religion. It suggests that popular religion is not only a useful instrument of resistance, but also a school of values that can be articulated and subsumed in terms of the gospel. Thus, popular religion can have not only a negative but also a *positive* role in the evangelization of the masses.[62]

In this, the second view merges with the third, the one that Scannone finds most congenial of all. He characterizes this option in these words:

> . . . this third approach gives a privileged place to unity rather than conflict. But it does so without totally ignoring the role of conflict. This approach also favors historical and cultural analyses over class analysis. Yet it does not fail to take class analysis into account.[63]

The basis of "unity" is the fountain of popular culture of which popular religiosity is a powerful ingredient. Scannone quotes the Document of Puebla regarding popular religiosity:

> That culture is imbued with faith yet frequently lacks an adequate catechesis. The culture is manifested especially in the religious attitudes of the people. Those attitudes are shot through with a profound sense of the transcendent and concomitantly of God's nearness. The culture translates itself into a popular wisdom with contemplative features. This wisdom sets the tone for our people's way of life especially in regard to their relationship with nature and with other men and women. It performs a similar function with regard to our people's understanding of human labor, celebration, solidarity, friendship, and kinship. This popular wisdom sets the tone for the people's sense of personal worth and dignity which, accordingly, is not diminished by the poverty and simplicity of their way of life.[64]

Scannone stresses this popular culture whose quintessential expression is religious. The concept "popular" and the reference to *pueblo* or the people is not meant to evoke notions of class conflict. Rather, it connotes the historical projects of the Latin American people who share many points in common: poverty, the Catholic faith, a colonial Iberian heritage, a strong *mestizo* presence, and so forth. He goes on to say:

In Latin America the poor and oppressed are the ones who more wisely have resisted cultural aggressions. It is they, as well, who preserve and condense the popular culture of Latin America. Their legitimate aspirations are better orientated toward the struggle for justice and the attainment of the common good. That is why they constitute the nitty-gritty of the process of social and cultural liberation.[65]

The point of departure for the evangelization of culture is the nucleus of values found in popular culture, especially popular religion. When evangelization, the announcement of the gospel, springs from the confrontation of ethos and gospel message, it may reach out and succeed in penetrating the other important areas of life—the social, political, and economic.

Scannone echoes the thought of the Document of Puebla:

At its core the religiosity of the people is a storehouse of values that offers the answers of Christian wisdom to the great questions of life. The Catholic wisdom of the common people is capable of fashioning a vital synthesis. It creatively combines the divine and the human, Christ and Mary, spirit and body, communion and institution, person and community, faith and homeland, intelligence and emotion. This wisdom is a Christian humanism that radically affirms the dignity of every person as a child of God, establishes a basic fraternity, teaches people how to encounter nature and understand work, and provides reasons for joy and humor even in the midst of a very hard life. For the common people this wisdom is also a principle of discernment and an evangelical instinct through which they spontaneously sense when the Gospel is served in the Church and when it is emptied of its content and stifled by other interests.[66]

The task ahead, then, is to create a new synthesis between the cultural heritage—human and Christian—and all that is good and valid in modern society and culture with a view toward their liberation. A pastoral program appropriate to this concept of evangelization must accompany historical processes with the light and the power of the gospel message. The starting point for this evangelization of today's culture must be the inculturation of the gospel faith that has *already taken place* in popular culture and religion. A kind of reculturation is necessary.[67]

In the case of Hispanics in the United States, it is important to keep in mind that popular culture/religion frequently exists in a secondary, not primary, form. That is, this culture is no longer exactly that of the rural families and communities of decades past. This secondary popular culture and religion is the result of migration to urban centers and across borders. Nonetheless, it continues to be the nucleus of values—personal and collective—of the people.[68]

If Scannone is right, the pastoral practice of many priests and other ministers in the United States must be revised. Frequently, that practice reflects, at best, the dichotomous view of the first option presented, namely, that individual conscience, individual conversion, must take place, and that popular religion must be programmatically replaced by the "separation of planes" concept. The end result of this pastoral approach is the destruction of the inner sense of solidarity characteristic of popular Hispanic cultures.

The importance given to the promotion of the standardized, rational Catholicism of the urban middle class is exaggerated. It is an unwise priority that in the long run renders the Hispanic people less rather than more disposed to hear and respond to the gospel message. Rather, this standardizing approach furthers, as can well be imagined, the assimilation of the Hispanic people to the North American urban middle-class culture, a process that often moves people away from the gospel instead of toward it.[69]

The evangelization of Hispanics must deal with two extremes, then. On the one hand, it must, as Scannone suggests, take its point of departure from Latin American popular culture, wisdom, and religion; on the other, evangelization of U.S. Hispanics must also take the middle-class urban culture—truly the most representative form of popular U.S. culture—as another point of departure. The convergence of these two very distinct starting points is precisely the question faced by those who would evangelize the cultures of immigrant peoples in the U.S. For creating a permanent Latin American Catholic subculture is not a viable alternative. Rather, evangelization of culture (and the personal and structural liberation it promises) is focused on a highly mobile and changing Hispanic population that, as the data in chapter one demonstrates, is assimilating into the mainstream.

In an immigrant nation such as the United States, therefore, the evangelization of culture becomes extremely complicated. For it must take into account both the cultural nucleus of the mother culture as well as that of the new (receiving) culture. At *this* point of mutual contact the gospel message must be brought to bear through dialogue, evaluation, and critical consciousness. The goal is a new way of being Church in an Hispanic and North American milieu that is in gestation.

Raimundo Panikkar provides an example of the movement from

traditional to modern to postmodern spirituality and religiousness in *Worship and Secular Man*. He is speaking about the encounter between East and West, but his observations are very helpful in dealing with the clash and conflicts in spirituality and religion taking place in the United States between Hispanics and other third world immigrants and assimilated North Americans. Panikkar refers to the traditional religious mindset as "heteronomy" which he defines as

> . . . a worldview, as well as an anthropological degree of consciousness which relies on a hierarchical structure of reality, which considers that the regulations in any sphere of being come from a higher instance, and are in each case responsible, so to speak, for the proper functioning of that particular being or sphere of being.[70]

Panikkar calls the mindset of modern humanity "autonomous" and by that he means

> . . . an understanding of the world as well as the human being to be *sui generis*, i.e., self-determined and determinable, each being a law unto itself. This autonomy means that any injunction from outside, even if it is said to come from above, is regarded as an abusive imposition.[71]

A third mindset is possible, one which appears in these latter times as a result of the dialectic between heteronomy and autonomy which Panikkar calls "ontonomy," and defines as

> . . . that degree of awareness, which, having overcome the individualistic attitude as well as the monolithic view of reality, regards the whole universe as unity so that the regulation of a particular being is neither self-imposed nor dictated from above, but a part of the whole discovering or following its destiny. Ontonomy is the realization of the *nomos*, the law of the *on*, being, at that profound level where unity does not impinge upon diversity but where the latter is rather the unique and proper manifestation of the former.[72]

Panikkar believes that these three mindsets are not only *or even mainly* three periods in the history of culture, but three fundamental religious and human attitudes corresponding to three anthropological degrees of consciousness.[73]

Panikkar's analysis comes out of his many years of study, teaching, and writing about the meeting of East and West. More than one author has noted the relevance of that issue to the meeting of Anglo American and Hispanic cultures in the Americas. The Mexican essayist José Vasconcelos expressed this concept more than sixty years ago in his book *Indología: Una Interpretation de la Cultura Ibero-Americana*, and his famous *La Raza Cósmica: Misión de la Raza Ibero-Americana.*[74]

The encounter of Hispanic popular Catholicism and religiousness with Anglo American Catholicism therefore should be characterized by the same respect and caution that Christian missioners are showing today toward non-Christian religions of the East. An analogy can be made between those ancient religions and the syncretistic popular Catholicism of the Hispanic in the United States. The end result of treating Hispanic popular Catholicism with more respect will be the creation of a spirituality and religiousness appropriate to cultures that are moving beyond traditionalism or nonmodernity and modernity to a postmodern world characterized by respect for ritual, symbol, and custom as well as religious dialogue and pluralism.[75]

5 | Searching for Pastoral Objectives and Strategies

The preceding chapter focused on four crucial issues that arise in the context of Hispanic ministry in the United States: (1) what it means to evangelize culture; (2) the importance of structural as well as personal conversion; (3) the impact of modernization and secularization on the Hispanic immigrant; (4) the fundamental importance of the Hispanic people's popular religiousness and the urgent need to distinguish it from the normative, more rationalized religion of the U.S. middle class. While many other issues were touched upon in the preceding pages, these were the ones that appear to have transcendent importance. In numerous ways these issues appear and reappear. They constitute an underground current extending in every direction in the varied, rich landscape of Hispanic culture, religion, and society in the United States.

In view of these crucial and admittedly complex issues, what practical pastoral responses are possible? Those responses—whatever form they take—are the sum total of goals, objectives, strategies, and resources developed in confronting the challenge of the Hispanic presence. This chapter is concerned, then, with identifying pastoral strategies that address at some depth the issues listed above. This chapter is a reflection on the pastoral reality outlined in chapter three in the light of the analysis of key issues provided in chapter four.

A review of the documents of the magisterium regarding the Christian community's understanding of its mission or goal in the world reveals, as has been seen, that "evangelization" is the umbrella concept under which the various pastoral/ministerial strategies are organized. The polyvalent nature of the concept, however, has led to a wide range of concrete approaches that reflect more or less the polarities inherent in the concept as developed by Pope Paul VI in *Evangelii Nuntiandi*. It is in relation to the broad concept of evangelization that inculturation, libera-

120

tion, modernity/secularization, and popular Catholicism were discussed in the preceding chapter. Now it seems appropriate to classify in some manner the more immediate objectives that in practice have been conducive to reaching the goal of evangelizing Hispanics in the United States.

There are eight objectives—often explicit, but sometimes implicit—in the pastoral action of ministers working among U.S. Hispanics today: (1) sacramentalization; (2) conscientization and empowerment; (3) the formation of basic ecclesial communities; (4) parish renewal; (5) the promotion of strong, ongoing conversion experiences; (6) the formation of lay leadership; (7) youth ministry; (8) *pastoral de conjunto* or coordinated pastoral planning. These objectives are not mutually exclusive nor incompatible. Nor are they the only objectives that one could identify from an analysis of the literature produced by the hierarchy and the Hispanic Catholic communities themselves. They are, nevertheless, the most persistent and frequently cited objectives in the pastoral service of U.S. Hispanics today.

The purpose of this final chapter, then, is to discuss these objectives with a view toward discovering their mutual relations. The neuralgic point will be precisely the correlation of the objectives to the goal which is evangelization, the Church's primordial task.

Sacramentalization

Dispensing the sacraments and maintaining the liturgical customs and rites of popular religiousness continue to be the more basic objectives of Hispanic ministry today. There is some discomfort with the degree and extent to which this kind of sacramentalization absorbs the energies of the Church's pastoral ministers. This is an emphasis that reflects continuity with the Church as it was before the Second Vatican Council. It is an approach that reaffirms the age-old tradition of the Church. The energies that are expended in providing this service may effectively eliminate other options and objectives in pastoral service.

Persons imbued with the spirit of *aggiornamento* as embodied in the Second Vatican Council may criticize this approach in that it does not stress the need for more active participation, more communion through viable community, and service on behalf of others. Sacramentalization can contribute to the persistence of mechanistic, ritualistic, or even "superstitious" aspects of traditional pre-Vatican II Catholicism. For these reasons there is some discomfort with this aspect of the Church's pastoral action among Hispanics—receiving, as it does, the major portion of time and effort in many if not most Hispanic pastoral settings.[1]

Yet the previous discussion about popular Hispanic Catholicism and the consequences of modernity and secularization for the Hispanic people of the United States seems to indicate that sacramentalization and an explicit orientation toward the sacred is a fundamental aspect of the Church's evangelizing mission, especially among Hispanics.[2] Langdon Gilkey, a Protestant theologian, has expressed profound admiration for Catholicism precisely because of the sacramental, ritual, mythic, and symbolic elements that thrive within it. In "Modern Myth-Making and the Possibility of a Twentieth Century Theology" Gilkey asserts that:

> (1) Secular existence, despite its heated denials, raises ultimate questions for which myth and symbolic language provide the only mode of conceptualization. (2) Mythic discourse is thus relevant to the life of secular culture, as evidenced by the myths borne out of this culture. (3) Secular myths, however, suffer from the inability of the secular mind to think symbolically and so are unable to comprehend the enigmas as well as the blessings of life. Thus they provide an impoverished and unsure base for secular existence. (4) What are lacking in order to thematize the actual experience of a secular culture are symbolic forms referent to mystery, to the transcendent and the sacred, and to the concrete experiences of dislocation and of fault. (5) In current secular mythology (with the exception of the cosmic myths of evolution and Marxism), the meaningfulness and creativity of destiny, of the given, is too radically denied, and the ambiguity of autonomy too easily overlooked. . . . We have argued for the necessity in our cultural life of a mode of mythical discourse that is both "secular"— that is, relevant to the questions and perplexities of our contemporary culture—and yet "theological"—that is, capable of giving consistent symbolic expressions to the human experiences of the transcendent and the sacred.[3]

Gilkey went on to write a book entitled *Catholicism Confronts Modernity*, as mentioned in chapter four. In this seminal work he develops the thesis that Catholicism is in a better position to confront modernity precisely because of the perdurance of sacrament, ritual, and symbol within it. He points to the strenuous effort of liberal Protestantism to deal with the historicity of doctrine—one of the consequences of taking modernity seriously. The result, according to Gilkey, was the emptying of Protestant Christianity of its inner fire and force. Catholicism, in contrast, resisted subjecting its doctrines to the onslaught of modernity and "modernism." Nevertheless, with the coming of Vatican II the Church in some ways did begin to take modernity more seriously. Gilkey's point is precisely that the Roman Catholic Church better not go down the same rationalistic path of liberal Protestantism. Rather, it must pay attention to the symbols preserved over the ages in the living faith of people embodied in the sacramental system, the liturgy and worship—formal and informal—of the faithful. He writes:

> What is called for desperately throughout the Christian churches is a synthesis of Christian revelation and modernity, of the Christian witness and life with the forms of our age, a synthesis with power and authenticity, and thus one as authentically true to the Gospel as it is relevant to modernity. . . . I mean to reinterpret, rethink, and reappropriate the traditional symbols of our Christian tradition in terms of modern experience. . . . Christian faith, then, is a conscious awareness of and committed relation to this continuous and healing divine presence of God the Father of Jesus Christ, *a presence that is experienced, understood, thematized, and so related to and enacted in terms of the symbols of our Christian tradition.*[4]

Gilkey's thought, therefore, bridges two key issues in Hispanic ministry—the highly sacramentalized world of Hispanic popular Catholicism and the powerful influence of modernity and secularization upon the Hispanic people. His call for a synthesis between faith and modern life mediated through the symbols of Christian tradition is especially relevant to the evangelization of Hispanics. The Hispanic communities in the United States continue to manifest the strong orientation of Hispanic Catholicism toward ritual, symbol, and myth. Yet these communities are experiencing an accelerated secularization and modernization. Gilkey's observations suggest that there is a way to synthesize the premodern, symbolic, ritualistic orientation and modern rationality and science. The fact that modernity is in decline, that a new postmodern period has dawned, one characterized by a certain disillusionment with science, technology, and rationality, makes it more likely that the synthesis Gilkey is talking about may come into existence.

Harvey Cox develops the theme of religion in a postmodern age in *Religion in the Secular City.* The famous author of *The Secular City* returns to his theme of secularization twenty-five years later. He points to two dramatic developments: (1) the rise of a vigorous fundamentalism in the

United States; (2) the growing vitality of Catholicism in the third world, especially in Latin America, through the agency of the basic ecclesial communities. In both cases Cox sees what he calls "people's religion" playing a role that "modern" liberal theologies of the past two centuries have not allowed:

> People's religion is not elite or clerical religion or the religion of the cultivated intellectuals. It is a resource for postmodern theology precisely because it is not any of these things. As the faith of those groups which have been least integrated into the premises of modern society, people's religion retains a living contact with those premodern intuitions and images which must become part of a postmodern world vision. People's religion also has a history of resisting and subverting the reign of modernity which will also be a useful resource in moving beyond it. . . . The postmodern enterprise requires a conscious and critical reappropriation of selected elements of the premodern, and this is clearly a critical theological task.[5]

Cox goes on to say that theology is not yet ready to take up this critical task for the reason that modern theology arose as a repudiation of folk piety and popular religion:

> The history of the antagonism (between modern rationality and popular religion) makes it hard for the modern theological enterprise to recognize and draw on people's religion as a key source in the building of a postmodern theology.[6]

In this connection Cox quotes Roger Chartier's study of the *fête* in France from the fifteenth to the eighteenth centuries:

> The festival is one of the privileged scenes where one may observe the popular resistance to normative injunctions as well as the restructuring, through cultural models, of the behavior of the majority.[7]

The point to make here, then, is that a pastoral response to the Hispanic presence must be grounded on an appreciation of the fact that a postmodern era has indeed dawned and that the persistent premodern tendencies of Hispanic, especially Mexican, Catholicism are not a problem; rather, those intuitions, rituals, symbols, and myths are part of the solution. They are essential elements in the restructuring of a Catholic Christianity that will be viable in the decades to come. The thorough training of priests, men and women religious, and lay ministers in "modern" theology explains—in part, at least—the ongoing conflict described in chapter three between the official ministers of the Church and the Hispanic people. Mary Douglas, writing in the context of English and Irish Catholicism, described the dynamics of this conflict in *Natural Symbols*. The Catholic clergy in England were quick to apply a rational concept of fast and abstinence in their pastoral labors:

> In their eyes [that of the clergy] the avoidance of meat on Fridays has become an empty ritual, irrelevant to true religion. In this argument the anti-ritualists are the clergy and the ritualists a type patronizingly known as the Bog Irish. Bog Irishism seems to be a highly magical, irrational, non-verbal culture.[8]

Douglas goes on to show how several modernist prejudices lie behind the clergy's adamant dislike for certain aspects of the ritualistic, symbolic, and mythic faith of these poor Irish immigrants in England. A similar scenario can be painted in the United States in the case of the pastoral encounter of Hispanic immigrants with the clergy.

What is needed, then, in Hispanic ministry is a new assessment of the organic relationship between sacrament in the broadest sense (not just the seven sacraments) and modernity, secularization, and the incipient postmodern age. The Hispanic communities in the United States, precisely because they are still grounded in premodern sensibilities, are key players in the elaboration of a postmodern Catholicism. Some of the fears and tensions formulated in terms of conservative-liberal polarities are expressions of this deeper current of change from premodern to modern and postmodern mindsets. The Hispanic communities and other tradition-based groups in the United States Catholic Church are sometimes not given a great deal of attention because of the historic discomfort of modern theology with forms of religion that are less rational, articulate, and literate.

A similar observation can be made with regard to how today's critical understanding of modernity and the reassertion of sacramentality grounded in popular religion and culture must be taken into account in efforts at conscientization and the promotion of social justice. This is another key objective for Hispanic ministry. The following section deals with precisely this issue.

Conscientization and Empowerment

The process initiated by the proclamation of the gospel message—evangelization—has many points in common with the pedagogy described by Paulo Freire in his highly influential writings. The process of change in one's attitude toward oneself and in one's relation with others and the world (another way of formulating the polarities in *Evangelii Nuntiandi's* definition of evangelization) has been formulated by Freire in his "pedagogy of the oppressed." He coined the Portuguese word *concientização* for this process. Freire's thought has been well received by pastoral agents in Latin America and the United States, even if the profound changes in approaches to education and ministry it implies have not come about as much as one would desire. Denis Collins summarizes the main features of this pedagogy in *Paulo Freire: His Life, Works and Thoughts:*

(1) Reality is experienced by men and women as a process.
(2) People can never be understood apart from their relationship with the world through thought-language.
(3) Men and women are different from animals.
(4) Some people only "live" and fail to "exist."
(5) Human existence is a task of praxis.
(6) Men and women, situated in history, are unfinished.
(7) Men and women have a two-fold ontological vocation: to become a subject and "to name the world." This is what it means to "be human."
(8) The relationship between men and women and the world reveals reality as a problem: the thematic universe and limit situations.
(9) To exist is to act politically for hominization.[9]

Freire's thought provides a compelling view of at least part of the process unleashed by an encounter with the message of Jesus Christ. That is why, no doubt, Freire's pedagogy has been so influential among missioners and evangelizers over the last twenty years. Developed in the context of a literacy program in the northeast of Brazil, Freire's approach became a standard tool of pastoral agents throughout Latin America and was read and commented upon widely in Hispanic ministry circles in the United States. Conscientization or consciousness raising became a stock word expressing the objective of pastoral ministry, namely, the promotion of the process by which people—especially socioeconomically and politically marginal people like the Hispanics—

opened their eyes to the reality around them and entered into a course of action calculated to overcome the dehumanizing situations in which they found themselves. This process necessarily implies the politicization of the people, since involvement in political policy-making is the necessary and inevitable result of taking the world and humanity's place in it seriously. That is why Freire's method was viewed with considerable suspicion. For it leads to all manner of questioning the status quo. Freire paid a heavy price himself, suffering exile from his homeland for more than a decade. [10]

In the context of the United States another social thinker/ practitioner was Saul Alinksy, the father of an approach toward social problems called "community organizing." Alinsky spelled out his principles in *Reveille for Radicals*. [11] Like Freire, Alinsky's thought has inspired a generation of pastoral agents working with Hispanics in the United States. Alinsky was more interested in practical action than in the theory behind the action. In this he is quite different from Freire. Moreover, working and writing in the North American context, Alinsky's underlying view was essentially reformist, that is, he took for granted that the basic political system of the United States was sound. His concept of community organizing is less utopian than Freire's, and in a certain sense it is more conservative. Alinsky dwells upon the criteria and *techniques* to be used in the determination of a community's issues and the strategies to be formulated in confronting an issue with a view toward obtaining the goal sought. [12]

Alinsky's community organizing methodology has been promoted by several national organizations that have significant involvements with Hispanics. The largest of these is the Industrial Areas Foundation in New York. Two of their projects have received considerable notoriety: the COPS project in San Antonio, and the UNO project in Los Angeles. The Industrial Areas Foundation pioneered the marriage between parish and community organization and is providing training for parish ministers in this empowerment methodology. Parishes and congregations, Catholic and non-Catholic, have banded together to define social, political, and economic issues that are of immediate concern in neighborhood, city, or region, to propose solutions and to strategize on how to win those issues. Community organizing, therefore, is one of the more dramatic and obvious ways in which the goal of transformation of unjust social structures is being addressed within the United States. For countless Hispanics, community organizing has provided the first experience of successful political participation. [13]

A third resource in the promotion of social awareness and justice among Hispanics in the United States is advocacy. By advocacy is meant the articulation of social justice issues by committed advocates or persons who study the issues and attempt to exert pressure on those policy-makers, politicians, and interest groups that have a key role in the decision-making process. Advocacy is especially necessary in those cases where the people and groups immediately concerned are unable to express their positions or defend their just interests. Such, for example, is the case of undocumented workers and refugees. Their "underground" status, inability to communicate effectively in English, and lack of political experience make it necessary for others to speak on their behalf. This aspect of advocacy, however, is always somewhat problematic in that it is obviously better for people to speak for themselves than depend on others. A certain paternalism toward the poor and powerless can sometimes insinuate itself in these kinds of situations.

The efforts of the Committee on Migration of the United States Catholic Conference to articulate the justice issues in the long-standing debate about immigration—legal and illegal—is, as mentioned above, a clear example of advocacy. The United States bishops have spoken out in pastoral letters and in testimony given before committees of the U.S. Congress. Regional Hispanic offices have been involved in various aspects of immigrants' rights issues.[14]

There are social justice issues of great import on which committed U.S. Catholics and the U.S. bishops themselves have taken a position: the reduction and eventual elimination of nuclear weapons, the transformation of the U.S. economy along the lines of Catholic social teaching from Pope Leo XIII to Pope John Paul II, the promotion of human life, respect for the unborn, and opposition to the widespread practice of abortion. But these issues and others about which the U.S. Catholic Church is concerned (for example, the rights of women in society and the Church, and pastoral care of persons whose sexual orientation is homosexual) generally do not arise in the context of Hispanic ministry. The sociopolitical and economic context of the Hispanic communities, their history and cultural orientations, are different from the middle-class Anglo American mainstream. Consequently, issues being advocated by Catholic activists are frequently unrelated to the immediate concerns of Hispanics. Cultural sensitivity, much dialogue, and mutual respect can bridge this gap, but it is not easy. Given the silence and consequent inarticulateness of many Hispanic communities and the very different world views of the Hispanic and Anglo American cultures, advocacy in Hispanic situations can become a rather extrinsic recourse in the promotion of social justice.[15]

Conscientization and community organizing are obviously more substantial ways of promoting evangelization understood as struggle for social change because they require an inner change in attitude and empower people to act as subjects rather than continue as passive objects. Advocacy, nevertheless, remains a necessary and useful complement in certain situations when those directly concerned are especially powerless and silent.

The discussion about specific ways to promote social change as a constitutive element of evangelization raises another issue of great importance. Luis Alberto Gómez de Souza has written an especially provocative article that deals with the question of the relationship between the traditional religious orientation of Latin American Catholicism and social change. He maintains, as already discussed above, that secularization and modernity are on the decline. While admitting the historical alliance of Church and power establishment over the years, Gómez de Sousa believes that

> The international character of the Catholic Church's power apparatus has made it one of the few forces capable of confronting the Latin American State in the authoritarian episodes of those States. . . . Religion which up to now has appeared to be one of the basic pillars of the official "established disorder" has now come to be viewed as subversive.[16]

In evaluating the implications of this new role for religion—official religion united to the people's popular religion and causes—Gómez de Souza notes that

> One of the more frequent observations is that religion in situations of social conflict loses its transcendent dimension, becoming enslaved to a kind of "historical flattening." Religion can turn into one more ideology among others reduced to a purely political function. We can begin, indeed, admitting that such a simplification is always possible and that religion has transformed itself into a political banner many times throughout history.[17]

The author goes on to say that "La irreductibilidad de la revelación cristiana no podría ser limitada a una opción histórica particular."

Gómez de Souza is pointing to one of the more obvious and important consequences of conscientization, commitment to social justice, namely the need to promote political responsibility as a fruit of effective ministry. Taking the social transformation element of evangelization seriously means precisely that. But it is not without problems and possible confusions. That is why the Brazilian sociologist's conclusion is so relevant:

> One has to always insist that political commitments arise out of practical involvement and social analysis. Religion—or the religions—ought not be the originating sources of the political option. Rather, fundamentally they ought to provide a critical and radical point of view from which all forms of domination can be opposed and hopes raised for the real transformation of the world.[18]

His point, then, is that the goal of social/structural transformation that is an integral element of evangelization means that faith and the gospel permanently retain a critical role and cannot be reduced to political projects, visions, schemes, or utopias of any kind without losing their integrity and originality. This point is well taken in regard to Hispanic ministry which most certainly has to do with the politicization of the Hispanic communities who, as chapter one demonstrated, lack sociopolitical and economic power, are often not treated with the dignity worthy of sons and daughters of God, and are not participating in the important decisions that affect them. Evangelization leads to the formation of persons and communities who are politically responsible. Conscientization and empowerment are objectives leading to that greater goal. But politicization carries with it a great risk, namely, it can subvert the authentic critical function of gospel faith. In that regard the formation of basic Christian communities, the next area to be treated, offers some hopeful possibilities.

Basic Ecclesial Communities

The interest of pastoral agents in basic ecclesial communities (BECs) as privileged instruments of evangelization—as an especially important objective for diocese and parish in the evangelization of Hispanics—has continued unabated over the past decade. The Tercer Encuentro National Hispano de Pastoral reconfirmed this orientation as mentioned in chapter three. Yet a review of the written reports and data on BECs in the United States, as mentioned in the same chapter, reveals that the BECs are not as widespread as the enthusiasm and commentary on them would indicate. Marcello Azevedo has written perhaps the most thorough assessment currently available in English of the origins and nature of these communities in the Brazilian context. A basic fact about these communities is that they have thrived in rural areas and in the peripheries of urban centers. They have generally not thrived in cities. As the demographic data in chapter one indicated, the U.S. Hispanic is massively an urban dweller, the second most urbanized minority in the U.S. after the Asians. Where the Church in the form of parish and clergy has not been present, the BEC finds a more propitious environment. Where those elements of Church are present it seems to have more difficulty in taking root.[19]

Nevertheless, the general interest in the promotion of small faith-sharing communities, whether they be called BECs or not, has become a basic characteristic of pastoral practice throughout the North American Church, not just among the Hispanic element in that Church. One excellent example of this is RENEW, the parish renewal process that began in the archdiocese of Newark and has promoted thousands of faith-sharing groups—organized within the parish—throughout the United States.[20]

The effort to move in the direction of BECs appears to be related to an insight about the nature of evangelization as understood today in the Church. These insights have already been discussed, but they need to be repeated here: (1) evangelization must be deeply rooted in culture (inculturated); (2) evangelization must lead to change in oneself and in the community, the environment, and the world and its concrete structures; (3) evangelization leads to political responsibility; (4) evangelization provides an ongoing (permanent) point of reference for critical analysis rooted in gospel imperatives that go beyond ideology.

Azevedo has shown how the BECs, at least in the Brazilian context, have effectively responded to these insights. They have also responded to other important features of the religious reality of the Brazilians, features that they share in common with U.S. Hispanics—a deep tradition of popular religion, a passive, nonparticipative orientation toward political involvement, a lack of familiarity with the Bible, and several other similarities. For that reason the relevance of these communities to the Hispanic context cannot be denied, even though the concrete form taken by them may depart in significant ways from the Brazilian pattern.[21] The potential of the BECs for evangelizing in the deepest and richest sense of that word is expressed by Azevedo in this brief summary of the achievements of the Brazilian communities:

> Without ceasing to be common "people," BECs have become one of the most valuable locales and means for evangelizing people in Brazil. This is so because BECs, operating within the religiousness of the people and remaining faithful to it, give it a new meaning. This results from a critical view of

popular religiousness (its passivity, fatalism, and so forth), and from the linkup of faith and life, projecting the demands of faith into the social sphere and overcoming the traditional dualism. In addition, BECs allow for the constant refueling of the evangelization process in and by the community itself. And this in a country where the presence of the priest is shrinking while the secularizing influence of the surrounding society is growing. BECs need the support and help of clergy and religious, but they are not dependent on them in any paralyzing way. Finally, in their own work of evangelization BECs link up word of God, sacrament, and action. Thus they give entirely new directions to an earlier type of evangelization in which these elements were frequently dissociated, absent, or simply nonexistent.[22]

The promotion of BECs, then, continues to be an objective of special importance in the evangelization of U.S. Hispanics. These communities provide a locus uniquely suitable for evangelization. For it is in the context of community and mutual support that the gospel message can take root in a people. In the impersonal and somewhat isolated context of the large urban parish it is impossible to create the conditions needed for evangelization understood as inculturation of the faith, personal/social conversion, or as political action on behalf of justice. That is why these communities continue to receive a great deal of attention among Hispanic Catholic leaders in the United States. For it is difficult to see how the Church's mission of evangelization can ever be achieved without creating the conditions of the BEC in some form or other.[23]

Parish Renewal

In chapter three, the fundamental importance of the parish in U.S. Church history was underscored. The vitality of this institution, especially in the United States, has been widely commented. The historical experience of Hispanics with the parish as basic instrument of evangelization and Church organization is limited in comparison with the Anglo American experience. Given the institutional strength of the parish in the United States, nevertheless, it must be given emphasis. The parish is the place where Hispanics come into contact with the gospel message. It provides a secure context for pastoral planning. The parish, moreover, makes continuity in evangelization possible in the long range. It provides an adequate base—financial and organizational—for carrying out any number of pastoral projects.[24]

In the Hispanic context the parish is especially linked with sacramental ministry. For that reason pastoral agents imbued with the spirit of the Second Vatican Council and Pope Paul VI's vision of evangelization sometimes find the parish frustrating and limiting. Rigid schedules and extensive pastoral duties can make the parish a kind of treadmill that is not conducive to the reform and renewal of this postconciliar period. The large number of Hispanics and the relatively small number of priests and other ministers qualified to serve Hispanics create a situation in which there is not enough energy to move beyond a "holding action" approach to parish ministry. Pastors are frequently reluctant to assume new commitments and projects, since their hands are full with what they have. More importantly, the lack of a clear focus on ministry within diocese and Church makes it difficult to truly prioritize. An endless flow of new projects and tasks promoted by diocesan offices without clear goals and objectives processed, assumed, and owned by the community at large creates the impression that "busywork" instead of serious evangelization is being promoted.[25]

In the specific case of the parish with a significant number of Hispanics there are several ways for the parish to respond, as was outlined in chapter three. In terms of the Church's task of evangelization as understood in the present study, the following observations can be made.

The celebration of the Sunday eucharist and the conferral of the other sacraments is not in itself an adequate emphasis for the parish. Access to good religious education for children and adults in conjunction with the reception of those sacraments is not enough either. In addition, offering a wide range of activities for youth, senior citizens, divorced, handicapped, and others is still not enough. Having excellent music and good opportunities to socialize is not enough. All of the above are good and contribute to the formation of a strong and viable parish. But the goal of evangelization is not necessarily achieved nor guaranteed by such activities. The process of conversion at the personal and structural levels requires an environment of community concern and interaction that none of the above activities necessarily imply. While there are exceptional parishes that have a focus outward toward service of the broader community, there is a tendency for parishes to be turned inward on their own inner dynamics and life. In such a context, ministry is conceived of as *parish or church* ministry and not as service in the world. In such a framework the parish can become a kind of monastery, the "city of God on earth." Moreover, the role of pastoral agents, especially the laity, can become clerical—focused on the institutional needs of Church rather than the needs of society. This in turn fosters confusion regarding the proper role of priests in distinction from the role of laity.[26]

When the locus of evangelization is displaced from parish to home and neighborhood, several benefits are gained. One of them is that the massified environment of today's urban parish—where the vast majority of Hispanics are found—is mitigated. Another is that the possibility of receiving personal testimony of God's action in the real life of flesh and blood people is enhanced. The Sunday homily in itself is not an adequate tool for the giving of testimony—limited as it is to priests and deacons. Women, professionals, workers, immigrants, and youth are the ones most suited to give the testimony that will move their peers to conversion. The extraordinary success of *cursillos de Cristiandad*, the charismatic renewal, and marriage encounter is due in large part to the central place given peer testimony in the dynamics of these movements.[27]

In addition to the personal changes that can come about within the context of small communities that meet in homes rather than at the parish, there is the possibility of conversion in the social or structural sense. Concretely that means a change in attitude about one's responsibility to others, especially the poor and marginal, in society. That means the politicization of the community not in the narrow partisan sense but in the sense of concern for public policy. The parish is not the most suitable place for that kind of action for several reasons. One of them is that the Church as institution (of which the parish is a basic unit) risks losing its tax-exempt status if it gets involved in direct political action. Nor is it appropriate for the clergy as clergy to be directly involved in politics. The large parish, moreover, must be a place of dialogue and pluralism where it is less likely that focused public policy positions will emerge. The small community, on the other hand, is a free association of citizens. They are not the institutional base in the same sense that the parish is. They have the greater possibility and responsibility of acting upon society and its structures on behalf of justice.[28]

The historical experience of promoting BECs among U.S. Hispanics in California reveals that there is need to avoid the tendency for these communities to become parallel churches imbued with the idiosyncracies of the leaders who initiate them. Interviews with Hispanic leaders in California, as mentioned in chapter three, indicate that many of the communities disintegrate within three to five years. Others evolve into charismatic prayer groups, and some become militant cells promoting social change in a manner that makes the group appear to be a kind of "underground" church with relation to the parish and diocese. Given the lack of financial and institutional security characteristic of BECs relative to the parish and diocese, there are considerable practical, organizational problems militating against their survival in the long run if they function apart from the parish.[29]

The BECs need to develop in a manner organically related to the broader life of the local Church—parish and diocese. How can that be done? The approach taken by RENEW is a good example. In this process the effort to establish ongoing small faith-sharing communities is integrated into a broader process of parish and diocesan renewal. The RENEW process tries to lay a firm foundation for the small faith-sharing communities by making sure that the local authorities—pastors and bishops—understand what is going to happen and, if not completely convinced, are willing to get out of the way to allow the process to unfold. Considerable time is given to articulating a clear, simple, and up-to-date theology of evangelization adequate to the systematic renewal of all aspects of Church life: liturgy, preaching, prayer, service, and even decision-making. The process is expressed in terms of sound biblical theology and takes as its point of departure the Second Vatican Council, never moving too far beyond its theological and disciplinary parameters.

As a result, the RENEW process defuses fears about small faith-sharing groups becoming parallel or underground churches. This is most helpful given the fragile character of BECs in their initial stages. A supportive environment from those in authority can obviously be very helpful. Efforts to establish BECs that prescind from, ignore, or oppose competent ecclesial authority at the parish level have been shown to be problematic. Generally they do not survive, especially in the urban context of most Hispanic ministry in the U.S., as well as in the larger Church that gives so much importance to the parish.

The RENEW process is only one way to proceed, but much can be said in its favor. No other process or movement has succeeded in initiating as many ongoing small faith-sharing communities in the United States among Anglo American or Hispanic communities. They number in the thousands.[30]

Another important consideration that relates directly to the renewed parish is the need to link the concepts of evangelization, community, and process/pilgrimage. One mindset in the Church emphasizes the sure and unchanging truths of Catholic faith and practice. Another mindset promotes transformation of practice and outlook in the service of justice. Between these two attitudes there is frequently a wide gulf. The parish can become the place where polarities of this type can be effectively faced. One of the reasons why these polarities can cause a great deal of difficulty is that western Christianity, in the view of Jacob Needleman and others, may have lost the sense of journey that is essential for a faith that proposes to transform individuals, societies, and indeed the whole world. A sense of journey is expressed through the articulation of stages or levels of growth, personal appropriation, and assimilation. Needleman is speaking of this lack in relation to eastern religions which, he claims, have maintained a vivid sense of religious commitment as journey and not as some finished achievement.[31] John Coleman, reflecting on the implications of Needleman's insight, writes that Needleman "sees Christianity as speaking the highest language of union with God without providing the necessary means to dispose towards it."[32]

Jesús Andrés Vela applies this observation to the context of evangelization in Latin America and to the conflicting views of what evangelization entails in that continent:

> There is a double danger: (1) to consider the Church merely an organization that "functions" with clear doctrines and obligations or (2) see her merely as a revolutionary force militating for social change. Such simplistic views involve making little of the Church's ancient effort to find concrete paths and methods for the progressive education of the person and the community in attitudes. The path begins with conversion and moves toward the full acceptance of Christ verified through the apostolate of Christian service and ministry. In either simplification the search for pastoral models with their specific processes is undervalued. These models and processes stress the development of a mature Christian personality in the context of community. When the institution is stressed the result can be an excessive concern for juridical and organizational aspects. When socio-political engagement is stressed the forces contributing to revolutionary changes are almost exclusively supported in detriment to the process by which Christian attitudes are really interiorized. Concern for the interiorization of attitudes can be dismissed as "intimistic and spiritualizing."[33]

Vela makes this observation in his exhaustive study of the relevance of the Rite of Christian Initiation of Adults (RCIA) to the cultural Catholicism or "sociological baptism" of Latin Americans. One of the major conclusions of the study is that the RCIA is an extraordinarily rich resource for integrating the various views of evangelization and the instrumentalities of parish, BEC, and sacraments. He indicates that there have been isolated efforts to integrate the RCIA with parish-based catechesis of children and adults in Latin America. But this effort has yet to bear much fruit.

The same can be said for the RCIA in the context of U.S. Hispanics. While it has made a considerable impact on Anglo American Catholics, it has hardly been implemented in any Hispanic context in the U.S. There has been some discussion about adapting it to those who are already baptized as a finely worked process for reevangelization and ongoing conversion, but this has hardly been done within an Hispanic setting in the United States.[34]

Vela believes that one of the difficulties of the BEC is the failure to relate the growth of the community, its stages, successes, failures, and goals, to the official liturgy of the Church. He believes that such an integration is quite possible. This deficiency has two serious consequences. One is that the unity of the small community with the larger Church is not expressed and symbolized as effectively as it should. Another is that the real need for symbolic and ritualistic expression of the community's faith is not being satisfied. The RCIA links community with symbol and ritual in a way that no normative document of the Church has done in centuries. It does so progressively in a manner that recognizes the need for plotting out the Christian journey in successive stages that are attainable for persons of flesh and blood.

The point to be made here, then, is that the RCIA provides a particularly powerful instrument for helping the renewed parish integrate the polarities in evangelization (personal change, social commitment) with the BEC. Moreover, the small community finds a framework for solidifying itself in prayer, liturgy, and celebration.

The RCIA becomes a powerful link bridging the institutional strength of the parish and wider Church with the energy radiated by small faith-sharing communities. In the case of U.S. Hispanics, popular religious expressions and the deep abiding sense of *fiesta* can complement the RCIA's already rich selections of celebrations and commissionings. Through the instrumentality of a "way" or journey like that proposed by the RCIA, the strengths of the parish and the small faith-sharing community are powerfully enhanced. It provides a comprehensive "package" and pedagogy that integrates all the elements in the Church's rich understanding of evangelization today. As such, the RCIA is unquestionably one of the most powerful resources available today for the renewal of parishes in the spirit of the Second Vatican Council.[35]

So the question must be asked why the RCIA has not gained

momentum within the context of U.S. Hispanics. It would seem that a useful tool in the renewal of parish as center of evangelization is being neglected. Similarly, the failure to link the resources of the RCIA with the promotion of BECs is perhaps one reason for the relative weakness of these communities in the North American context. Perhaps the answer to the question about the neglect of the RCIA has something to do with the persistence of dichotomous, selective thinking on the part of pastoral agents. One of the polarities in evangelization, one concept of Church, one favorite instrumentality, is stressed while others are ignored. Consequently, long-range, organic models are shunned in favor of more immediately satisfying ones.

A more inclusive and "catholic" way of looking at the pastoral challenge of Hispanic ministry at the parish level suggests that a more comprehensive view of goals, methods, and strategies must be adopted. Accordingly, the BEC should not be viewed necessarily as a threat to the viability of the larger parish. Quite the contrary, the existence of small faith-sharing communities is essential if the parish is to truly become a center of evangelization as the magisterium understands that term. By the same token, the small faith-sharing communities should not view the parish as a massified, deadening institution that holds back the small community. The BECs in the U.S. context do not appear to be surviving to any great extent outside the protective and potentially empowering mantle of the parish.[36]

Ongoing Conversion

The influence of evangelical and charismatic religion upon society in the United States has been well documented. This kind of religion gives great importance to the encounter of the individual with God and God's grace as experienced through the person of Jesus Christ. This emphasis contrasts with the calmer, less dramatic approach characteristic of Catholicism, especially the cultural Catholicism of U.S. Hispanics. Notwithstanding the calmness of traditional Catholicism compared to charismatic religion, there are certainly points of contact between popular Hispanic Catholicism and evangelical religion.[37]

One of the features of the new charismatic religion is its level of affectivity. Feeling, movement, and drama are given expression in a relatively spontaneous way. Standard Catholicism mediated through the somewhat austere Roman rite preserves a decorum and coolness that is appealing to some, but limited in certain cultural contexts.[38]

In Hispanic America the limitations of the standard Roman Catholic style of liturgy, prayer, and worship were mitigated, as was seen in previous chapters, by medieval, baroque, and indigenous influences. In the United States the mitigating function of popular religious expressions is compromised by the spirit and mood of Anglo American styles of liturgy, worship, and prayer which, like the Roman rite, are perceived as cool and at times "hygienic" by Hispanics. The unease and occasional conflict experienced by both U.S. Hispanics and Anglo Americans when brought together in worship—even in the same Catholic church—is worth noting. There seems to be a need for more colorful, dramatic, and emotive religious and liturgical expressions among Hispanics. The charismatic emphasis on conversion and in the giving of testimony about that conversion establishes a level of emotivity that can be attractive to U.S. Hispanics. This is one of the factors which attracts Hispanics to the evangelical and/or charismatic style.

In a related manner the appeal of strong weekend conversion experiences such as the *cursillo* as noted in chapter three derives from the need for persons who are "culturally" Catholic or Christian to appropriate that faith in a more profound and personal way. No statistics exist with regard to the impact of *cursillo* on Hispanic Catholics in California or elsewhere, but it is generally conceded that a large percentage of laity involved in leadership positions including clergy involved in Hispanic ministry are *cursillistas*.

The appeal of evangelical/charismatic religion and strong weekend conversion experiences is especially strong among second and third generation Mexican Americans or Chicanos. This group, more than the native Mexicans or Latin Americans, has experienced ongoing rejection. This group, more than their parents, has experienced the confusion characteristic of the children of immigrants. They are not totally accepted by their parents because they are "different," nor are they accepted by the new culture for similar reasons. The personal experience of God's love and unconditional acceptance is the hallmark of the first stage of conversion. That experience, then, is fundamental for the healthy religious development of Hispanics, especially the second and third generations among whom there is an understandable thirst for acceptance.[39]

The ongoing flirtation of Hispanic Catholic communities in the U.S. with Pentecostal sects and Protestant evangelicalism is a consequence of several factors:

(1) a personal conversion experience—strongly fostered by the sects—which has not been a feature of Hispanic Catholicism rooted as it was in culture and in the collectivism of rural societies;[40]
(2) nostalgia for the more dramatic, graphic, and emotive popular religiousness that existed in the homeland;
(3) the systematic diminution of this popular religiousness by Catholic priests and pastoral agents in the United States.

That belittling, misunderstanding or outright opposition has in turn two major explanations: first, the cultural differences between Anglo American Catholicism rooted in northern Europe and Ireland versus Hispanic American Catholicism rooted in the pre-Columbian, medieval and baroque worlds; second, the efforts to apply the liturgical renewal as understood in Vatican II across the board without taking popular religiousness and the need to inculturate very seriously. This effort is yet another instance of the tendency to impose more rational, middle-class frameworks upon the religious reality of a people. The result is bewilderment, misunderstanding, and resentment on the part of the people, and frustration on the part of the pastoral agents.[41]

An emphasis on ongoing conversion contributes to the overcoming of this impasse between the people's religion and the official, middle-class religion. The conversion experience personalizes the faith and provides a foundation *other than custom and tradition* for Christian life. That foundation is an adult, personal encounter with Jesus Christ mediated in a new way through the dynamics of a weekend retreat or prayer group. The problem, as already discussed, is that the concept of conversion is frequently too narrow and does not readily result in the insertion of the person into viable faith-sharing communities committed to service of the world. What is lacking is a sound pastoral strategy, a pedagogy that enshrines the experience in a "way" that is attainable in stages and in the long term. A sound view of the conversion process, moreover, suggests that the rich patrimony of popular religiousness should not be discarded (as is the practice of evangelical Protestants) but that it be subsumed into a more integral and organic Christian faith—the gospel faith that the magisterium's rich and nuanced concept of evangelization aims to promote.

That nuanced concept of evangelization incarnated into a pedagogy has at its very heart the notion of ongoing conversion. That means conversion at the affective, intellectual, moral, religious, and political levels. It is not a once and for all change of heart, but rather a progressive change, a human process, not some miraculous superevent. There are certainly strong moments of conversion experience deeply felt. There are strong moments of insight when the truths of faith are perceived with unusual clarity. There are activities of service and commitment to social change when the human will reveals a high level of conformity to the conviction and truth of one's faith in Christ. There may be mystical moments, as well, of numinous presence and union with God. All of these experiences are important and all in some way are necessary as expressions of conversion to the Lord. But none of them should be absolutized and all of them must be encouraged lest the goal of evangelization be obscured, deformed, or bypassed.

One of the consequences of taking the concept of ongoing conversion seriously within the context of Hispanic ministry is evaluating every movement, organization, agency, catechetical, liturgical, educational, and social program of the Church among Hispanics in terms of the five stages of conversion and the magisterium's complete concept of evangelization which those levels of conversion complement. The failure to view ongoing conversion in relation to the Church's holistic concept of evangelization is the source of considerable confusion and loss of energies in pastoral ministry across the board, not just in Hispanic ministries.

The Formation of Lay Leadership

One of the more constant appeals heard in the field of Hispanic ministry is the need to train or form lay leaders. Two of the ways to achieve that goal have already been discussed, namely, the community organizing and the BEC models. Both of them are excellent sources for the transformation of laity from passive bystanders in the Church to active ministers and leaders. In this section the objective of lay leadership formation will be viewed more broadly in terms of some of the issues raised in previous chapters.

The very use of the word "leader" in the Hispanic context—certainly in the Mexican or Mexican American context—is somewhat problematic as was seen in chapter four in the section dealing with social change and empowerment. A recent study of Mexican parents by the Centro de Estudios Educativos shows that training children to be leaders is considered to be one of the *least* important qualities to be promoted in childrearing. In Mexico, to be a "leader" frequently implies involvement in abuse of power and for that reason can hardly be a virtue.[42] The persistence of *caudillismo, caciquismo,* and the rigid sense of hierarchy that has characterized Mexican society since the Aztecs means that the promotion of "leadership" within this cultural context is more complicated than it may appear at first.

Illustrative of this need for adaptation of terminology and sensitivity to cultural background is the process of forming leaders for BECs or small faith-sharing groups. If one says that leaders are being formed, some Hispanics may take that to mean that some persons are being selected to assume great responsibility over the group, to make the major decisions, carry the brunt of activities, and become the *jefes* or "bosses." In an historically nondemocratic world of leaders and followers like the Hispanic one, the more subtle, participative form of leadership expressed by the words "coordinator," "moderator," and "facilitator" are difficult to grasp. Indeed there is an even deeper issue. Harry

Eckstein has studied the efforts made over the past century to promote participation of working-class people in sociopolitical action. He has studied the efforts of democratic societies such as those of Great Britain and the United States to promote the participation of disenfranchised groups from the lower socioeconomic class in decision-making. He calls this civic inclusion. Part of that process consists precisely in the creation of responsible leaders among groups that had little or no power in society. He writes:

> There are dramatic discrepancies between what was expected to follow from civic inclusion and what has in fact happened. . . . My proposed explanation of these discrepancies rests on the notion that there exists an authority culture of the lower-classes of society—the beneficiaries of civic inclusion—that has been poorly understood by the higher-class proponents of inclusion. . . . I consider lower-class authority to be a positive and adaptive response to the defining trait of poverty: being compelled to live with and manage high scarcity. The authority-culture of the poor is all the more resistant to change because of this.[43]

The point to be made here is that the supposition that greater participation in the life of society and the overcoming of structural injustices will occur by simply opening society up to more participation by the powerless is too simple. There are many examples of previously oppressed, marginated groups being as oppressive or possibly more oppressive than the groups they replaced. The violent and repressive political machines of second generation Irish and Italians in some parts of the United States are examples of this.

The idea that leadership understood as service in the Christian tradition can be effectively promoted among poor and marginated groups such as the Hispanic without taking into account the deeply embedded historical experience of the people and their vigorous authority-culture needs to be questioned. But questioning that proposition is especially difficult in the "enlightened," culturally liberal society of the United States that naively presumes (against a great deal of evidence) that social progress automatically results from opening up opportunities for participation and leadership to previously excluded groups. There are many complex issues raised by Eckstein's work and the final word obviously cannot be given here. The point is that within pastoral circles there must be more awareness of the complexity of the issue about leadership formation and empowerment of previously excluded groups. For the opportunities for leadership in the Church could conceivably reinforce oppressive leadership styles and work against broader and truer participation. There is a need to promote truly participative structures and constantly evaluate them.[44]

It would be a mistake to infer from these remarks that leadership formation is not an appropriate objective in Hispanic ministry. It is essential, a form of ministry whereby the life of the Christian community is structured, and takes form and substance. The majority of leaders being formed at various levels from ordained ministers to laymen and women in parish, catechetical, social, and liturgical ministries are undoubtedly viewing their leadership roles as nothing more than service in the unique Christian understanding of what power, influence, and authority in the Church serve. Concern for Hispanics and the preferential option for the poor ought not to be, nevertheless, a naive, romantic, unanalyzed conviction that fails to deal with the ongoing efforts in the social sciences to grasp these cultural, socioeconomic, and historical trends in all their vexing complexity. Not everything that purports to advance the well-being of the poor or that springs from a sincere commitment to promote the well-being actually does so. That is why diachronic and synchronic studies of the reality are so necessary, lest important aspects of the truth be sacrificed on the altar of unanalyzed myth or sentiment.

Finally, there is a more basic point to be made about leadership formation in the Hispanic context. There is some frustration among Hispanic laity due to the resistance of some priests and bishops to allowing the laity to truly function as leaders. The magisterium itself has insisted on the proper role of laity in the Church, and the Extraordinary Synod on the Laity held in October of 1987 exemplifies the Church's keen interest in this theme. Efforts to open up parish and diocesan structures to more lay participation have been uneven. There continues to be considerable concern about the sincerity and seriousness of the call for lay leadership formation when sometimes those leaders are not accepted by the hierarchical ministers and their role is minimized, ignored, or eliminated.[45]

Underlying the issue of leadership is the prior issue of ministry—hierarchical and nonhierarchical. Leadership will have a tendency to model or reflect hierarchical ministry. It will reflect on the one hand an openness and orientation to service if hierarchical ministry reflects these values. It may reflect, on the other hand, concern for power, prestige, and status to the extent that hierarchical ministry does. Consequently the authority-culture of nondemocratic societies may be reinforced or replicated by leadership and lay ministry in the Church.

These are matters that go beyond the scope of this study. They indicate a need to establish more clearly the mutual relationship between concepts of ministry—ordained and nonordained—and concepts of leadership in the Church.[46]

Youth Ministry

The Hispanic population of the United States is the most youthful of all ethnic groups in the country. The Mexican origin part of that population is the youngest of all. The average Hispanic of Mexican origin is ten years younger than the average Anglo American.[47] Hispanic ministry is therefore ministry with youth to a degree and extent beyond other Catholic groups. The importance of youth was stressed in the Latin American context at the Puebla Conference in 1979. Along with the preferential option for the poor, Puebla also expressed a preferential option for youth.[48] The Tercer Encuentro also emphasized the need for more organized, consistent participation of youth in the Church, for more services and more recognition of youth at every level of the Church's life and action in the United States.[49]

In 1977 a National Youth Task Force was established at the Segundo Encuentro Nacional Hispano de Pastoral. Today it is called the Comité Nacional Hispano de Pastoral Juvenil. This committee works with the Secretariat of Hispanic Affairs in Washington, D.C. At the various regional levels other youth committees are working to coordinate and support diocesan Hispanic youth ministry initiatives. There are directors of Hispanic youth ministry in many dioceses of the United States and there are many Hispanic youth ministers working in parishes throughout the country. Given the massive numbers of Hispanic youth—at least 43 percent are under the age of twenty-five— there continues to be an urgent need to address the special circumstance of this massive presence of Hispanic youth.[50]

There are several issues that impact the functioning of Hispanic youth ministry in the U.S. context. The first is sociocultural in nature. The concept of "youth" is generally different in the Hispanic community than in the Anglo American community. For Hispanics, youth is the time from puberty to marriage. Therefore it is defined more in terms of being married or not, rather than in terms of age. Among Hispanics of the lower socioeconomic class—the vast majority of U.S. Hispanics—the number of years in school are fewer. In the case of the immigrant youth the level of schooling is very low. That group represents about half the population of Hispanic youth in California. What that means is that a significant percentage of the immigrant youth, frequently the undocumented immigrant youth, are workers, not students. Their attitudes, needs, and expectations are therefore much different from the average high school or college youth, whether Hispanic or otherwise. In a sense these young workers are adults. They are responsible wage earners. They are away from home and their need to make important decisions and "carry their weight" in family and society has not been postponed. If anything, it has been accelerated. They are living much like young adults. Comparable youth in middle-class Anglo American society are being "nurtured" in school and the time for their "carrying their own weight" postponed sometimes for years as they go through high school, college, and graduate or professional school.

The kinds of programs and issues that concern high school youth ministry are relevant to first generation Hispanic youth who are in U.S. high schools. Generally they are not relevant to working immigrant Hispanic youth who are in a much different psychosocial environment. Moreover, the distinction between youth and young adult ministry is more difficult to make in the Hispanic context because of the Hispanic tendency to marry earlier, the pressures against being single, and the involvement of so many young people in full-time employment and not in school. In the Anglo American context the socioeconomic and cultural pressures are on prolonging the period of youth, while in the Hispanic context they are on shortening the period of youth. Consequently it becomes difficult to relate youth ministry as it is conceived and practiced in Anglo American and middle-class environments with the needs of Hispanic youth, especially the immigrant youth.[51]

An even more important observation to make is that the cultural approaches to the education and formation of youth in their religion can take many different forms. In this connection Michael Warren's *Youth, Gospel, Liberation* is very helpful. Warren traces the historical evolution of youth ministry in the United States. He shows how it comes out of the Protestant experience that transferred religious formation from the family context to professional religious educators who would intervene decisively in the life of youth to promote a deeper conversion in them and to instill Christian moral values. The public school—despite the fact that it was to be religiously neutral—was supposed to perform the second task of instilling Christian and American moral values. As the children were given the opportunity for increased schooling the institutions that worked with youth assumed increasing control over youth vis-à-vis parents. Joseph Ketts describes the state of affairs at the end of the nineteenth century:

A common thread which ran through college "life," the high
school extra-curriculum, and the Christian youth organizations was hostility to precocity, to adult behavior in youth. As
it acquired institutional forms, the long-standing fear of precocity changed its shape. The avoidance of precocity no
longer entailed merely the removal of intellectual pressures
and social stimulants from youth, but the creation of a self-
contained world in which prolonged immaturity could sustain
itself.[52]

Warren believes that there was a shift from the *nurturing* of youth
for religious purposes to the *education* of youth for civic and religious
purposes. One consequence of this was the postponing of maturity and
the creation of an unreal atmosphere of nurturing and comforting of
youth in school settings. Whatever be the merits of this development in
U.S. society, the point is that comforting youth rather than challenging
them became the function of youth ministry.[53]

For Warren, one of the most important features of youth ministry
today is

. . . replacing the nineteenth century legacy of programs limited to trivial concerns—programs which offered youth a
largely privatized view of their own lives and extended their
dependence on adults. So persistent and taken-for-granted is
this legacy that many have difficulty seeing it.[54]

One of the consequences of this legacy for Warren is the silence of
youth. Since they are not yet ready to contribute to society because
their education goes on and on and they are not "ready," youth are not
expected to have anything particularly important to say. They may
complain, protest, and occasionally even riot. But what else can one
expect of youth? They are not taken seriously.

Gregory Baum, in the introduction to Warren's book, articulates
the issue that is crucial especially for Hispanic youth ministry in the
U.S. context. He praises Warren for attempting

. . . what few Christian educators have dared to do: he seeks
to apply the prophetic stance of Christian faith to the education of young people. It is no longer possible to propose a
positive message to young people in the naive hope that they
are ready to hear what is being said to them. What is required
first is a critique of the prevailing culture and of the social

conditions society has created for young people of different classes. It is necessary to uncover the myths and illusions in which society brings up young people to disguise from them the inequality, the injustice, exploitation, and violence that characterize the present age. Faith is here first a critique of culture.[55]

According to Warren, the most urgent need of youth ministry, whether in the Anglo American middle-class context or in the Hispanic context, is politicization. By that he means not its manipulation by ideologies or partisan interests but a sound orientation toward the transformative action constitutive of evangelization in the fullest sense. When youth ministry is identified too closely with nurturing and comforting, it becomes an obstacle rather than support for evangelization.[56]

Youth ministry must be conceived in intimate relation with the Church's goal of evangelization. It cannot be a stop-gap activity, much less a gesture to anxious, neglected, or angry youth. Youth ministry must be integrated with pastoral planning that includes all the dimensions of evangelization and sees youth as playing a responsible role in the life of the Church and society from the earliest ages. Youth efforts organized independently of the other ministries can unwittingly contribute to the alienation of youth and suggest to them that their role is less serious, less important, than that of other groups in the Church. Youth ministry carried out in isolation from the pastoral options of the local Church, of the adult ministers and leaders of the community, is counterproductive. For that reason youth ministry must be integrated into all the other ministries in some manner through sound pastoral planning. Given the urgent pastoral, sociopolitical, and economic needs of Hispanics and their youthfulness, finally, a vigorous youth ministry must take as its point of departure the Church's understanding of evangelization. It must challenge youth to a change of heart and to struggle for change of unjust social structures.

These considerations lead to the last section of this chapter, a discussion about the place of pastoral planning in the effort to prioritize and effectively order pastoral objectives in the pursuit of the evangelization of U.S. Hispanics.

Pastoral de Conjunto: Organized Pastoral Planning

One of the more powerful instruments for renewal in the Church after the Second Vatican Council is organized pastoral planning, a concept which first achieved official recognition by the Church in Latin

America under the term *pastoral de conjunto*. This expression received wide currency after the Second General Conference of the Latin American bishops held in Medellín, Colombia, in 1968.[57] The emergence of the concept was due to the profound revision of goals and ecclesial structures undertaken by the Latin American Church in response to the call of the Second Vatican Council.[58] A conference given by Bishop Leónidas E. Proaño of Riobamba, Ecuador, at the Medellín assembly and entitled "Pastoral Coordination" was a catalyst for the elaboration of the concept of pastoral planning in a special sense. José Camps summarized Proaño's influential formulation of the problem of inadequate pastoral planning in these words:

> Monsignor Proaño delivered a critical and somewhat sarcastic description of traditional pastoral practice. He took for his point of departure a run-of-the-mill parish. The reality of our pastoral practice which is currently not at all renewed requires a change in mentality (fidelity to the human reality and to the Gospel, solidarity with the poor who struggle, pastoral audacity and team ministry). It also demands a reorganization of activities (know the reality, set goals and objectives, choose the appropriate action steps, organize and sustain the pastoral activities with ongoing theological reflection and periodic evaluations).[59]

Bishop Proaño's statement included almost all the elements that subsequently have come to characterize pastoral planning as it is understood in Hispanic ministry in the United States. The Secretariat for Hispanic Affairs has more recently described the pastoral planning process in these terms:

> By pastoral planning we understand the effective organization of the total process of the life of the Church in fulfilling her mission of being a leaven for the Kingdom of God in this world. Pastoral planning includes the following elements:
>
> —analysis of the reality wherein the Church must carry out her mission;
>
> —reflection on this reality in the light of the Gospel and the teachings of the Church;
>
> —commitment to action resulting from this reflection;
>
> —pastoral, theological reflection on this process;

—development of a pastoral plan;

—implementation;

—celebration of the accomplishment of this life experience;

—and the ongoing evaluation of what is being done.[60]

The Secretariat for Hispanic Affairs defines *pastoral de conjunto* as:

> . . . co-responsible ministry involving coordination among pastoral agents of all of the elements of pastoral life, and the structures of the same in view of a common goal: the Kingdom of God.[61]

Underlying the national pastoral planning process for Hispanics called Tercer Encuentro Hispano Nacional de Pastoral discussed in chapter three is a serious commitment to pastoral planning as it was formulated at Medellín and confirmed in the documents of Puebla.[62] This concept of method in pastoral planning is potentially another way of pursuing the goal of evangelization. The comprehensive nature of the method offers the possibility of establishing an effective relationship between the goal of ministry—evangelization in the fullest sense—and the manifold objectives, strategies, and resources that are conducive to its attainment. It is important, however, to highlight some of the factors that make it difficult to apply this general method of pastoral planning in the North American context.

Perhaps the first observation to be made is that the interest in pastoral planning or *pastoral de conjunto* as it comes down from Medellín is different from pastoral planning as it is conceived of in the United States. Articulating that difference is not easy, for it appears to be a matter of tone more than substance, but a difference nonetheless. Planning in the U.S. context—and many dioceses have pursued very serious pastoral planning—has a different *intentionality*. That intentionality relates to the functionalist and conformist social science vision of North Americans. Pastoral planning in the United States is geared toward making the Church institution function more effectively within the broader context of society. The intention behind the analysis of reality and all the subsequent steps is pragmatic.[63] It is not generally concerned with *transformative* action. There is an unspoken understanding that the *structures* (whether of Church or society) are basically sound. Pastoral planning, therefore, has as its primordial function *making the system work more efficiently*. Pastoral planning in the Latin American sense—the one assimilated by many Hispanic ministry leaders in the

United States—has another intentionality. Like much of the social reflection of Latin America it reveals an indebtedness to Marxist analysis.
Not that it accepts inevitable class conflict or dialectical materialism,
but, rather, pastoral planning is viewed as a method of praxis ultimately
concerned with bringing about serious, if not radical, change in conformity with a vision, a utopia. The code word for that vision in the Latin
American context is the kingdom of God. Pastoral planning leads to
historical praxis—action geared to the transformation of society.⁶⁴

There are those who would argue, perhaps, that *some* pastoral
planning in the U.S. context has a more radical underlying vision and
intentionality. Certainly the concern for the role of laity in the Church,
the question of equality of women in Church and society, the right of
theologians to dissent in some way from official Church teachings, and
concern for more participative, democratic approaches in Church life
and polity are all instances of an agenda with serious structural implications for the Church as well as for society in general. The context
within which these pastoral concerns are voiced, nevertheless, is very
much the context of U.S. society. They are concerns that flow out of
the desire to somehow conform the life of the Church to the existing
egalitarian, modern society of the United States with its strong emphasis on *individual* rights and liberties. The intentionality behind planning
influenced by these kinds of concerns is not structural in the same sense
understood in some U.S. Hispanic or Latin American contexts.⁶⁵

The intentionality behind planning in the U.S. Hispanic and Latin American contexts, as distinguished from the Anglo American one,
seems to better reflect the structural critique, the critical theory implicit
in the magisterium's understanding of evangelization. In this connection a conference given by Gregory Baum at the June 1986 convention
of the Catholic Theological Society of America is relevant. Baum
speaks about the social context of U.S. Catholic theology. One point he
makes about U.S. theology expresses the differences *mutatis mutandis*
between the intentionality of pastoral planning in the U.S. and in the
Hispanic context:

> . . . the question raised is whether post-conciliar American
> Catholic theology has surrendered to liberal values and the
> liberal political philosophy associated with the American
> dream? . . . Has a certain sense of discontinuity made post-
> conciliar theologicans forget the cautions against liberalism
> contained in pre-conciliar theology? Has the entry into ecume-
> nism . . . encouraged Catholic theologians to join the cultural
> mainstream? Is American theology generated out of an identi-

fication with the middle class? . . . The question must, therefore, be asked whether and to what extent American Catholic theology has become part of the liberal ideology that legitimates American society as the land of freedom and offers it as a model to the rest of the world?[66]

Baum's observations point to the fact that even the more progressive forms of theological reflection and the more controversial dogmatic and/or moral issues—the ones that may be more problematic for Church authorities—are in a sense less radical than concepts advanced in the magisterium itself. Baum is convinced that the magisterium advances a critical theory of society, that it insists on the need to do a critique of socioeconomic structures as well as of culture:

> While a radical critique of modern society is found only in a minority of American Catholic theologians, it is found more frequently in ecclesiastical documents on social justice, including the U.S. pastorals on peace and economic justice. The impact of the Latin American Church, especially the Medellín and Puebla Conferences, is here undeniable. The radical critique of capitalism (and communism) has been endorsed and further developed in John Paul II's remarkable *Laborem exercens.*[67]

Baum proceeds to show how the pastorals of the U.S. bishops reflect a serious effort to do structural analysis along the lines promoted by the magisterium. However, he shows that there is a conflict between that effort and the fundamentally liberal, progressive orientation of many theologians and laity alike in the United States:

> In my judgment, the U.S. pastoral has a clearer sense than the major trend of American (and NATO) Catholic theology that the problems of personal spirituality, personal ethics, and personal well-being cannot be understood and overcome without an analysis of the material factors of domination and an historical commitment to emancipation.[68]

The reflection to be made here is that possibly something similar to what occurs in theology occurs in pastoral planning. Pastoral planning in the U.S. context reflects the prevailing milieu, stresses continuity, and tends to become an exercise in efficiency, in making affairs run more smoothly. Thus it becomes an instrument in promoting the modern, progressive agenda of personal freedom and well-being. But pastoral planning in the Hispanic context more appropriately ought to deal with the "material factors of domination" that are grasped principally through structural analysis. Pastoral planning, therefore, in the context of U.S. Hispanics and other marginated groups properly promotes a critique of the status quo and stresses evangelization as struggle for socioeconomic and political change.

In this connection it must be said that within the Hispanic context there can be a variety of approaches to pastoral planning while still following the steps as outlined by Bishop Proaño and by the Secretariat for Hispanic Affairs. One can talk about pastoral planning or *pastoral de conjunto* and mean very different things. One can conceive of the stages in planning, for instance, within a theological framework similar to that of the Puebla Conference. The key concepts there were "communion, participation, and liberation."[69] These words correspond to concepts rooted in sacred scripture, Church tradition, and the magisterium. They provide a solid framework for discussing the goal of evangelization and how to achieve it. But one's point of view and ideology influence the order in which one thinks of them and the emphasis given to one aspect with relation to another. One can conceive of the "reality" taken as the starting point in pastoral planning as a global reality—for instance, the Hispanic in the United States or the urban working class and *campesinos* of Mexico. In such a macroanalysis the extreme aspects of inequality and injustice will most probably be cast in sharp relief. This concern for the macro level of socioeconomic and political reality naturally encourages pastoral planning that places "liberation" first. Another "analysis of the reality," one that is more modest and focuses on the micro level of affairs such as the reality of one neighborhood, parish, or community in southern California or in Honduras, may, without necessarily overlooking the structural problems, spotlight the lack of cooperation and mutual trust within this unit of Church and society. Consequently "communion" and "participation" will, within a certain logic, appear to provide a more immediately relevant framework for pursuing pastoral planning. "Liberation" will be given third place. More precision is needed, then, in using the tool of pastoral planning than frequently is the case. There needs to be awareness about the options, priorities, and intentionality already present in the pastoral agents before they ever begin the planning process. This point relates to the ongoing tensions, the polarities within evangelization itself—and differing interpretations of it—factors seen more than once in this present study.

Finally, it is obvious that the level of serious commitment to evangelization (change or conversion) is a fundamental requisite for pastoral planning. That means that the community, parish, diocese, or Church doing the planning must presume a high degree of detachment or "indifference" in the Ignatian sense of that word among those doing the planning and on the part of the groups impacted by the process. Serious planning impinges upon vested interests. It cannot move forward in a climate of provincialism and parochialism. Unfortunately that climate exists in many areas of the Church's and society's institutional life reflecting as it does the insecurities and foibles of human nature.[70]

The specifically "team" aspect of pastoral planning is also very important. The planning is coordinated and reflects a commitment to coresponsible action on the part of all those concerned in the process. In an atmosphere of rigid authoritarianism such a climate simply cannot exist. Dialogue, the give and take of vigorous discussion, and a certain level of pluralism are indispensable elements in *pastoral de conjunto*. Finding the path for that creative revision of priorities and means while simultaneously affirming the hierarchical qualities of the Church is not easy. Pastoral planning as affirmed by the Medellín and Puebla Conferences and by the U.S. bishops in the Document of the Tercer Encuentro requires precisely this skill. Without commitment to substantive change in policy and direction on the one hand, and respect for the unifying and coordinating context of competent authority on the other, pastoral planning will lose its efficacy as a viable instrument of evangelization in the Catholic Church. Achieving this balance in the U.S. Hispanic context as well as in the Church generally is a practical need if pastoral planning and team ministry are to succeed.

This chapter must end, therefore, in an open-ended manner. Not only are the critical issues complex, but the range of responses are likewise varied and open to considerable debate. Some indications have been given regarding practical ways to respond to the Hispanic presence. These observations and suggestions flow from the critical analysis of the Hispanic reality made in previous chapters. This type of discussion needs to be promoted if Hispanic ministries are to bear fruit for the kingdom of God.

Conclusion

David C. Leege states the implications of the growing Hispanic presence in the U.S. Catholic Church with these words:

> We must pay attention to the Hispanics and the Asians. The ancestors of the Hispanics were within the Church in the United States well before most of us other Catholics were. Most Hispanics today, however, are recent immigrants. While they share a single language, they are many peoples with great cultural diversity. . . . The Hispanics are beginning to come of age in America. Consider the forecast that before the turn of the century, over half of all Catholics in Chicago will be Hispanic or non-white. . . . Just at a time when the dominant element in American Catholicism is white, well educated and middle class, we become aware that large parts of this Church are not white, not well educated and not middle class.[1]

The preceding pages have attempted to trace if only in broad strokes the outline of Hispanic ministry, the Church's response to the Hispanic presence described by Leege. That has meant providing a description of several aspects of their complex realities and analyzing them in light of scripture and tradition. Pope Paul VI's understanding of evangelization in *Evangelii Nuntiandi* is a distillation of the manifold biblical and doctrinal sources available for expressing the Church's mission in the world today. As such, the pope provides an effective instrument for theological reflection.

This study has taken seriously the need to attend to the concrete, human existence of U.S. Hispanics. That task has been hindered by three circumstances:

154

(1) the relative lack of serious social science analyses of the Hispanic Catholic communities of the United States in terms of their participation and interaction within the ecclesial context;

(2) the inadequacy of the word Hispanic for covering such diverse groups and hence the difficulty in specifying the particularity of the people in question;

(3) the lack of theologians and theological studies that take the concrete existence of U.S. Hispanics as their point of departure.

The juxtaposition of a wide range of issues in this study has been an attempt to "see the trees." Hopefully others will undertake the arduous task of "seeing the forest," that is, developing a more rigorous, methodologically consistent approach for Hispanic ministry as a branch of pastoral theology. The elements of such an undertaking have been presented here if only in a seminal manner. Basically it has to do with method—moving back and forth from theory to praxis.

The September 1987 pastoral visit of Pope John Paul II to the United States dramatized the urgency of the Hispanic question in the United States Catholic Church. Many commented upon the very different tone and texture between the pope's encounters with the dominant "mainstream" Catholics on the one hand, and the Hispanic community on the other. The *National Catholic Reporter* made this observation:

> The Pope appeared most at ease in settings that included the less educated, the poor, the immigrants. And yet that meant he did not equally communicate with those who have questions and seek dialogue rather than only answers based on previous answers.[2]

The dichotomy implied in this statement is symptomatic of the problem posed by the Hispanic presence in the bosom of the U.S. Church. This dichotomy between progressive, enlightened, modern people (such as the U.S. middle class) and the tradition-bound "unprogressive" third world peoples (the Hispanic immigrants) is exacerbated by the failure of mainstream North Americans to acknowledge their ideological presuppositions. Without disputing totally the point of view of this NCR editorial, it is obvious that progressive, mainstream U.S. Catholics have not assimilated the spirit of the Church's "preferential option for the poor" as much as they might think. They may have difficulty in grasping all the implications of what is meant when the magisterium of the Church affirms that the poor are *evangelizers* as well as evangelized.[3]

Harvey Cox puts his finger on the wound when he explains the difficulty of modern theology in dealing with all forms of popular religion as discussed in chapter four. He suggests that the Hispanic presence in the form of lived popular religiousness is an important ingredient in the elaboration of postmodern religion. The cogency of this view has yet to impact large segments of mainstream Catholicism in the U.S., for the Hispanic presence in the United States, if Cox is correct, is a force *shaping the future* as well as recalling the past. The ongoing tendency of U.S. Catholics to impose the paradigm of previous Catholic immigrants may be blinding them to the broader and more original implications of *this* immigration at this particular point in time.

Gregory Baum, as mentioned in chapter five, points to another but related source of ideological interference that limits the ability of mainstream U.S. Catholics to grasp the implications of the Hispanic presence. The conscious or unconscious project of many U.S. Catholics and their theologians is the reconciliation of traditional aspects of Catholic thought with the modern, progressive and democratic North American experience. Such an effort gives special importance to those aspects of Catholic thought which deal with personal rights and morality. An effort to reconcile Catholic thought with global realities, however, stresses other aspects of Catholic thought, most especially the serious structural difficulties at the worldwide socioeconomic and political levels. The comfortableness of the pope's interaction with Hispanics and other marginated groups in the United States may be an expression of the Church's effort to reconcile its concerns and interests with those of the great masses of Catholics throughout the world whose cultural milieu is profoundly different from that of mainstream America. If this be the case, then, the Hispanic presence in the U.S. and worldwide Catholicism mediated through the role of Peter is a powerful force at the service of a critical theory of U.S. culture today. The Hispanic presence and the role of Peter in relation to that presence is potentially a fruitful alliance at the service of a truly global awareness.

Further study of the Hispanic presence and the Church's response to it offer the hope of shaping the outline of a new way of being Catholic, Hispanic, and American. That new way has something to do with the way one understands Christian existence in the world. It means attention to the human and respect for the received traditions of the faith. The social sciences provide insight into the human, while a theological hermeneutics grounded in the critical correlation of theory and praxis provides the pattern for dealing with the Christian and Catholic heritage respectfully and efficaciously in a world moving away from modernity to postmodernity.

In addition to the complex theological issues that the present study has evoked in reference to the issue of Hispanic ministry, there are more mundane issues that have also been surfaced. They too require more reflection on the part of practitioners seeking guidelines for loving and effective service of their Hispanic communities. As such, this work is a kind of bridge between the lofty heights of theory and the mundane concerns of pastoral praxis.

Important issues have been left out. One of them is the role of Hispanic women in the forging of the new U.S. Catholic. It is hoped that Hispanic women will take the issues and points raised here and critique them from their unique perspectives. Similarly, the central role of family in Hispanic cultures has been developed only tangentially. A rigorous concept of family and data clarifying Hispanic family concerns ought to figure prominently in future studies.

If this work has advanced the critical dialogue about the evangelization of U.S. Hispanics and encouraged discussion and even a little controversy, this writer will be more than satisfied. The important thing is that Hispanic ministry be recognized as one of the most crucial elements of the U.S. Church's life as it enters the twenty-first century. Much needs to be done if the response to this monumental challenge is to be at once intelligent, loving, and effective.

Notes

Introduction

[1]Margarita Melville, "Los Hispánicos: Clase, Raza o Etnicidad?" (Berkeley: University of California at Berkeley, Chicano Studies Department, 1987), pp. 1–32; and by the same author, "Ethnicity: An Analysis of Its Dynamism and Variability Focusing on the Mexican/ Anglo/Mexican American Interface," special issue, *American Ethnologist* (1983); 272–289.

Chapter I

[1]See *Gaudium et Spes* ##4–10, in Austin P. Flannery (ed.), *Documents of Vatican II* (Grand Rapids: Eerdmans, 1975), pp. 903–1014.

[2]U.S. Department of Commerce, Bureau of the Census, Current Population Reports, Population Characteristics, Series P-20, #403, December 1985, *Persons of Spanish Origin in the United States*, March 1985 (Advance Report). The U.S. Bureau of the Census estimated the Mexican origin undocumented in 1980 to be approximately three million. Cf. Wayne Cornelius, Leo Chávez, and Jorge G. Castro, *Mexican Immigrants and Southern California: A Summary of Current Knowledge* (San Diego: Center for U.S.-Mexican Studies, UCSD, 1982), p. 14.

[3]Ibid.

[4]U.S. Department of Commerce, "1980 Census Population Totals for Racial and Spanish Origin Groups Announced by Census Bureau," *U.S. Department of Commerce News*, February 23, 1981.

[5]Frank D. Bean, Elizabeth H. Stephen, and Wolfgang Opitz, "The Mexican Origin Population in the United States: A Demographic View," in *The Mexican American Experience* (Austin: University of Texas Press, 1985), pp. 58–59.

[6]Leobardo F. Estrada, "The Dynamics of Hispanic Population: A

Description and Comparison," in *Social Thought* 11 (Summer 1985): 34–35.

[7]Bean et al., p. 63.

[8]Estrada, p. 31.

[9]Ibid., p. 32.

[10]Ibid.

[11]Bean et al., pp. 67–68. Despite the convergence of mortality rates between Hispanics and Anglos, there is a significant difference between the mortality rate of young Mexican origin men and young white males. Young Mexican origin men die more frequently from diseases related to alcoholism such as cirrhosis of the liver. Cf. Francis P. Gillespie and Teresa A. Sullivan, *What Do Current Estimates of Hispanic Mortality Really Tell Us?* Texas Research Center, No. 5.010 (Austin: University of Texas), 1983.

[12]U.S. Department of Commerce, Bureau of the Census. Cf. also Daniel Patrick Moynihan, *Family and Nation* (New York: Harcourt Brace Jovanovich, 1986). Moynihan discusses the feminization of poverty in the U.S. and how unfair tax structures perpetuate it.

[13]U.S. Department of Commerce, Bureau of the Census, *1980 Census of Population Supplementary Reports*, PHC 80-SI-1, Provisional Estimates of Social, Economic and Housing Characteristics (March 1982), pp. 47, 100.

[14]Ibid.

[15]Ibid.

[16]U.S. Department of Commerce, Bureau of the Census, *1980 Census of Population and Housing, General Social and Economic Characteristics*, PC 80-1-C1 (Washington, D.C.: U.S. Government Printing Office, 1983).

[17]Ibid., Table 170. Cf. also National Commission on Employment Policy, *Hispanics and Jobs: Barriers to Progress* (Washington, D.C.: National Commission for Employment Policy, 1982) and Cordelia W. Reimers, "The Wage Structure of Hispanic Men: Implications for Policy," in *The Mexican American Experience*, pp. 118–132.

[18]*The Official Catholic Directory* (Wilmette, IL: P. J. Kenedy & Sons), 1986. For estimates of the percentage of Hispanics of Mexican origin who are Catholic see Lawrence J. Mosqueda, *Chicanos, Catholicism and Political Ideology* (Lanham: University Press of America, 1987), p. 10.

[19]*The Official Catholic Directory* lists the Catholic population of the Los Angeles archdiocese at 2,650,000. The Hispanic population of that area, according to the 1980 census, is 2,065,000. It is true that not all

Hispanics are Catholic, but a conservative estimate is that 80 percent are. Hence the estimate of an Hispanic Catholic population well in excess of 1,800,000.

[20]Kevin F. McCarthy and R. Burciaga Valdez, *Current and Future Effects of Mexican Immigration in California*, Executive Summary (Santa Monica: Rand Corporation, 1985), pp. 6–7.

[21]Ibid., p. 9. For a compelling fictionalized account of the experience of undocumented immigrants that evokes the reality, see Ted Conover, *Coyotes: A Journey Through the Secret World of America's Illegal Aliens* (New York: Vintage Books, 1987).

[22]McCarthy and Burciaga Valdez, p. 9.

[23]As this work is being written, the U.S. Congress has passed the Immigration Reform Act of 1986. Aliens in the country illegally before January 1982 may apply for legalization, but it will now be illegal for employers to knowingly hire undocumented persons. Agricultural interests obtained special consideration for the bringing in of farm laborers. It remains to be seen what real impact this new legislation will have on undocumented Mexican immigration. The ongoing economic and political crisis of Mexico, together with the need for cheap labor in the U.S., makes it unlikely that this immigration will be significantly reduced.

[24]McCarthy, pp. 6–7.

[25]Ibid., pp. 27–28.

[26]Ibid., p. 15. The Rand report estimates the Mexican born and their minor children to be 45 percent of the total Mexican origin population of California.

[27]In addition to the Rand report, there are many others which demonstrate the generally positive effect of immigrants on society, especially the economy. The series of publications by the U.S.-Mexican Studies Center at the University of California, San Diego has documented that contention. Cf. especially Wayne A. Cornelius, "The Future of Mexican Immigrants in California: A New Perspective for Public Policy," in *Working Papers in U.S. Mexican Studies* (San Diego: University of California, 1981).

[28]Cornelius, Chávez, and Castro, p. 11. Cf. also Wayne A. Cornelius, Richard Mines, Leo R. Chávez, and Jorge G. Castro, *Mexican Immigrants in the San Francisco Bay Area: A Summary of Current Knowledge* (San Diego: University of California, Center for U.S.-Mexican Studies, 1982).

[29]Cornelius, Chávez, and Castro, p. 84.

[30]McCarthy, p. 27.

[31]Ibid., pp. 30–31.

[32]Ibid., p. 34.

33Cornelius, Chávez, and Castro, p. 13.

34Ibid.

35*Southern California: Region in Transition*, vol. 3: *Locational Patterns of Ethnic and Immigration Groups* (Los Angeles: Southern California Association of Governments, 1984), p. 8.

36Ibid., p. 10.

37Ibid.

38Joseph P. Fitzpatrick, S.J., "Cultural Change or Cultural Continuity: Pluralism and Hispanic Americans," in *Hispanics in New York: Religious, Cultural and Social Experiences* (New York: Archdiocese of New York, Office of Pastoral Research, 1982), p. 68.

39A recent collection of monographs on Mexican immigration to the U.S. concludes saying, "Given the great concern that the authors in this book have demonstrated toward unique features of the Mexican American community, perhaps the greatest surprise is the consensus among them that the data demonstrate that the Mexican Americans are following an integrationist pattern not qualitatively dissimilar from that followed by earlier immigrant groups. Although not ruling out the possibility of significant deviation in the future, the authors suggest that alterations in the pattern have thus far reflected differences of tempo rather than direction." See Walker Connor, *Mexican Americans in Comparative Perspective* (Washington, D.C.: The Urban Institute, 1985), p. 360.

40Fitzpatrick, pp. 79–82.

41Horace M. Kallen, *Americanism and Its Makers* (New York: Bureau of Jewish Education, 1944), pp. 13–14.

42Milton Gordon, *Assimilation in American Life* (New York: Oxford, 1964), passim. For a detailed account of the assimilation process of Mexican immigrants, see Alejandro Portes and Robert L. Bach, *Latin Journey* (Berkeley: University of California Press, 1985).

43S. Dale McLemore and Ricardo Romo, "The Origins and Development of the Mexican American People," in *The Mexican American Experience*, p. 25.

44Ibid., pp. 25–26.

45Fitzpatrick, pp. 79–82.

46New Mexico had a large Hispanic population in the 1850s when Mexico ceded it to the United States. The Hispanics remained a sizable percentage of the population throughout the following decades to the present day. In other parts of the southwest and California the original Hispanic populations were overwhelmed by Anglos migrating from the east. Only now is the Hispanic population becoming once again a political force in those areas.

⁴⁷McLemore and Romo, p. 25. For a deeper analysis of Mexican American political participation and Catholicism's impact on it, see Mosqueda, pp. 105–122.

⁴⁸McLemore and Romo.

⁴⁹Rodolfo Acuña, *Occupied America: The Chicano's Struggle Toward Liberation* (San Francisco: Canfield Press, 1972), p. iii.

⁵⁰Frank Bonilla and Robert Girling, *Structures of Dependency* (Palo Alto: Nairobi Press, 1973).

⁵¹Ronald Bailey and Guillermo Flores, "Internal Colonialism and Racial Minorities," in *Structures of Dependency*, pp. 149–160.

⁵²Guillermo V. Flores, "Race and Culture in the Internal Colony: Keeping the Chicano in His Place," in *Structures of Dependency*, pp. 189–190. Another exposition of the internal colony concept is Mario Barrera's *Race and Class in the Southwest* (Notre Dame: University of Notre Dame Press, 1979). Barrera's is the most complete treatment available of Mexican American social history from a Marxist social science perspective. David T. Abalos provides a new interpretation of the Hispanic presence in *Latinos in the United States* (Notre Dame: University of Notre Dame, 1986).

⁵³Franz Fanon, *Black Skins, White Masks* (New York: Grove Press, 1967); and by the same author, *The Wretched of the Earth* (New York: Grove Press, 1968). Albert Memmi, *The Colonizer and the Colonized* (Boston: Beacon Press, 1965).

⁵⁴Evelina Dagnino, "Cultural and Ideological Dependence: Building a Theoretical Framework," in *Structures of Dependency*, pp. 129–148.

⁵⁵Tomás Almaguer, "Historical Notes on Chicano Oppression: The Dialectics of Racial and Class Domination in North America," in *Aztlán*, 3 (1974): 28.

⁵⁶Orlando Fals Borda, "El Problema de Como Investigar la Realidad Para Transformarla," in *Crítica y Política en Ciencias Sociales*, Tomo I (Bogotá: Punta de Lanza, 1978), pp. 209–249. Examples of *investigación-acción participativa* are found in Fals Borda, *Conocimiento y Poder Popular* (Mexico, D.F.: Siglo Veintiuno Editores, 1985).

Chapter II

¹Thomas Groome, "Shared Christian Praxis," in *Lumen Vitae*, vol. 31 (1976): 199. Emphasis added.

²See Manuel Ballesteros Gaibrois' *Cultura y Religion de la América Prehispánica* (Madrid: BAC, 1985).

³Miguel León-Portilla, *Native Mesoamerican Spirituality* (New York: Paulist Press, 1980), cf. pp. 13–26.

4Jacques Soustelle, *Daily Life of the Aztecs* (Stanford: Stanford University Press, 1961), pp. xiii–xxiv.

5Burr Cartwright Brundage, *A Rain of Darts: The Mexica Aztecs* (Austin: University of Texas Press, 1972), p. xv.

6León-Portilla, p. 29.

7José Luis Guerrero, *Flor y Canto del Nacimiento de México* (México, D.F.: Alfa Offset, 1980), pp. 37–38.

8Miguel León-Portilla, *The Broken Spears: The Aztec Account of the Conquest of Mexico* (Boston: Beacon Press, 1962), pp. xviii–xxix.

9Soustelle, p. 12.

10See Bernal Díaz del Castillo, *Historia verdadera de la conquista de la Nueva España* (Mexico, 1942). For a fascinating explanation of Aztec cannibalism based on the need for protein in an ecology severely strained by population, see Marvin Harris, *Cannibals and Kings* (New York: Random House, 1977), pp. 107–110.

11Octavio Paz, *The Labyrinth of Solitude: Life and Thought in Mexico* and *The Other Mexico* (New York: Grove Press, 1985).

12Paz, *The Other Mexico*, pp. 314–315.

13Ibid., pp. 294 and 297.

14Ibid., p. 298.

15See Jacques Lafaye in *Quetzalcóatl and Guadalupe* (Chicago: University of Chicago Press, 1976), who develops the idea of Guadalupe as *the* national myth and symbol of Mexico. Eric Wolf's anthropological analysis of the Guadalupan event affirms that the tradition links together family, politics, and religion: colonial past and independent present; Indian and Mexican. Cf. Eric Wolf, "The Virgin of Guadalupe: Mexican National Symbol," *Journal of American Folklore*, 71 (1958): 34–39. Victor and Edith Turner also analyze the Guadalupe event from an anthropological perspective in *Image and Pilgrimage in Christian Culture* (New York: Columbia University Press, 1978), pp. 76–103.

16Peggy K. Liss, *Mexico Under Spain: 1521–1556* (Chicago: University of Chicago Press, 1975), especially the closing chapter, "Reflections on an Era," pp. 144–157. See also Colin M. MacLachlan and Jaime E. Rodríguez O., *The Forging of the Cosmic Race: A Reinterpretation of Colonial Mexico* (Berkeley: University of California Press, 1980), and Rodríguez, *Down From Colonialism* (Los Angeles: Chicano Studies Research Center, UCLA, 1983).

17Paz' analysis of the role of Cortés' Indian adviser and lover Malinche and the origins of the word *chingar* (to sexually violate) in the Mexican vocabulary shows how the initial violence of the Conquest has left deep, indelible marks. See Paz, *The Labyrinth of Solitude*, pp. 77–88.

¹⁸One may conceive of today's theology of liberation as an example of this deeper concern for social justice issues going back to the beginnings of Christianity in Latin America. See Enrique Dussel, *Historia de la Iglesia en América Latina* (Barcelona: Editorial Nova Terra, 1972), pp. 91–101.

¹⁹Dussel, p. 97. See also Francisco Javier Clavigero, *Storia antica del Messico* (Cesena: Per Gregorio Biasini, 1780).

²⁰See José Luis Guerrero, *Flor y canto del nacimiento de México*, pp. 221–224. Also, Virgilio Elizondo, *La Morenita: Evangelizer of the Americas* (San Antonio: Mexican American Cultural Center, 1980), pp. 49–53.

²¹See Franz Fanon, *The Wretched of the Earth*, and Albert Memmi, *The Colonizer and the Colonized*.

²²Elizondo has also written a theological reflection on the origins of Mexican American culture titled *Mestizaje: The Dialectic of Cultural Birth and the Gospel* (San Antonio: Mexican American Cultural Center, 1978). He builds on these reflections in a later work, *Galilean Journey* (Maryknoll, NY: Orbis Books, 1983).

²³See Jody Brant Smith, *The Image of Guadalupe: Myth or Miracle* (New York: Image Books, 1984). The English translation of the Nican Mopohua is provided on pages 121–135. Also, Donald V. Kurtz, "The Virgin of Guadalupe and the Politics of Becoming Human," *Journal of Anthropological Research*, 38 (1982): 194–210.

²⁴See J. Vicens Vives, *Historia social y económica de España y América* (Barcelona: Editorial Vicens-Vives, 1977), pp. 324–336.

²⁵Dussel, p. 97. Elizondo in *La Morenita*, p. xiii, shows how the prophecies of Joachim de Fiore influenced the first missioners to the Americas. De Fiore had prophesied a new age that would come about through discovery and this would be the beginning of an age of blessedness. See also J. L. Phelan, *The Millennial Kingdom of the Franciscans in the New World* (Berkeley: University of California Press, 1956).

²⁶Elizondo, *La Morenita*, pp. 60–62.

²⁷Elizondo develops the notion of rejection (*rechazo*) as a formative experience of the Mexican and Mexican American in *Mestizaje: The Dialectic of Cultural Birth and the Gospel*, p. 360, and in *The Galilean Journey*, pp. 100–102.

²⁸Vicens Vives, *Historia de España y America*, pp. 364–374.

²⁹Allan F. Deck, *Francisco Javier Alegre: A Study in Mexican Literary Criticism* (Rome: Historical Institute of the Society of Jesus, 1976), pp. 6–30. Also, Hans-Jurgen Prien, *La Historia del Cristianismo en América Latina* (Salamanca: Ediciones Sígueme, 1985), pp. 353–356.

³⁰Dussel, *Historia de la Iglesia en América Latina*, pp. 163, 171. Also, Prien, p. 377.

[31]John Eagleson and Philip Scharper, *Puebla and Beyond* (Maryknoll: Orbis Books, 1979), p. 116. In the introduction to the Document of Puebla the bishops state: "For all our faults and limitations we pastors, too, ask pardon of God, our brothers and sisters in the faith, and humanity." In No. 209 of that document the Conference participants add: ". . . the wayfaring Church humbly acknowledges its mistakes and sins, which obscure the visage of God in his children." See p. 150.

[32]The enormous contrast between the starting point or origin of the two civilizations, the Anglo American and the Hispanic American, is seen in a comparative reading of works like Max Weber's *The Protestant Ethic and the Spirit of Capitalism* (New York: Charles Scribner's Sons, 1958) with Samuel Ramos' *Profile of Man and Culture in Mexico* (Austin: University of Texas Press, 1962). Jeffrey W. Barrett gives the most compelling description of the enormous contrasts between the Hispanic American and Anglo American worlds. He includes data from historical, cultural, and economic analyses in chapter two, "Modernization: Impeding Values" in *Impulse to Revolution in Latin America* (New York: Praeger, 1985), pp. 8–51. Barrett quotes Alexis de Tocqueville's observation that "One cannot but be astonished at the influence which the point of departure has on the good or ill destiny of peoples." See Alexis de Tocqueville, *Journey to America*, ed. J. P. Mayer, trans. George Lawrence (London: Faber & Faber, 1959), p. 263.

[33]Lee Soltow and Edward Stevens in *The Rise of Literacy and the Common School in the United States* (Chicago: University of Chicago Press, 1981), explain the literacy of early Anglo American settlers in terms of religious interest: "The close relationship between religious instruction and the achievement of literacy was manifest in the concern of the early New England colonists that their children learn to read the Scriptures" (see p. 28). Such an interest in popular reading of the scriptures and in spreading literacy did not exist in colonial New Spain. On the contrary, reading of the scriptures by anyone but clergy was frowned upon. See also Kenneth A. Lockridge, *Literacy in Colonial New England* (New York: W. W. Norton, 1974), p. 13.

[34]See Walter J. Ong, S.J., *Orality and Literacy: The Technologizing of the Word* (London: Methuen, 1982). Ong develops the cultural and theological implications of the contrast between orality and literacy in *The Presence of the Word* (New York: Simon & Schuster, 1970).

[35]See Ong, *Orality and Literacy*, especially chapter three, "The Psychodynamics of Orality," pp. 31–77.

[36]Ong, *The Presence of the Word*, pp. 5–6.

[37]Reginald Horsman, *Race and Manifest Destiny* (Cambridge: Harvard University Press, 1981), p. 9.

[38]Ibid., p. 209.

[39]Herbert E. Bolton, *The Spanish Borderlands: A Chronicle of Old Florida and the Southwest* (New Haven: Yale University Press, 1921).

[40]See John Francis Bannon, S.J., *The Spanish Borderlands Frontier, 1513–1821* (New York: Holt, Rinehart & Winston, 1970). Carey McWilliams develops the story up to the 1940s in *North From Mexico* (New York: Greenwood Press, 1968). Another excellent introduction to the borderlands history of Mexican Americans is David W. Weber's *Foreigners in Their Native Land* (Albuquerque: University of New Mexico Press, 1973). Paul Horgan has evoked the spirit of borderlands culture in *The Heroic Triad* (New York: World Publishing, 1971).

[41]One of the more insightful studies of the encounters between Hispanics and Anglos on the vast borderlands is that of Cecil Robinson entitled *With the Ears of Strangers: The Mexican in American Literature* (Tucson: University of Arizona Press, 1963).

[42]McWilliams, p. 54.

[43]See Richard L. Nostrand, "The Hispanic American Borderland: Delimitation of an American Culture Region," in *Chicano: The Evolution of a People* (Minneapolis: Winston Press, 1973), pp. 23–25.

[44]McWilliams, pp. 102–105.

[45]See Dussel, pp. 154–155, 171. See also David C. Bailey, *Viva Cristo Rey!* (Austin: University of Texas Press, 1974), p. 9. Bailey provides an excellent summary of Church-state conflict in Mexico from colonial times to the Cristero Revolt of the 1920s. Also see Herbert Herring, *A History of Latin America*, 3rd ed. (New York: Alfred A. Knopf, 1968), pp. 325–334.

[46]Bailey, p. 13. See also A. J. Hanna and K. A. Hanna, *Napoleon III and Mexico* (Chapel Hill: University of North Carolina Press, 1971), pp. 88–89.

[47]Ibid., p. 19. Bailey shows how significant changes had occurred in the Church in Mexico at the beginning of the twentieth century due to the influence of Pope Leo XIII and the Catholic social doctrines he promoted.

[48]Ibid., pp. 21–22.

[49]For a concise summary of the Cristero Revolt see Servando Ortoll, "Faccionarismo Episcopal en México y Revolución Cristera," in *Religión y Política en México* (Mexico, D.F.: Siglo XXI Editores, 1985), pp. 27–41. The most thorough study of the Cristero experience is the three volume work of Jean Meyer titled *La Cristiada* (Mexico, D.F.: Siglo Veintiuno Editores, 1973).

[50]For various views regarding the Mexican Revolution and where it

got off track see Stanley R. Ross (ed.), *Is the Mexican Revolution Dead?* (New York: Alfred Knopf, 1970).

[51]See Luis del Valle, S.J., "Conciencia Cristiana y Compromiso Político," *Religión y Política en México*, p. 332.

[52]See Wayne A. Cornelius, *Immigration, Mexican Development Policy and the Future of U.S.-Mexican Relations* (La Jolla: Center for U.S.-Mexican Studies, 1981).

[53]Rosaldo, Calvert, and Seligman, *Chicano: The Evolution of a People*, especially the section entitled "Acquiescence and Adjustment," which deals with the first fifty years of Anglo domination in the southwest, pp. 59–146.

[54]See Antonio Blanco, *La Lengua Española en la Historia de California* (Madrid: Ediciones Cultura Hispanica, 1971).

[55]For the story of the forced repatriation of Mexican nationals in the 1930s see Abraham Hoffman, *Unwanted Mexican Americans in the Great Depression: Repatriation Pressures, 1929–1939* (Tucson: University of Arizona Press, 1974).

[56]Acuña, pp. 168–172.

[57]Ibid., p. 233.

[58]The literature of the Chicano movement is abundant. An example of the militant spirit of this period and its concerns and interests is Armando B. Rendon's *Chicano Manifesto* (New York: Collier Books, 1971).

Chapter III

[1]The most complete, authoritative statement on Hispanic ministry is the U.S. bishops' pastoral letter entitled *The Hispanic Presence: Challenge and Commitment* issued on January 10, 1984 in *Origins*, 13 (January 19, 1984): 530–541. For a synthesis of Hispanic ministry, especially the pastoral context, see Allan Figueroa Deck, S.J., "Hispanic Ministry Comes of Age," *America* (May 17, 1986): 400–402.

[2]For examples of this conflict see Moisés Sandoval (ed.), *Frontera: A History of the Latin American Church in the United States Since 1513*, especially part two, "The Church in Conflict" (San Antonio: Mexican American Cultural Center, 1983), pp. 141–221. See also Allan Figueroa Deck, "El Movimiento Hispano y La Iglesia Catolica de los Estados Unidos," *Cristus* (marzo, 1983): 320–324. For a detailed analysis of the conflict between the Church and some Hispanics in the United States, especially during the decade of the 1960s and 1970s, see Juan Hurtado, *An Attitudinal Study of the Social Distance Between the Mexican American*

and the Church (San Antonio: Mexican American Cultural Center, 1975).

[3] Virgilio Elizondo, *Christianity and Culture* (San Antonio: Mexican American Cultural Center, 1975), pp. 124–128, 156–157.

[4] José Oscar Beozzo, "Evangelization and History," *Lumen Vitae,* 33 (1978): 277–312. Beozzo writes a summary of the history of evangelization in Latin America on the occasion of the convening of the Conference of the Latin American Bishops at Puebla in 1979. See pp. 281–282.

[5] Ibid., p. 287. "The structure of the *padroado,* i.e., *Patronato Real,* system was such that Trent could not exercise the function that the conciliar Assembly and the Holy See wished to insure for it." Enrique Dussel in *Historia General de la Iglesia en América Latina* (Salamanca: Ediciones Sígueme, 1983), p. 482, quotes Rodríguez Valencia's *Toribio de Mogrovejo* in reference to the Second Council of Lima which attempted to implement the decrees of Trent: "The holy Council of Trent was not applied in the majority of cases relevant to church reforms."

[6] For further background on the relationship between Church and state in Latin America and some comparison with that issue in the United States, see J. Lloyd Mecham, *Church and State in Latin America* (Chapel Hill: University of North Carolina Press, 1966), especially pp. 23 and 42. For the origins and spirit of American Catholicism in the nineteenth century, see Dolan, especially pp. 190–191 where he explains how effective clerical control gradually overcame strong lay influence (what Dolan calls congregationalism) in the American Church at the beginning of the nineteenth century due to the initial lack of priests. In the case of Mexico the trend was just the opposite, namely, the ranks of the clergy did not increase through the nineteenth century as Prien discusses at length (pp. 486–492).

[7] Prien points out that a trend toward the privatization of religion took place in the nineteenth century. This occurred around the time of the rise of the urban bourgeoisie and Protestantism's first inroads through U.S. presence; see p. 509. Also, the Brazilian Church historian Riolando Azzi explores the Romanization of Latin American religiosity in several of his studies. See Azzi's manuscript, "Evangelização e Presença Junto Ao Povo: Aspectos Da Historia Do Brazil" (Rio de Janeiro: IBRADES, 1981), pp. 15–16. See also P. A. Ribeiro de Oliveira, "Catolicismo popular e romanização do catolicismo brasileiro," *Revista Ecclesiastica Brasileira* (March 1976): 131–141. Enrique Dussel treats of this period in *The History of the Church in Latin America* (San Antonio: Mexican American Cultural Center, 1974), pp. 28–30.

[8] Elizondo, *Christianity and Culture,* especially the chapter "Popu-

lar Religious Practices of the Mexican American and Catechesis," pp. 174–194.

[9]See the summary of Luis Maldonado's workshops on popular religion entitled *Faith Expressions of Hispanics in the Southwest* (San Antonio: Mexican American Cultural Center, 1977).

[10]Dolan says, "When immigrant Catholics came to the United States, the vast majority of them headed for the neighborhoods of urban America. The city was where they had their best chance of finding a job; it was also where they could find relatives and friends," p. 195. For a careful description of the Americanization of the Catholic clergy of the U.S. in the urban environment of the nineteenth century, see John Tracy Ellis (ed.), *The Catholic Priest in the United States* (Collegeville: Saint John's University Press, 1971), especially "The Formation of the American Priest: An Historical Perspective," pp. 3–110.

[11]See Luis Leñero Otero and Manuel Zubillaga V., *La pastoral en el México de hoy* (Brussels: Pro Mundi Vita, 1984), pp. 8–9.

[12]Ibid.

[13]Juan Carlos Scannone, *Teología de la liberación y praxis popular* (Salamanca: Ediciones Sígueme, 1976), has stressed popular culture as the starting point for doing theological reflection in Latin America. See pp. 72–73.

[14]Cardinal Luis Martínez Aponte, *Hispanic American Pastoral Studies* (New York: Northeast Catholic Center for Hispanics), 1 (June 1986): 11.

[15]For the assimilation of American Catholics and the decline of the national parishes after World War II and especially in the 1960s, see Dolan, p. 426. For a general discussion of the national parish in the U.S., see W. Nessel, "The National Parish Revisited," *The Jurist*, 28 (1968): 82–92.

[16]Archbishop Robert Lucey of San Antonio was deeply concerned about the lack of attention being given Mexican American Catholics in the southwest in 1947. See Appendix B, "Religious Assistance to Mexicans in the United States," in Stephen A. Privett's *Robert E. Lucey: Evangelization and Catechesis Among Hispanic Catholics*, doctoral dissertation at the Catholic University of America, Washington, D.C., 1985, pp. 362–366.

[17]See J. A. Coriden, T. J. Green, and D. E. Heintschel, *The Code of Canon Law: A Text and Commentary* (New York: Paulist Press, 1985), pp. 418–419.

[18]Andrés Guerrero in *A Chicano Theology* (Maryknoll: Orbis Books, 1987) summarizes the reasons for the lack of clergy among the Mexican immigrants (see p. 20).

[19]Pope Piux XII summarizes the history of the Holy See's concern for the care of immigrants in his Apostolic Constitution *Exul Familia*. He mentions the Holy See's concern for Italian immigrants in the U.S. See *Acta Apostolica Sedis* 34 (September 30, 1952): 649–701.

[20]Daniel O'Neill, "St Paul's Priests 1850–1930: Recruitment, Ethnicity and Americanization," in David J. Alvarez (ed.), *An American Church* (Moraga, CA: Saint Mary's College, 1979), p. 34.

[21]In addition to Andrés Guerrero's resume of this issue in *A Chicano Theology*, especially in the section on the dispute between Archbishop Lamy and Father Martínez and other native clergy, see Paul Horgan, *Lamy of Santa Fe: His Life and Times* (New York: Farrar, Straus & Giroux, 1975), p. 127; and James H. Defouri, *Historical Sketch of the Catholic Church in New Mexico* (San Francisco: McCormick Brothers, 1887), pp. 67, 122. For the absence of Mexican priests during the period immediately after the Mexican American War, see Sandoval, *Fronteras*, where he quotes the statistics from the archives of the archdiocese of San Francisco which indicate that in the period from 1848 to 1945 out of a total of 693 priests there was not one who had received his training in Mexico (see p. 244).

[22]Juan Romero, *Reluctant Dawn, Historia del Padre A. J. Martínez* (San Antonio: Mexican American Cultural Center, 1976).

[23]The history of tensions between Hispanic clergy whether native born Mexican Americans or from Spain and Latin America and Anglo American priests is documented in Antonio M. Stevens Arroyo's *Prophets Denied Honor* (Maryknoll: Orbis Books, 1980). In the same book see Juan Romero's article "PADRES: Who They Are and Where They Are Going," pp. 130–140. ASH, the Association of Hispanic Priests, especially of the New York and Miami areas, is mentioned on pp. 211, 270, and 283.

[24]Manuel J. Rodríguez, ed., *Directorio de Sacerdotes Hispanos en los Estados Unidos de America* (Forest Hills, NY: Herencia Española, 1986), p. 4.. Rev. Frank Colborn has written an unpublished manuscript entitled *Reflections on Pastoral Ministry Among Hispanics*. In the section "Pastoral Ministry: Cultural Integration," he discusses the different types of parish (pp. 19–23).

[25]In contrast to Americanization, the Hispanic communities have advanced the notion of "unity in pluralism." See the official conclusions of the Segundo Encuentro Nacional de Pastoral (Washington, DC: Secretariat for Hispanic Affairs, 1977), p. 42.

[26]Report of Rev. Msgr. Michael Driscoll, Chancellor of the Diocese of Orange, on diocesan statistics for 1983.

[27]Colborn, p. 22.

²⁸Allan Figueroa Deck, "Hispanic Ministry Comes of Age," p. 400.

²⁹Colborn, p. 20.

³⁰Ibid.

³¹Joseph P. Fitzpatrick, S.J. has written a comprehensive study of the main issues confronting the U.S. Catholic Church in the service of Hispanics. Of relevance here is chapter four, "The American Experience," which gives a synthetic view of the entire process of assimilation of Catholic immigrants and the Church's role in that process. See *One Church Many Cultures* (Kansas City: Sheed & Ward, 1987), pp. 95–124.

³²Dolan, p. 176.

³³Azzi develops the theme of the conflict between the *cofradías* and the clergy in Brazil. The same theme is developed by J. J. Tamayo Acosta in "Dios en la religiosidad popular," in *Misión Abierta*, 5–6 (November 1985) in regard to *hermandades* or *cofradías* of the colonial period (p. 189).

³⁴Dolan, p. 177.

³⁵Sara Marie Murrieta, *The Role of Church Affiliated Hispanic Organizations in Meeting Some Significant Needs of Hispanic Americans in the United States*, doctoral dissertation at United States International University, 1977. Murrieta analyzes three important movements in the San Diego, California, area: the cursillo de Cristiandad, the Asociación Guadalupana, and the *comunidades de base*.

³⁶With respect to Acción Católica, see Donald J. Mabry, *Mexico's Acción Nacional* (Syracuse: Syracuse University Press, 1973), p. 19. For background information on Catholic Action see J. Fitzsimmons and P. McGuire, *Restoring All Things: A Guide to Catholic Action* (New York, 1938), or Theodore Hesburgh, *The Theology of Catholic Action* (South Bend: University of Notre Dame Press, 1942).

³⁷Meyer, pp. 257–271.

³⁸The powerful impact of the Cristero movement on at least two generations of Mexicans—many of them immigrants to the United States—is attested to by the review *David: Revista mensual ilustrada, órgano oficial de la Legión de Cristo Rey y Santa María de Guadalupe—veteranos de la Guardia Nacional* (*Cristeros*) which was published from 1952 to 1969 in Mexico D.F. The collection is found in the Library of the Centro de Reflexión Teológica, Colección Cuevas.

³⁹Pope Paul VI commended the practice of eucharistic adoration in his address to the U.S. bishops in Rome on June 15, 1978. See *Acta Apostolicae Sedis* 70 (1978): 419–423.

⁴⁰Murrieta, pp. 73–74. Manuel Velázquez in "El Fenómeno Social del Guadalupanismo," *Servir* (Mexico, D.F.), 12 (1976) has character-

ized the various types of *guadalupanos* in terms of their level of awareness regarding history, social justice, and oppression. Generally, their critical awareness is limited (see p. 123).

⁴¹E. Bonnin, "The Essential, the Important and the Accidental in the Cursillo Movement," mimeograph, 1968. See J. Hervás, *Cursillos in Christianity—Instrument of Christian Renewal* (Phoenix: Ultreya Press, 1965). For an appraisal of the *cursillo* movement from a social anthropological point of view see Marcene Marcoux, *Cursillo: Anatomy of a Movement* (New York: Lambeth Press, 1982). A historical study of the *cursillo* is Ivan Rohloff, *The Origins and Development of Cursillo* (Dallas: National Ultreya Publication, 1976).

⁴²Donald L. Gelpi provides a convincing account of the linkages between the various levels or stages of conversion. See "The Converting Jesuit," *Studies in the Spirituality of Jesuits*, 18 (January 1986): 9–25.

⁴³For a fuller discussion of the appeal of fundamentalism to Catholics including Hispanics in the United States, see "Vatican Report on Sects, Cults and New Religious Movements," *Origins*, 16 (May 22, 1986): 1–10. Also see José Armando Nuñez and Allan Figueroa Deck, "Religious Enthusiasm and Hispanic Youth," *America* (January 23, 1982): 232–234, and Allan Figueroa Deck, "Fundamentalism and the Hispanic Catholic," *America* (January 26, 1985): 64–67. For the background to the charismatic renewal see Kilian McDonald, *Charismatic Renewal and the Churches* (New York: Seabury, 1976); William Samarin, *Tongues of Men and Angels* (New York: Macmillan, 1970). Peter M. J. Stravinskas' monograph "Proselytism Among Today's Immigrants: A Preliminary Report," published by the Bishops' Committee on Migration (Washington, D.C.: USCC, February 1987): 1–30, is one of the more comprehensive studies available with bibliography.

⁴⁴"The Hispanic Presence: Challenge and Commitment," p. 538.

⁴⁵"National Pastoral Plan for Hispanic Ministry," *Origins*, 17 (December 10, 1987): 450–463.

⁴⁶National Federation of Priests' Councils, *Developing Basic Christian Communities* (Chicago: NFPC, 1979), p. 32.

⁴⁷Pope Paul VI, Apostolic Exhortation *Evangelii Nuntiandi* (Washington, D.C.: United States Catholic Conference, 1976), no. 58, pp. 40–42.

⁴⁸A telephone survey of the dioceses of California in March 1987 revealed that there are very few BECs functioning in California. Many of the groups originally initiated have gone out of existence; some have become charismatic prayer groups. A lack of clarity as to what the BEC is and inadequate leadership to accompany and sustain the BECs are given as reasons for their disappearance. Another serious charge is that

they sometimes operate outside the parish system and even compete with it or are mistakenly perceived as doing so.

[49]To this writer's knowledge, the only report on a project to implant and sustain BECs available in California is Cecilio J. Morales' *Retrato de Evangelizacion Hispana—Centro de Evangelización y Catequesis* (Washington, D.C.: NCCB Committee on Evangelization, 1981).

[50]For a detailed study of the BEC in Brazil, see Marcello de Carvalho Azevedo, *Basic Ecclesial Communities in Brazil* (Washington, D.C.: Georgetown University Press, 1987). In Spanish, *Comunidades eclesiales de base alcance y desafío de un nuevo modo de ser iglesia* (Madrid: Soc. Educ. Atenas, 1986). See also Alvaro Barreiro, *Basic Ecclesial Communities: The Evangelization of the Poor* (Maryknoll: Orbis Books, 1982). For a view of the BEC as it is understood in various places throughout the world, see *Basic Christian Communities*, a special issue of *Christianity and Crisis*, 41 (September 21, 1981).

[51]Marcelo de Carvalho Azevedo, "Basic Ecclesial Communities: A Meeting Point of Ecclesiologies," *Theological Studies*, 46 (1985): 601–620.

[52]For an evaluation of RENEW see James Kelly, "The Renew Process: Strengths and Areas for Improvement," *America* (March 7, 1987): 547–549.

[53]Rev. Thomas Dowd of the RENEW coordinating team in Newark, New Jersey, reported on March 4, 1987, that clusters of parishes have gone through the RENEW process in the archdiocese of Los Angeles. There is a cluster in the diocese of Oakland. The archdiocese of San Francisco will begin the process in the fall of 1988.

[54]Carmen M. Cervantes, *Catholic Education for Ministry Among Hispanics in California*, doctoral dissertation (Stockton: University of the Pacific, 1987).

[55]*Guidelines for the Formation and Certification of Catechists and Master Catechists* (Sacramento: California Catholic Conference, Office of Hispanic Affairs, 1980). For a summary of the key issues in the catechesis of U.S. Hispanics, see María de la Cruz Aymes and Francis J. Buckley, "Case Study: Catechesis of Hispanics in the United States Today," in *Effective Inculturation and Ethnic Identity* (Rome: Centre "Cultures and Religion" Pontifical Gregorian University, 1987), pp. 3–28.

[56]Frank H. Bredeweg, C.S.B., *United States Catholic Elementary and Secondary Schools 1985–1986* (Washington, D.C.: National Catholic Educational Association, 1986), pp. 15–16.

[57]In the *Proceedings of the Segundo Encuentro Nacional de Pastoral* there is a section entitled "Evangelization and Integral Education," where stress is given to the education of the family and of the adults who in turn can educate the children. See no. 6, p. 78.

⁵⁸See Virgilio Elizondo, *Religious Practices of the Mexican American and Catechesis* (San Antonio: Mexican American Cultural Center, 1974). For approaches on adaptation of the liturgy to the Hispanic community, see Ricardo Ramírez, *Fiesta, Worship and Family* (San Antonio: Mexican American Cultural Center, 1981); also Ricardo Ramírez, "Is the Prophet Speaking Spanish? Hispanic Gifts and Needs in Liturgy," *Living Worship*, 13 (December 1977): 23–26.

There is a growing body of literature on Hispanic popular religion. See Luis Maldonado, *Religiosidad Popular* (Madrid: Ediciones Cristiandad, 1975); and by the same author, *Introducción a la Religiosidad Popular* (Santander: Ediciones Sal Terrae, 1985); Segundo Galilea, *Religiosidad Popular y Pastoral* (Madrid: Ediciones Cristiandad, 1979); by the same author, *Religiosidad Popular y Pastoral Hispano-Americana* (New York: Northeast Catholic Pastoral Center for Hispanics, 1981); *Iglesia y Religiosidad Popular en América Latina* (Bogota: CELAM, 1977); Diego Irarrázaval, *Religión del Pobre y Liberación* (Lima: CEP, 1978); by the same author, *Navidad en la Tradición de los Pobres* (Lima: CEP, 1981); Eduardo Hoornaert, *Guadalupe: Evangelización y Dominación* (Lima: CEP, 1977). Enrique Dussel, "Religiosidad popular Latinoamericana," *Christus* (diciembre 1986): 14–20; Gilberto Giménez, *Cultura Popular y Religión en el Anáhuac* (Mexico: CEE, 1978). One volume of *Concilium* was devoted entirely to popular religion: Norbert Greinacher and Norbert Mette (eds.), *Popular Religion* (Edinburgh: T. & T. Clark, 1986). This is the August 1986 volume of *Concilium*. Orlando Espín outlines a method for doing American Hispanic theology in "Toward a Hispanic-American Theology" (Boynton Beach, FL: St. Vincent de Paul Regional Seminary, 1987), using Hispanic popular religion as the point of departure (pp. 1–23).

⁵⁹Robert O. González and Michael La Velle, *The Hispanic Catholic in the United States: A Socio-Cultural and Religious Profile* (New York: Northeast Hispanic Pastoral Center for Hispanics, 1985), p. 134.

⁶⁰These guidelines were published in *Noticias*, the official publication of the Office of Hispanic Affairs of the California Catholic Conference in Sacramento (Summer 1986).

⁶¹A report from the National Conference of Catholic Bishops states that there are more than 1,000 Hispanic permanent deacons in the U.S., or 13 percent of the total. See "Results of New Diaconal Study for 1986," *Deacon* (Spring 1987): 1. For worldwide statistics on the permanent diaconate, see "The Diaconate Worldwide," *Deacon Digest* (February 1987): 9.

⁶²See Office of Hispanic Ministry, Diocese of Orange, "Report on

the Hispanic Ministry in the Diocese of Orange, 1983–84," and in the *Diocesan Directory* (1986), p. 74.

⁶³Juan A. Estrada, *La Transformación de la Religiosidad Popular* (Salamanca: Sígueme, 1986), pp. 83–87.

⁶⁴The very great diversity between the pastoral norms for reception of the sacraments in Mexican dioceses, for example, and in U.S. dioceses has, to this writer's knowledge, never been studied.

⁶⁵The traditionalism of the residually oral culture and the unsecularized, premodern mindset is part and parcel of the Hispanic reality. David J. O'Brien in "The American Laity: Memory, Meaning and Mission," *America* (March 7, 1987): 189–194, describes how pre-Vatican II ethnic parishes in the United States did gradually contribute to the immigrant group's giving up its Old World views. It did so by promoting a "bottom-up" process of Church formation.

⁶⁶One of the more influential efforts to call attention to the diverse psychologies of the Hispanic and Anglo American is Joe L. Martínez, *Chicano Psychology* (New York: Academic Press, 1977). Also Alberto Hernández Medina and Luis Narro Rodríguez, *Como Somos los Mexicanos* (Mexico, D.F.: Centro de Estudios Educativos, 1987). For a complete bibliography see Frank Cota-Robles Newton, Estéban L. Olmedo, and Amado M. Padilla, *Hispanic Mental Health Research* (Berkeley: University of California Press, 1982).

⁶⁷A California diocese's marriage tribunal reported to this writer that in 1984 it dealt with 380 annulment applications. Of those, 51 were cases in which one or both of the parties were Hispanic. In 1985, 67 out of 454 were Hispanic and in 1986, 64 out of 423 were Hispanic. More than half of the Catholics in that diocese are Hispanic, but only 15 percent of the petitions for annulment are Hispanic.

⁶⁸For the centrality of conversion understood in its several stages, see Gelpi. Also Paulo Freire, *Pedagogy of the Oppressed* (New York: Seabury Press, 1974), and *Education for Critical Consciousness* (New York: Seabury Press, 1973).

⁶⁹See chapter one, note 26.

⁷⁰Allan Figueroa Deck, "A Christian Perspective to the Reality of Illegal Immigration," *Social Thought*, 4 (Fall 1978): 39–53.

⁷¹For a current summary of the situation of the undocumented immigrants in the U.S., see David M. Reimers, *Still the Golden Door: The Third World Comes to America* (New York: Columbia University Press, 1986). Also see *The Church and the Undocumented Immigrant: Perspectives of the Church in Mexico Regarding Undocumented Immigrants in the United States*, an instruction by the bishop of Tijuana (Tijuana: Obis-

pado, 1979); and *Letter to the Episcopal Conferences on the Church and People on the Move*, from the Pontifical Commission for the Pastoral Care of Migrant Peoples (Washington, D.C.: USCC, 1978).

[72]Sheldon Maram,⁻ "Survey of Immigrant Workers at Orange County Parish" (unpublished, Fullerton: California State University at Fullerton, 1979).

[73]There is a long list of statements of the United States Catholic bishops as well as regional conferences of bishops on issues of immigration. See, for example, *Quest for Peace* (Washington, D.C.: National Conference of Catholic Bishops, 1981), and *Chiesa e mobilitá umana* (Rome: Centro Studi Emigrazione, 1985), pp. 755–889. This compilation provides the texts of all Pope John Paul II's pronouncements on migration from the beginning of his pontificate (1978) through 1983.

[74]For reflections on the need for a more receptive, affirming environment for Hispanics in the Church, see *Colleción Mestiza Americana*. Especially relevant is Archbishop Patricio Flores' article, "The Church: Diocesan and National," where the archbishop outlines the implications of the Hispanic presence at every level of Church (pp. 70–81).

[75]Ellis, *The Catholic Priest in the United States*, p. 429, speaking of the attitudes of U.S. priests to social action, states: "American Catholic social action was primarily shaped by two sometimes conflicting forces: by the demands made on the Church to conform its values and ideals to those of American culture, demands increasingly assimilated and internalized by the Church and its leaders, and by the needs and aspirations of the Catholic people themselves."

[76]The California Department of Education, Division of Migrant Education, Sacramento, California, issues periodic reports on the status of the migrant workers.

[77]In this connection it is important to note that *pastoral de conjunto* was repeatedly stressed as an essential component in planning for Hispanic ministry. In addition to the *National Pastoral Plan for Hispanic Ministry*, see *Prophetic Voices* (Washington, D.C.: United States Catholic Conference, 1986), p. 6. See also Allan Figueroa Deck, "Rural Hispanic Minstry," *Rural Roots* (May/June 1986): 1–3.

[78]The best source for information on the varying structures and organizational models of the Hispanic ministry offices is the Office of Hispanic Affairs of the California Catholic Conference, Sacramento, California.

[79]See *Noticias*, 7 (November 1986) and 8 (December 1986) for a description of the Catholic Hispanic Institute of California.

[80]See *Prophetic Voices* and *National Pastoral Plan for Hispanic Ministry*.

[81]See *Celebration '86: Plan Pastoral Para la Comunidad Hispana de la*

Arquidiócesis de Los Angeles en California (Los Angeles: Office of Hispanic Apostolate, 1986).

[82]*Prophetic Voices.*

[83]The lack of written sources on the mass media and evangelization in Spanish or among persons of Hispanic origin is notable. For an overview see *Acta* or Proceedings of the Hispanic Catholic Communications Conference held at the Marywood Center, diocese of Orange, from November 1–3, 1986. The Proceedings are available at Hispanic Telecommunications Network, San Antonio, Texas. For an example of one medium's appeal (radio) to Hispanics, see *Radio Today: The Hispanic Listener* (San Francisco: Arbitron Ratings, 1985).

Chapter IV

[1]For a general treatment of evangelization in the U.S. context, see David Bohr, *Evangelization in America* (New York: Paulist Press, 1977); and Kenneth Boyack, C.S.P., *Catholic Evangelization Today* (New York: Paulist Press, 1987).

[2]See English translation of *Evangelii Nuntiandi, On Evangelization in the Modern World* (Washington, DC: United States Catholic Conference, 1976), No. 18.

[3]The *Instruction on Christian Freedom and Liberation* of the Congregation for the Doctrine of the Faith (Vatican City, 1986) is an attempt to clarify some of the disputed points in the way evangelization is understood. No. 64 of this document deals with the relationship between evangelization and human promotion. Returning to this theme, the 1985 Extraordinary Synod of Bishops in their "Message to the People of God" wrote: "The salvific mission of the Church in relation to the world must be understood as an integral whole. Though it is spiritual, the mission of the Church involves human promotion even in its temporal aspects. For this reason the mission of the Church cannot be reduced to a monism, no matter how the latter is understood. In this mission there is certainly a clear distinction—but not a separation—between the natural and the supernatural aspects. This duality is not a dualism. It is thus necessary to put aside the false and useless oppositions between, for example, the Church's spiritual mission and *diaconia* for the world." See *Origins*, 15 (no. 27): 450.

[4]*Evangelii Nuntiandi*, No. 36.

[5]In this context it is helpful to review the various concepts of Christian conversion. Certainly Bernard Lonergan was a pioneer with his characterization of the process in terms of affectivity, intellect, morality, and religion. See Bernard Lonergan, *Method in Theology* (New York: Seabury Press, 1972), pp. 236–244. Donald L. Gelpi provides a

trenchant synthesis of the different momenʋ of conversion and explicates the relationship of sociopolitical conversion to the other kinds in "The Converting Jesuit," in *Studies of the Spirituality of Jesuits,* op. cit.

⁶J. Gómez Caffarena reviews the various kinds of "humanisms" in his article "Humanismos" in *Conceptos Fundamentales de Pastoral* (Madrid: Ediciones Cristiandad, 1983), pp. 426–437.

⁷See Gregory Baum, *Religion and Alienation* (New York: Paulist Press, 1975), p. 196.

⁸The letter of Pope John Paul II to the Brazilian bishops exemplifies the "both/and" approach of the magisterium with respect to the polarities of personal and social or structural conversion. The Holy Father speaks of the Church's mission in these words: "the *mysterium salutis* is essentially religious because it is born of God's initiative and finds its completion in the Absolute of God. It is at the same time service to man—the person and society—to his or her spiritual or temporal needs, fundamental human rights and civil life in common." See *L'Osservatore Romano* (English Language Edition) ("Pope's Letter to Brazilian Episcopal Conference") 28 April 1986, p. 6. See also Bonaventure Kloppenburg, *Christian Salvation and Human Temporal Progress* (Chicago: Franciscan Herald Press, 1979).

⁹For a resume of the anthropological concept of culture as understood in the contemporary magisterium see Paul Cardinal Poupard, "El Magisterio de la Iglesia y la Pastoral de la Cultura," in *Apostolado de la Cultura,* No. 28 (1981): 25–45; and in the same number, "El humanismo cristiano de Juan Pablo II," pp. 46–62.

¹⁰*Evangelii Nuntiandi,* No. 20, p. 16.

¹¹For background on the Church's understanding of culture and the term "inculturation," see Marcello de Carvalho Azevedo, S.J., *Inculturation and the Challenges of Modernity* (Rome: Pontifical Gregorian University, 1982), especially pp. 3–8. Robert J. Schreiter, C.PP.S., develops the theological implications of the new sensitivity toward culture in *Constructing Local Theologies* (Maryknoll: Orbis Books, 1985), especially chapter three, "The Study of Culture," pp. 39–74. Michael Amaladoss provides an assessment and valuable critique of the concept of inculturation as it currently is understood in "Inculturation and Dialogue," *Centrum Ignatianum Spiritualitatis,* 17 (1986): 151–176.

¹²The series titled *Inculturation: Working Papers on Living Faith and Culture,* edited by Ary A. Roest Crollius, S.J., studies the implications of the dynamic relationship between Christian faith and the various human cultures. See especially Ary A. Roest Crollius, *What Is So New About Inculturation?* (Rome: Pontifical Gregorian University, 1984). In a compact, insightful monograph, Gerald A. Arbuckle stresses symbol

as the central issue linking cultures and action. See "Communicating Through Symbols," in *Human Development*, 8 (Spring 1987): 7–12.

[13]See Azevedo, *Inculturation and the Challenges of Modernity*, p. 25. Very Reverend Pedro Arrupe, S.J., former superior general of the Society of Jesus, issued a "Letter to the Whole Society on Inculturation" (May 14, 1978).

[14]*Evangelii Nuntiandi*, No. 20.

[15]See Louis J. Luzbetak, S.V.D., "The Beneficiaries of Evangelization," *Catholic Evangelization Today*, ed. by Kenneth Boyack (New York: Paulist Press, 1987), p. 72. For the text of Rahner's talk see *Theological Studies*, 40 (December 1979): 716–727.

[16]Ibid.

[17]See Joe Holland, "Faith and Culture: An Historic Moment for the American Catholic Laity," a background paper for the Pillar Faith and Culture Project (Seton Hall University: Pallottine Institute for Lay Leadership and Apostolate Research, 1987).

[18]The *New Oxford Review* sponsored a "Symposium on Roman Catholicism and 'American Exceptionalism.' " Joe Holland discusses the negative and positive aspects of Anglo American culture and its influence in the world. See *New Oxford Review* (March 1987): 8. The *New Catholic World* also devoted an entire issue to the question of North American culture and evangelization. See especially John Coleman, "The Substance and Form of American Religion and Culture," *New Catholic World* (May–June 1987): 106–111. In the same issue, Michael Warren treats the same theme in "Questioning Culture," pp. 100–105.

[19]Robert Schreiter shows how scriptural and doctrinal traditions are themselves "local theologies," necessarily wedded to the culture that gave them expression. See Schreiter, *Constructing Local Theologies*, pp. 93–94. G. Rupp develops the impact of culture on the formulations of Christological doctrines in *Christologies and Cultures* (The Hague, 1975). See also B. Secondin, *Messagio Evangelico e Cultura: Problemi e dinamiche della mediazione culturale* (Rome, 1982); and J. Stott and R. T. Coote (eds.) in *Gospel and Culture* (Berkeley: University of California Press, 1979); J. Neusner, *Judaism and Christianity in the Age of Constantine* (Chicago: University of Chicago Press, 1987).

[20]Taken from the Fourth Book and the twelfth chapter of *De Doctrina Christiana* and quoted in Boyack (ed.), *Catholic Evangelization Today*, p. 69.

[21]Ibid. Emphasis added.

[22]There is a substantial amount of literature on the Anglo American spirit, modernity, and religion. See Max Weber, *The Protestant Ethic and the Spirit of Capitalism* (New York: Charles Scribner's Sons, 1976),

and S. N. Eisenstadt, *Protestant Ethic and Modernization* (New York: Basic Books, 1968). Ernst Troeltsch raised issues relevant to the relationship between American Protestantism and modernity in *Protestantism and Progress* (Boston: Beacon Press, 1958). Finally, Robert Bellah et al. in *Habits of the Heart: Individualism and Commitment in American Life* (Berkeley: University of California Press, 1985) have synthesized copious material on this subject and given a contemporary interpretation of Anglo American culture.

[23]Bellah, p. 334.

[24]Ibid., p. 335.

[25]Joseph Cardinal Ratzinger provides a stimulating assessment of Catholic social thought, the several ways in which it parts company with liberal capitalism and collectivism, and its focus on ethical concerns in "Freedom and Liberation: The Anthropological Vision of the Instruction *Libertatis Conscientia*," *Communio*, 14 (Spring 1987): 55–72. In the Fall 1986 issue (vol. 13) of the same review he speaks of the practical consequences of Catholic social thought—distinct from that of liberalism or collectivism—on the global economy in "Church and Economy: Responsibility for the Future of the World Economy," pp. 199–204. Rupert J. Ederer stresses the strong corporativist and solidarist current of Catholic social thought in "Who Was Heinrich Pesch?" *New Oxford Review* (November 1986): 21–25.

[26]John Francis Kavanaugh, *Following Christ in a Consumer Society* (Maryknoll: Orbis Books, 1984); and Dean Brackley, "Downward Mobility: Social Implications of St. Ignatius's Two Standards," *Studies in the Spirituality of Jesuits*, 2 (January 1988): 1–48.

[27]John A. Coleman, *An American Strategic Theology* (New York: Paulist Press, 1982). The author struggles with the tensions between fidelity to the gospel and the need to contextualize.

[28]Joe Holland, "Faith and Culture," makes the point that the central question is precisely how to be Catholic and American in the current postmodern period. For a most original perspective on the Americanization of U.S. Hispanics from a long-time Spanish visitor to the United States, see Alberto Moncada, *La Americanización de los Hispanos* (Barcelona: Plaza y Janes Editores, 1986).

[29]See U.S. bishops' pastoral letter on war and peace, *The Challenge of Peace: God's Promise and Our Response* (Washington, D.C.: United States Catholic Conference, 1983), and *Economic Justice for All: Catholic Social Teaching and the U.S. Economy* (Washington, D.C.: United States Catholic Conference, 1986). See Paul Steidl-Meier, *Social Justice Ministry: Foundations and Concerns* (New York: LeJacq Publishing, 1984), p. 232.

³⁰Rogelio Díaz-Guerrero, *Psychology of the Mexican: Culture and Personality* (Austin: University of Texas Press, 1967); Santiago Ramírez, *El Mexicano: Psicología de Sus Motivaciones* (México, D.F.: Editorial Grijalbo, S.A., 1977); Oscar Lewis, *The Children of Sanchez* (New York: Vintage Books, 1961); Octavio Paz, *The Labyrinth of Solitude* (New York: Grove Press, 1961) and *The Other Mexico: Critique of the Pyramid* (New York: Grove Press, 1972); Carlos Fuentes, *Where the Air Is Clear* (New York: Farrar, Straus & Giroux, 1971) and *The Death of Artemio Cruz* (New York: Panther, 1974) and *Tiempo Mexicano* (México, D.F.: Joaquín Mortiz, 1973); Joaquín A. Peñalosa, *El Mexicano y los 7 Pecados Capitales* (México, D.F.: Ediciones Paulinas, 1972).

The cultural values and disvalues of the Mexican American ought not be overlooked either. See, for instance, Rodolfo Alvarez, "The Psycho-Historical and Socioeconomic Development of the Chicano Community in the United States," *Social Science Quarterly* (March 1973): 920–942; Nathan Murillo, "The Mexican American Family," in *Chicanos: Social and Psychological Perspectives* (St. Louis: C. V. Mosby, 1976), pp. 97–108. In this connection it is worth mentioning the controversial works of Richard Rodríguez who has attempted to get underneath the surface of the bilingual Mexican American reality in *Hunger of Memory* (Boston: Grodine Publisher, 1982), and in "Mexico's Children" *The American Scholar* (Spring 1986): 161–177.

³¹Arthur F. Corwin in "Mexican American History: An Assessment" provides a critique of the nationalist anti-American tendency among some Mexican American historians in *The Chicano*, edited by Norris Huntley, Jr. (Santa Barbara: Clio Press, 1975), pp. 1–40.

³²Various Marxist interpretations of Latin American culture, especially those inspired on the theory of dependency, exemplify this tendency to conceive of Latin American culture as almost totally dependent and hence somehow lacking its own authenticity and originality.

³³See Paul Papajohn and John Spiegel, *Transactions in Families*, especially chapter eight, "The Ethnic Family and Culture Change" (San Francisco: Jossey-Bass, 1975), pp. 268–291.

For the low self-image of Hispanics of Mexican origin see Díaz-Guerrero, *Psychology of the Mexican*, pp. 27–30. For the historical background to the low self-image of California Hispanics, see Leonard Pitt, *Decline of the Californios* (Berkeley: University of California Press, 1966), especially "The Schizoid Heritage," pp. 291–296. Edward Casavantes explores the origins of the Hispanic self-image in "Pride and Prejudice: A Mexican American Dilemma," *Civil Rights Digest* (Winter 1970): 22–27. Spencer Kagan has studied the origins of different self-images between Anglo Americans and Hispanics of Mexican origin in "Field

Dependence and Conformity of Rural Mexican and Urban Anglo American Children," *Child Development*, 45 (1974): 765–771; also by the same author, "Development of Adaptive Assertiveness in Mexican and United States Children," *Developmental Psychology*, 11 (1975): 71–78; and "Mother-Directed Achievement of Children in Two Cultures," *Journal of Cross-Cultural Psychology*, 4 (June 1973): 221–228.

[34]Robert Schreiter, *Constructing Local Theologies*, p. 8.

[35]See "Justice in the World," Synod of Bishops Second General Assembly, November 30, 1971, in *The Gospel of Peace and Justice*, p. 514, No. 6. For a study of the phrase "constitutive dimension of the preaching of the gospel," see Francis R. Smith, "Liberation Theology: The Roman Reaction," in the collection of papers on Church and state in Latin America on file at the U.S.-Mexico Studies Center, University of California at San Diego.

[36]*Gaudium et Spes, Pastoral Constitution on the Church in the Modern World*, No. 1.

[37]For a concise review of this issue see J. García Roca, "Ideología," in *Conceptos Fundamentales de Pastoral*, p. 443.

[38]For a bibliography representative of the reflection on the Hispanic presence in the U.S. and its implications, see *Integral Education: A Response to the Hispanic Presence* (Washington, D.C.: NCEA, 1987), pp. 79–80. One of the more thoughtful pastoral letters on Hispanics in the Church is Archbishop Roger M. Mahony's "El Ministerio de la Iglesia Local de Stockton a Nuestros Hermanos y Hermanas Hispanas," diocese of Stockton (October 18, 1982).

[39]The Tercer Encuentro process has emphasized a praxis-oriented reflection process for the Hispanic community in the U.S. A pastoral plan for U.S. Hispanics has been approved by the U.S. bishops. For a resume of this process as it has unfolded in California, see *Encuentro Regional Hispano de Pastoral Region XI* (Sacramento: Office of Hispanic Affairs of the California Catholic Conference, 1985).

[40]Philip W. Powell, *Tree of Hate* (New York: Basic Books, 1971). Powell subtitled his book "Propaganda and Prejudices Affecting United States Relations with the Hispanic World."

[41]See Ramon Dubert, "La Masa," in *Manual del Presidente de Asamblea* (Santiago de los Caballeros: Obispado, 1976), p. 36. Fromm and Maccoby in *Sociopsicoanálisis del Campesino Mexicano* discuss the diffidence characteristic of the *campesino*; see pp. 62 and 276. Also Luis del Valle, "Conciencia Cristiana y Compromiso Politico" in M. de la Rosa and C. A. Reilly (eds.), *Religión y política en México*, p. 328.

[42]Daniel H. Levine, *Religion and Politics in Latin America* (Princeton:

Princeton University Press, 1981) describes the changing role of the Church as institution and religion in social and political affairs in Colombia and Venezuela. See especially pp. 29–55; also Peter Worsley, *The Trumpet Shall Sound* (New York: Schocken Books, 1968).

[43]See Martin C. Needler, *Politics and Society in Mexico* (Albuquerque: University of New Mexico Press, 1971), pp. 75–76.

[44]See Daniel Cosio Villegas, *El Sistema Político Méxicano* (México, D.F.: Cuadernos de Joaquín Mortiz, 1975).

[45]Alan Riding expresses the implications of Mexico's geographical relation to the United States in these words: "Contiguity with the United States has proved a permanent psychological trauma. Mexico cannot come to terms with having lost half of its territory to the United States, with Washington's frequent meddling in its political affairs, with the U.S. holding on its economy and with growing cultural penetration by the American way of life." See *Distant Neighbors* (New York: Alfred A. Knopf, 1984), p. 316.

[46]Given the Catholic character of the Mexican and Mexican American people, especially the popular masses, it is appropriate to mention here an observation made by José Míguez Bonino regarding the failure of revolutionary ideology to move the Latin American masses. He argued that groups militating for social change have not understood "the depth to which Christianity—as a sociological entity—has penetrated and still moulds Latin American consciousness, at a visceral level where theoretical, rational explanation fails to make an impact. . . . People 'live' their economic and social alienation in a world of mythical representation which political ideology is not able to pierce." See *Christians and Marxists* (Grand Rapids: Eerdmans Publishing, 1976), p. 26.

[47]Pope John Paul II's recent encyclical on social justice, *Sollicitudo Rei Socialis* (Washington, D.C.: USCC, 1988), leaves little room for doubt regarding the magisterium's critical stance toward both dominant economic systems.

[48]Archbishop Thomas Kelly, O.P., former general secretary of the National Conference of Catholic Bishops, *Quest for Justice* (Washington, D.C.: United States Catholic Conference, 1981): p. v.

[49]Juan Luis Segundo in *Faith and Ideologies* (Maryknoll: Orbis Books, 1984), p. 3.

[50]Harold Wells in "Ideology and Contextuality in Liberation Theology" studies the influence of Marxist ideology in the theology of liberation. Wells states the issue this way: "The question is not whether the theologian has an ideological bias, but rather whether that bias is congruent with faith, i.e., with the Gospel." See pp. 14–16 of the paper

delivered at the Symposium on Church and Politics in Latin America on September 30, 1986, at the U.S.-Mexico Studies Center, University of California at San Diego.

⁵¹See Marcello Azevedo, *Inculturation and the Challenges of Modernity*, pp. 30–52. Harvey Cox explores the status of the debate about secularization that his 1965 book *The Secular City* initiated in *Religion in the Secular City: Toward a Postmodern Theology* (New York: Simon & Schuster, 1984). Mary Douglas and Steven M. Tipton explore religion in a secular age in *Religion and America* (Boston: Beacon Press, 1982).

⁵²See Cyril Black, *The Dynamics of Modernization* (New York: Harper & Row, 1966). For the application of a theory of modernity to the Hispanic situation in the United States, see Alfredo Castañeda, "Traditionalism, Modernism, and Ethnicity," in Joe L. Martinez, Jr. (ed.), *Chicano Psychology*, pp. 355–360. Also, A. Inkeles, "Becoming Modern: Individual Change in Six Developing Countries," *Ethos* (1975): 323–342.

⁵³Modernity as a culture identified with the United States is explored by Theodore F. Zuern, Joseph Tetlow, and Peter Schineller in *On Being Church in a Modern Society*, part of the series Working Papers on Living Faith and Cultures (Rome: Pontifical Gregorian University, 1983).

⁵⁴Norman Perrin has explored the core teaching of Jesus as reflected in the parables in *Rediscovering the Teaching of Jesus* (New York: Harper & Row, 1976).

⁵⁵See Leonardo Boff, *Jesus Christ Liberator* (Maryknoll: Orbis Books, 1978); also Johannes Nissen, *Poverty and Mission: New Testament Perspectives* (Leiden-Utrecht: Interuniversitair Institut Voor Missiologie, 1984), and Norbert Lohfink, *Option for the Poor* (Berkeley: Bibal Press, 1987).

⁵⁶See Langdon Gilkey, "Modern Myth-Making and the Possibilities of Twentieth-Century Theology," in L. K. Shook (ed.), *Theology of Renewal*, vol. 1 (New York: Herder & Herder, 1968), pp. 283–312. Gilkey also develops these ideas further in *Catholicism Confronts Modernity* (New York: Seabury Press, 1975). According to Gilkey, postmodernity builds on modernity dialectically by adding and stressing other ways of knowing beyond science, correcting and enhancing the narrow rationalistic and technological frameworks of modernity. But in no way does postmodernity cancel out modernity's substantial contributions. See chapter one, "The Nature of the Crisis."

⁵⁷Robert Bellah writes: "It [modernity] is itself more and more evidently incapable of giving the alternative system of meaning that the Enlightenment thought it would." In Douglas and Tipton, *Religion in America*, p. xii. For a detailed description of the crisis of U.S. Catholi-

cism in the face of modernity see Coleman, *An American Strategic Theology*, pp. 156–165.

⁵⁸Juan Carlos Scannone, "Influjo de Gaudium et Spes en la Problemática de la Evangelización de la Cultura in America Latina—Evangelización, Liberación y Cultural Popular," *Strómata* (julio–diciembre 1984); 87–103. Scannone develops his theory about the relationship between liberation and popular culture in *Teología de la liberación y praxis popular* (Salamanca: Sígueme, 1976). He expands and systematizes his views in *Teologia de la liberación y doctrina social de la iglesia* (Madrid: Cristiandad, 1987).

⁵⁹Scannone, "Influjo de Gaudium et Spes, p. 91.

⁶⁰Ibid., p. 93.

⁶¹For an evaluation of Gramsci's understanding of the relationship between popular religiosity and revolutionary change, see V. Fagone, "La religione populare in Gramsci," *La Civiltà Cattolica*, 3 (1978): 119–133; by the same author, "Marxismo e Cristianesimo negli Scritti Giovanili di A. Gramsci," *La Civiltà Cattolica*, 1 (1978): 530–546. Regarding popular religiosity as a form of cultural resistance, see J. L. González, "Teología de la Liberación y Religiosidad Popular," *Páginas*, 7 (1982): 4–13.

⁶³Scannone, "Influjo de Gaudium et Spes," p. 96.

⁶⁴Ibid., pp. 96–97.

⁶⁵Ibid., p. 97.

⁶⁶*The Document of Puebla*, No. 448.

⁶⁷J. J. Mueller in "Teaching for the 21st Century: Teaching as Reculturator," *Milltown Studies*, 18 (Autumn 1986): 61–72 traces the development of the words acculturation, inculturation, reinculturation, and reculturation. He prefers the word reculturation as most expressive of the evangelizer's task.

⁶⁸Segundo Galilea has described the characteristics of secondary popular religiosity in *Pastoral Popular y Urbana en America Latina* (Bogotá: CLAR, 1977), especially pp. 23–26.

⁶⁹George Gallup comments on the impact of upward mobility on U.S. Hispanics in *The American Catholic People* (New York: Doubleday & Co., 1987): "It would appear that as Hispanic-Americans become more assimilated into American society and more affluent, religion will become a less important factor in their lives." See p. 143.

⁷⁰See Raimundo Panikkar, *Worship and Secular Man* (Maryknoll: Orbis Books, 1973), pp. 28–29.

⁷¹Ibid., p. 28.

⁷²Ibid., p. 29.

⁷³Ibid.

[74]See José Vasconcelos, *Indología: Una Interpretación de la Cultura Ibero-Americana* (Paris: Agencia Mundial de la Librería, 1927); and by the same author, *La Raza Cósmica* (Madrid: Aguilar S.A. de Ediciones, 1961).

[75]See Raimundo Panikkar, "Dios en las Religiones," *Misión Abierta* 5–6 (November 1985): 85–102.

Chapter V

[1]For a discussion regarding sacraments and sacramentals in the Hispanic American religious experience see Consejo Episcopal Latinoamericano (CELAM), *Iglesia y Religiosidad Popular en América Latina* (Bogotá: Secretariado General del Celam, 1977).

[2]See note 58 for chapter three.

[3]Gilkey, "Modern Myth-Making," pp. 308–309.

[4]Gilkey, *Catholicism Confronts Modernity*, pp. 9–11.

[5]Cox, pp. 240–241.

[6]Ibid., p. 241.

[7]Roger Chartier, "Discipline and Invention: The Fête in France S. XV–XVIII," *Diogenes* 110 (Summer 1980): 24.

[8]Mary Douglas, *Natural Symbols* (New York: Pantheon Books, 1970), p. 3.

[9]Denis E. Collins, *Paulo Freire: His Life, Works and Thought* (New York: Paulist Press, 1977), pp. 44–53.

[10]Ibid., p. 13. A collection of essays stresses the application of Freire's pedagogy in U.S. educational settings. See Ira Shor (ed.), *Freire for the Classroom* (Portsmouth, NH: Boynton Books, 1987).

[11]Saul D. Alinsky, *Reveille for Radicals* (New York: Random House, 1969).

[12]For a study of Alinsky's life and work, see P. David Finks, *The Radical Vision of Saul Alinsky* (New York: Paulist Press, 1984).

[13]See Ed Chambers, *Organizing for Family and Congregation* (Huntington, NY: Industrial Areas Foundation, 1978) for an outline of the methods of Church-based community organizing. Peter Skerry analyzes IAF projects in San Antonio and Los Angeles in "Neighborhood Cops: The Resurrection of Saul Alinsky," in *New Republic* (February 6, 1984): 21–23.

[14]The National Conference of Catholic Bishops has produced several statements and taken positions over the years on immigration issues. A recent example is *Together a New People: Pastoral Statement on Migrants and Refugees* (Washington, D.C.: National Conference of Catholic Bishops, 1986). Diocesan bishops have also spoken out on behalf of undocumented immigrants and refugees. See, for example, Los An-

geles Archbishop Roger M. Mahony's Pastoral Letter, "Welcoming the New Immigrants," in *Origins* (January 16, 1985): 518–520.

[15]An important movement linking advocacy with the empowerment of the Hispanic people—in this case Central American refugees—is the international Sanctuary Movement. For a review of Sanctuary's activities on behalf of refugees and social justice in Central America, see Michael McConnell, "Movement Building: Civil Rights to Sanctuary," *Basta!* (September 1986): 11–16.

[16]Luis Alberto Gómez de Sousa, "Secularización en declive y potencialidad transformadora de lo sagrado," *Páginas* 12 (84): 9.

[17]Ibid.

[18]Ibid., p. 10.

[19]See chapter one on urbanization of U.S. Hispanics.

[20]See Kelly, p. 548.

[21]Marcello de Carvalho Azevedo, *Basic Ecclesial Communities in Brazil* (Washington, D.C.: Georgetown University Press, 1987). Chapter three of Azevedo's work describes the popular Catholicism, socioeconomic conditions, and historical patterns of the Brazilians that have much in common with Hispanic America. See pp. 119–129.

[22]Ibid., pp. 136–137.

[23]For further descriptions and analyses of the BECs see James O'Halloran, *Living Cells: Developing Small Christian Community* (Maryknoll, NY: Orbis, 1984); National Secretariat and Hispanic Teams, *Basic Ecclesial Communities: An Experience in the United States* (Liguori, MO: Liguori Publications, 1980); François Francou, *Ante Todo Evangelio: Piedra Angular de las Comunidades de Base* (Mexico, D.F.: Buena Prensa, 1980); Thomas Maney, *Basic Communities: A Practical Guide for Renewing Neighborhood Churches* (Minneapolis: Winston Press, 1984); Casiano Floristán, *La Comunidad Cristiana de Base* (San Antonio: Mexican American Cultural Center, 1976).

[24]The Final Report to the Bishops of the United States by The Parish Project is titled *Parish Life in the United States* (Washington, D.C.: National Conference of Catholic Bishops, 1982), p. 83. An earlier statement on parish life in the U.S. also issued by the National Conference of Catholic Bishops is *The Parish: A People, A Mission, A Structure* (Washington, D.C.: National Conference of Catholic Bishops, 1980). For a general treatment of parish renewal as it has developed in the U.S., see *Parish Renewal: A Resource Book for Dioceses* (Washington, D.C.: National Conference of Catholic Bishops, 1983).

[25]See Archbishop Daniel Pilarczyk, "Does the Church Flourish in Its Parishes?," *Origins* (March 12, 1987): 681–686.

[26]See "An Expanded View of Ministry," December 13, 1986 State-

ment of the Cincinnati Archdiocesan Pastoral Council, *Origins* (January 15, 1987): 553–557. The view of ministry as focused more or less narrowly on Church or on service in the world impacts one's notion of the parish and one's concept of the role of priests and laity alike. See also Allan Figueroa Deck in "Ministry and Vocations: Going Back to the Drawing Board," *America* (March 14, 1987): 212–218.

[27]Andrew M. Greeley discusses the importance of preaching in attracting youth in "Parish, Priest and the Young Catholic," *The Parish Project Reader* (Washington, D.C.: National Conference of Catholic Bishops, 1982), pp. 18–22. Allan Figueroa Deck and José Armando Nuñez, "Religious Enthusiasm and Hispanic Youths," *America* (October 23, 1982): 232–234, believe that part of the difficulty in effectively reaching youth is due to the limited style and kind of preaching in the Church.

[28]Maney develops the idea that small faith-sharing communities can and should become vehicles of social change (see pp. 62–68).

[29]O'Halloran discusses the relationship of BECs to the parish and the diocese in *Living Cells*, pp. 51–58.

[30]Kelly, p. 548.

[31]Jacob Needleman, *Lost Christianity* (New York: 1980).

[32]John Coleman, "The Religious Significance of New Religious Movements," *Concilium* (January 1983): 10.

[33]Jesús Andrés Vela, *Reiniciación Cristiana, Respuesta a un Bautismo "Sociológico"* (Bogotá: Pontificia Universidad Javeriana, 1985), p. 261.

[34]Bishop Ricardo Ramírez, "El Redescubrimiento del Tesoro Más Rico en la Liturgia: El Rito de la Iniciación Cristiana Para Adultos" (October 1986), published at the Instituto de Liturgia Hispana, Miami, FL, pp. 1–10. The Department of Education of the United States Catholic Conference has produced a paper titled "The Process of Christian Initiation for the Hispanic Community in the United States" (Washington, D.C.: U.S.C.C., 1986).

[35]Vela's study is devoted to showing the relevance of the RCIA model to evangelization in areas where cultural or sociological Catholicism is strong.

[36]For a summary statement of the actual condition of parish life in the United States see *The Parish in Transition*, *Proceedings of a Conference on the American Catholic Parish* (Washington, D.C.: United States Catholic Conference, 1986). The Institute for Pastoral and Social Ministry at the University of Notre Dame has been conducting a massive study of Catholic parish life. For the present, the Hispanic parish has not been included in this study. One of the major topics to be considered in such a future study is the functioning of BECs within Hispanic parish structures.

[37]The work of Protestant evangelicals in Latin America needs to be

surveyed in terms of how the charismatic element in their approach is linked to structural analysis and liberation. In this connection the work of the Latin American Evangelical Center for Pastoral Studies (CELEP) in San José, Costa Rica, is especially significant. See *Occasional Essays* of CELEP, "A Decade in the Service of Jesus Christ" (December 1985). In this issue of *Occasional Essays* an example of this inquiry within the Latin American context is "Consultation on Pentecostalism and Liberation Theology," pp. 150–155.

[38]The issue of inculturation and liturgy has been addressed by Michael Amaladoss, an Indian liturgical scholar, in *Do Sacraments Change?* (Bangalore: Theological Publications in India, 1979). See also "Inculturation: Necessary and Urgent," *Origins* (October 31, 1985): 342–343.

[39]See Deck and Núñez, "Enthusiastic Religion and Hispanic Youths."

[40]Juan A. Estrada, *La Transformación de la Religiosidad Popular* (Salamanca: Ediciones Sígueme, 1986), p. 115, deals directly with the issue of personal appropriation of faith among rural Andalucians imbued with popular Catholicism.

[41]See *Sacrosanctum Concilium*, The Constitution on the Sacred Liturgy, in *The Documents of Vatican II*, Austin P. Flannery (ed.), especially nos. 21, 23, 37, and 38.

[42]Alberto Hernández Medina, *Cómo Somos los Mexicanos*, p. 80.

[43]Harry Eckstein, "Civil Inclusion and Its Discontents," *Daedalus* (Fall 1984): 107.

[44]For a commentary on Eckstein's view regarding the historical results of the empowerment of the lower socioeconomic classes, see Walter Dean Burnham, "A Commentary on Harry Eckstein," in the same issue of *Daedalus*, pp. 147–160.

[45] Philip Murnion, "Parish Leadership," *The Parish in Transition*, pp. 58–65. An eloquent statement of the reality of lay participation in U.S. Church life is the speech of Donna Hanson, president of the Bishops' Lay Advisory Council, in the presence of Pope John Paul II at St. Mary's Cathedral in San Francisco on September 28, 1987. See *The National Catholic Reporter* (September 25, 1987): 33.

[46]Speaking of the emergence of lay leadership in U.S. parishes, David C. Leege makes the revealing observation: "There is a tendency toward recognizing lay responsibility through providing credentials to graduates of training programs. Thus there is a credentialed liturgist or a credentialed minister of adult education. . . . Some pastors and leaders are seeing, however, that these programs give individuals such a distinctive set of skills that they intimidate other parishioners, creating

new splits in the parish. Just as the priest has had to learn how to be sensitive, so the credentialed lay minister must remember that the parish is the people of God that must be encouraged and affirmed. Otherwise, we have merely traded a hierarchical dominance based on ordination for one based on training credentials." See *The Parish in Transition*, p. 17.

⁴⁷See chapter one on the average age of U.S. Hispanics.

⁴⁸See John Eagleson and Philip Scharper (eds.), the Document of Puebla, in *Puebla and Beyond*, especially nos. 33, 71, 95, 127, 865, and 1166ff.

⁴⁹See *Prophetic Voices*, pp. 11–13.

⁵⁰See Teresita Basso, "Ministry to Hispano Mexicano/Chicano Youth," in Michael Warren (ed.), *Resources for Youth Ministry* (New York: Paulist Press, 1978), pp. 190–201.

⁵¹Ibid., pp. 193–194. Basso outlines the specific differences between Anglo American and Hispanic youth..

⁵²Joseph F. Ketts, *Rites of Passage: Adolescence in America, 1790 to the Present* (New York: Basic Books, 1977), p. 68.

⁵³Michael Warren, *Youth, Gospel, Liberation* (San Francisco: Harper & Row, 1987), pp. 1–11.

⁵⁴Ibid., p. 12.

⁵⁵Ibid., p. xiv.

⁵⁶Michael Warren, *Youth and the Future of the Church* (New York: Seabury Press, 1982), especially "Youth Ministry: Toward Politicization," pp. 89–102.

⁵⁷The Document of Medellín in *Iglesia y Liberación Humana* (Barcelona: Editorial Nova Terra, 1969). See the section on "*Pastoral de Conjunto*," no. 15, pp. 229–242. It seems that a serious commitment to coordinated pastoral planning first appeared in Brazil in the First Joint Pastoral Plan of the Brazilian Bishops in 1965. See Azevedo, *Basic Ecclesial Communities*, pp. 27–28; also note no. 21 on p. 46.

⁵⁸Eagleson and Scharper, *Puebla and Beyond*, nos. 1306 and 1307, p. 284.

⁵⁹The Document of Medellín, p. 25.

⁶⁰See *National Pastoral Plan for Hispanic Ministry* (draft), p. 2.

⁶¹Ibid.

⁶²The Puebla Conference insisted on the need to conceive of ministry in a comprehensive, coordinated manner. Eagleson and Scharper, *Puebla and Beyond*, no. 1204, p. 272.

⁶³Joe Holland and Peter Henriot, *Social Analysis: Linking Faith and Justice* (Maryknoll: Orbis Books and the Center of Concern, 1983), provide a cogent explanation of the tendency to resist coordinated plan-

ning that leads to real, creative change. They quote Gibson Winter on the root metaphor behind modernity, namely, the machine. In the postmodern era a new *artistic* root metaphor more open to break-throughs and real innovation is arising. See pp. xvi–xviii.

[64]Gustavo Gutiérrez in *A Theology of Liberation* (Maryknoll: Orbis Books, 1973) develops the notion of historical praxis as an *indispensable* feature of pastoral ministry (see p. 81). José Míguez Bonino develops the correlation between pastoral activity and historical praxis in "Historical Praxis and Christian Identity," in Rosino Gibellini (ed.), *Frontiers of Theology in Latin America* (New York: Orbis Books, 1974), p. 262. Rebecca S. Chopp summarizes the discussion of theology and praxis as it has developed in Latin American theologies and in European political theology in *The Praxis of Suffering* (Maryknoll: Orbis Books, 1986), pp. 134–148.

[65]Bernard Lonergan in *Method in Theology* (New York: Seabury Press, 1972), pp. 340–344, develops the concept of intentionality analysis that distinguishes different levels of conscious and intentional operations. Jesús Andrés Vela has incorporated Lonergan's understanding of intentionality in his article titled "Planificación y Evaluación Pastoral," *Cursos de Iglesia y Vocación* 107 (1982): 1–26.

[66]See Gregory Baum, "The Social Context of American Catholic Theology," in the Catholic Theological Society of America, *Proceedings of the Forty-First Annual Convention* (June 1986): 94.

[67]Ibid., p. 98.

[68]Ibid., p. 99.

[69]Eagleson and Scharper, *Puebla and Beyond*. The concepts "communion, participation, and liberation" provide a thread for understanding the work of the Puebla Conference. See for example nos. 189, 211, 212, 215, 281, 326, 452, 475, 480, 696, and 895.

[70]Dody Donnelly, *Team: Theory and Practice of Team Ministry* (New York: Paulist Press, 1977), provides a detailed outline of the dynamics of team ministry as it has developed in the United States.

Conclusion

[1]Leege, *The American Parish in Transition*, p. 14.

[2]"He Confirmed the Church He Came to Condemn," *National Catholic Reporter* (September 25, 1987): 40.

[3]The Document of Puebla in *Puebla and Beyond* states: ". . . it is of the utmost importance that we pay heed to the religion of our peoples. Not only must we take it as an object for evangelization. Insofar as it has already been evangelized, we must accept it as an active, evangelizing force." See no. 396.